A Frontline Worker's Manifesto

A Frontline Worker's Manifesto

Lessons Learned in Good Company

by **DANIEL OUDSHOORN**
with a Foreword by **NICKY DUNLOP**

CASCADE *Books* • Eugene, Oregon

A FRONTLINE WORKER'S MANIFESTO
Lessons Learned in Good Company

Copyright © 2025 Daniel Oudshoorn. All rights reserved. Except for brief quotations in critical publications or reviews, no part of this book may be reproduced in any manner without prior written permission from the publisher. Write: Permissions, Wipf and Stock Publishers, 199 W. 8th Ave., Suite 3, Eugene, OR 97401.

Cascade Books
An Imprint of Wipf and Stock Publishers
199 W. 8th Ave., Suite 3
Eugene, OR 97401

www.wipfandstock.com

PAPERBACK ISBN: 979-8-3852-2780-8
HARDCOVER ISBN: 979-8-3852-2781-5
EBOOK ISBN: 979-8-3852-2782-2

Cataloguing-in-Publication data:

Names: Oudshoorn, Daniel, author. | Dunlop, Nicky, foreword author.

Title: A frontline worker's manifesto : lessons learned in good company / Daniel Oudshoorn ; with a foreword by Nicky Dunlop.

Description: Eugene, OR : Cascade Books, 2025 | Includes bibliographical references.

Identifiers: ISBN 979-8-3852-2780-8 (paperback) | ISBN 979-8-3852-2781-5 (hardcover) | ISBN 979-8-3852-2782-2 (ebook)

Subjects: LCSH: Social workers—Canada. | Burn out (Psychology). | Social isolation. | Mental Health. | Mental Health—Canada.

Classification: HD8039.S45 .O93 2025 (paperback) | HD8039.S45 .O93 (ebook)

03/26/25

For
everyone barred, and banned, and restricted, and suspended, and issued a "step away," and told they are trespassing, and disciplined, and punished, and locked-up, and locked-out, and shot-down, and shot-up (by cop-shots, by hot-shots), and misdiagnosed, and over-prescribed, and under-treated and cut off from their medicines, and blamed, and overworked, and underpaid, and broken-hearted, and beat-down, and despairing because you've been treated like you are the problem when you care about yourself and others and persist in thinking that others should, too.

And, also, against
bosses and bureaucrats who claim to care—and who get paid a lot of money to do so—but who continue to cause grievous bodily, emotional, mental, and spiritual harm to others. You have always known what you are doing.

"What is the relationship of beauty and atrocity in a landscape such as this?"[1]

–Robert MacFarlane

---

1. MacFarlane, *Underland*, 229.

Contents

Foreword by Nicky Dunlop | *ix*

Introduction: Good Company | *xiii*

1. Welcoming | 1
   A. Inviting | 7
      i. Making Safe Space | 14
   B. Acknowledging | 27
      i. Greeting | 33
      ii. Prioritizing (Wasting Time Together With) | 37
      iii. Listening | 46
      iv. Remembering | 51

2. Honoring | 54
   A. Trusting | 65
   B. Working Together With (Collaborating) | 71
      i. Meeting | 78
      ii. Guiding | 81
      iii. Mutual Caring | 87
   C. Affirming | 96
      i. Specialness (Belovedness) | 99
      ii. Worthiness | 107
      iii. Inter- and Intra-Connectedness | 114

- D. Celebrating | 122
  - i. Marveling | 134
  - ii. Thanking | 137
  - iii. Grieving | 142

3. Being | 148
   - A. Honest | 152
   - B. Gentle | 165
   - C. Affectionate (Tender-hearted) | 171
   - D. Kind | 176
   - E. Comforting | 183

4. Parting | 188
   - A. Murdered and Disappeared | 192
     - i. Not Knowing | 197
     - ii. Commemorating | 201
   - B. Battered Company (Destructive Companions) | 207
     - i. Alternate Courts of Justice | 212
     - ii. Restoring Ecosystem Thriving | 220
     - iii. Exiling | 228
   - C. Leaving | 237
     - i. Suffering | 240
     - ii. Convalescing | 245
     - iii. Choosing When to Stay and When to Go | 249

Conclusion: Loving and Raging in the Mean Time | 257
Postscript | 264
Bibliography | 269

Foreword
Nicky Dunlop

You have no doubt heard the phrase "to give the shirt off your back." It denotes generosity, going without so someone else may go with. It conveys selflessness, kindness, and compassion. Love. Before I tell you how my life and Dan's came together, I have a much more recent story to share about the author of this book.

In the fall of 2019, I was diagnosed with breast cancer. A fluke really. A fiftieth birthday gift to myself to book my first scan. It would be routine they told me. A good baseline for future scans they said. And then there it was. My treatment included surgery, chemo therapy, radiation, and bags of treatments dripping slowly from an IV pole for the next five to ten years. But my gratitude for the treatment options offered to me and the life I have been given is abundant. The start of the treatment was rough on my body and tough on my pride. Weakness sets in and I began to rely on people and that is not a comfortable place for me to be. To ask for help. And more so, to not be able to help others. I've never been someone who fussed about myself. I've been called "low maintenance" and I've taken it as a compliment whether it was meant to be or not. When I began to lose my hair, I was a bit shocked and perhaps disappointed in myself. The first clump came out in my hand one day and my reaction didn't feel very "low maintenance." I felt like I was spinning. I tried to be careful with it like washing it gently would stop it from all coming out. I realized I had no control over it. In fact I didn't have control over my cancer at all, other than the choice to accept or refuse treatment, but from there it was left to statistics and my body to sort out. I realized one day that although I couldn't control whether I lost my hair or not, I could control when. And I could control how. I threw a head-shaving party with friends! Complete with a photographer to capture it. It was a celebration! A small foothold on a tiny bit of control. It was a beautiful day and Dan played an immense part of my celebrating this part of my cancer.

He wasn't there on the day. He was 4,000 kilometers away. What arrived in my mailbox one cold day was a toque. A toque with dreadlocks Dan had cut off of himself and sown into it. It was quite possibly the most disgusting and beautiful gift I have ever received in my life. I sat, parked at the mail box and laughed as tears poured down my cheeks. He is one of the brightest lights in my life and I have no doubt he will always give me the hair off his head or the shirt off his back.

Now let's go back to the beginning. Our lives came together when we worked at the same large organization on the fringe of the Downtown Eastside of Vancouver around 2005. Our work was driven by statistics and service delivery models and it all had to align with the Christian foundation of the organization. This top-down organization provided a rigid framework which we as "youth workers" and "team leaders" had to operate within to structure plans for these kids and young adults to meet program expectations so they could keep a bed under them, a roof over them and food in them, while trying to survive their trauma, addiction, illness, and exhaustion. We were tracking and reporting statistics. Program success was measured by meeting targets and outcomes. It wasn't program outcomes that we stayed awake at night worrying about or cried rivers of tears for when they died too young. We were not there because of our love of outcomes and performance indicators, yet it was what was driving our work.

Dan speaks openly about how on many occasions he chose to do what was needed when "program plans" went off the rails. What was needed to save lives and keep those we cared about from harm, as opposed to what we were authorized to do within the limits of our "role." He put his own security to maintain housing and meet his needs at risk when he chose to put his job on the line. I wish I'd had the bravery and love to follow him. I wish I had read this book back then, or in school, or before I ever set foot in the world of social service work. To even think of it as some sort of "manual" or "textbook" as to how we need to build the foundation of the work we do, seems to diminish it somehow and gives it a rigidity that is so far from what it is. Yet I think of the impact it would have on every single person who reads it, regardless of their role or position.

My varied gigs in the "social service" field have involved wearing such hats as "life skills coach," "youth worker," "legal advocate," "training facilitator," and "executive director." My current focus is on building the capacity of front-line workers through the creation of an online community for them to network, share, collaborate, and address systemic inadequacies together. It's ironic that although I rely on online tools to build community, I also believe strongly that the digital divide is becoming a canyon within which those trying to access services are being driven off the edge and blamed for their choice to jump. I believe reliable and accessible internet access should be a human right, along with housing and a basic income sufficient to thrive and not just survive.

Dan is an accomplished academic, author, lecturer, convener, collaborator, poet, and activist. In this book Dan speaks from his heart. He shares his lived experience, joys, and personal traumas. His openness and vulnerability come through as lessons and gifts for us all. A gift of self-reflection and growth. An opportunity if we are open to accept it, to grow with intention, love, and compassion and become better company.

This book has changed how I will live and work. I hope it creates a shift in your life and makes you think about the kind of world you want to not only live in but be part of creating.

Maybe it's the Virgo in me that makes me so opposed to bumper stickers, but if I had one, it would inevitably read "WWDD."

Nicky Dunlop

Introduction
Good Company

I was seventeen years old when I joined the company of other children and teens who were abandoned and left for dead by their parents. I did not choose to join this company. I was cast out into it one January evening as an ice storm was passing through the city (and much of what we refer to as eastern Canada). I had an hour to "get [my] things and go" knowing that "anything [I] leave behind will be thrown into the garbage." The large black plastic bags I was given to carry my belongings well-represented what my dad felt like he was doing—taking out the trash, ridding himself of the living excrement, the *human waste*, that contaminated the purity of his domain. "Just get out of my life," is what he said to me when I asked: "Should I phone or anything?" Years of sustained and multi-faceted manipulation, cruelty, and abuse made this seem normal to me, made me accept it, made me think I was at fault, and made me think I deserved to be treated that way.

I am now forty-four years old (not yet old, no longer young, solidly middle-aged), and I have yet to leave the company of the abandoned and left-for-dead. Over the last twenty-seven years, I have realized how vast this company is—not only abandoned children but also adults who have been forcibly deprived of housing, people whose medicines or whose ways of obtaining or taking their medicine have been criminalized, people who engage in physical forms of labor that a bourgeois moralizing discourse disallows; people who have been disabled, handicapped, delayed, formed, institutionalized, diagnosed, sterilized, manipulated, photographed, studied, and medicated by ableist and sanist experts and norms; racialized and colonized peoples who, simply because they exist and are who they are, have been targeted by all the arms and hands and fingers and mouths and dicks and assholes of the carceral state; queer, trans, and gender-nonconforming folx who are barred from experiencing the fullness, abundance, and wonderful richness of life by the diffuse, capillary networks of those who enforce misogyny and trans-antagonism—these are my friends and companions. These are those whom I have sought out and who, in turn, have come looking for me. Because, while I was thrown into this company through no choice of my own, I deliberately made the choice to remain within it (and that, itself, reflects how different my experiences as a cishet, White, somewhat able-bodied and passably able-minded male from a middle-class background, are different from the experiences of others who never have the choice of leaving). I wouldn't trade this company for the world—at least not for the world as it is.

Because here's the thing: it is in this company that I have learned about the possibilities of other worlds. And more than being possibilities, these worlds are already a reality, occurring and persisting in the interstitial spaces that have not yet been cleared, caulked, and filled by neoliberalism, surveillance, law and order, gentrification, and business plans. Now, I know, I know, people in interstitial spaces can also be violent, life can be very hard, and poverty qua poverty, dispossession qua dispossession, and abandonment qua abandonment are nothing to be celebrated or valorized. Among those who write about these things (especially academics, ethnographers, and spiritual-but-not-religious do-gooders) the observation that "we should not romanticize poverty" has become an oft-repeated truism. But, here's the thing about that observation—it's usually made by outsiders looking in (or those who were once insiders who fled to the outside, and who have found ways to profit from advancing the sort of narrative that outsiders prefer—I don't begrudge them their hustle but I do contest their truth if they want to make it universal). As for insiders, of course fuck poverty, fuck violence, fuck oppression and dispossession, but, I'll tell you what, those who are finding ways to bring life out of the most severe death-dealing circumstances, those who are queering oppressive norms in creative, playful, and exuberant ways, those who are laughing in the face of unjust laws, and those who, day after day, are doing the work of caring for one another while others care for them, are the very best goddamned people in the world. That's not romanticism—that's just facts.

But I am not writing this text to convince you of any of this or, at least, I'm not trying to convince you of any of this in the usual ways in which texts are deployed to do this. Plenty of literature like that already exists and it's there to be found if you go looking for it. And these other-worldly communities are also there, they're not hard to find, we get glimpses of them all the time (from street pharmacists who don't dispense meds during the hours when kids are walking to and from school, to the music rising next to a fire made by people making a home for themselves down by the river, to the unused rigs that are sometimes stashed in certain places in public

INTRODUCTION

bathrooms for those who might need them). If you're a safe enough person, you can be invited in.

This, then, is what I want to share in this text: lessons I have learned from these companions regarding how to be good company to and with others. Most of us were never taught how to be good company. So-called "civilization" itself was founded upon making bad company honorable, normal, enforceable, and ubiquitous, and this trend has only deepened as "civilization" has expanded and developed into its current world-encompassing neoliberal iteration. This is where the forced march of progress has brought us: to a world where it is so easy to be bad company that we hardly notice what miserable companions we are to others—from those who are driving on the highway beside us, to those who are panhandling outside the grocery store, to those who mess up our drink orders at the bar, to those who are eviscerated by drone strikes funded by our tax dollars, to those who are so invisible to us that we never even notice when they are murdered or disappeared (from Indigenous women and girls, to transgendered sex workers, to isolated seniors who have been forcibly deprived of housing). We can be miserable companions and we are also accustomed to others being miserable companions to us. From teachers who are too swamped to attend to our needs, to parents who are working three part-time, unbenefited jobs or who are trend-setting CEOs, doctors, and lawyers, working eighty-hour weeks, and who end up being too exhausted to play with us; to employers who exploit us in bullshit jobs; to powerful men who literally manhandle us; it seems nobody has the time and energy needed to be good company. All of us, regardless of where we are situated, are so exhausted, so full of unprocessed pain and grief, so absorbed in finding immediate distraction from loneliness and angst, that we frequently feel incapable of being good company and, when tested (even just a little), end up acting in ways that later cause us to feel shame—which also accumulates because we feel too overwhelmed to address it!

To me, this calls to mind Peter Maurin's compelling observation that we need to create the kind of world where it is *easier to be good*—although I would modify this to say we need to create the kind of world where it is easier to be *good company to and with others*.[1] As we will see, this can perhaps be summarized by saying that we need to create the kind of world where it is easier to be honest, gentle, affectionate, kind, and comforting—and where it is also easier to both welcome people into relationships where we act in this way towards one another, and where it is easier to part well

---

1. See Maurin, *Easy Essays*. I am suggesting, then, that "goodness" is not so much a static attribute we possess as it is a dynamic way in which others experience us as we develop relationships with them.

with one another when the time comes for us to part. To achieve this world, we need to explore different ways of being together with others. All of us already exist in various kinds of relationships with others. All of us already are responsible to and for some others, accountable to and for some others, connected to and with some others. We may be lonely, but we are not alone (which, of course, is part of what makes our loneliness so tragic). So, of necessity, we begin where we are.

In what follows, I offer what I have learned about being good company and what I have learned from good companions. I offer this text to any who are going out to try and be good company to and with others, especially anyone going to work in the so-called caring professions (social services, healthcare, and so on) as well as anyone who desires to contribute to our mutual thriving. This is not a be-all, end-all presentation of how to be together with others. Rather, it is a suggestion of some foundational elements we must have in place if we are going to alter our collective trajectory and journey to a better place together. What I share is not everything that is needed to get us there, but, I believe, it is one way to start going in that direction. I share personal stories and details, not to offer exact models for imitation, but to inspire creativity and experimental engagement on the part of the reader. I have structured this text so that each section can be read as a short daily meditation. Each section stands alone but, as you will see from the table of contents, each section is also very much connected to the sections that come before and after as we move through the process of meeting one another, creating spaces where it is easier to be good company to and with one another, and also parting from one another. Thus, while it is possible to read this text in whatever order you wish, you may find the experience to be richer if you read it in the order it is written. That said, please know that these are words written from my heart and, as you read them, I hope you also open your heart to hearing them. If you wish, you can write me heart-words in return. I'll read them (and respond, if you desire, and as I am able to do so). Bonne chance et bon courage!

Dan
daniel.oudshoorn.london@gmail.com

1. Welcoming

The origins of the VERB "to meet" connote coming into physical contact with others, uniting or joining together with others, and coming to an agreement together.[1] Today, we say, "it's nice to meet you," but we frequently say it as a throw-away comment—a polite remark made to demonstrate our politeness as we go through the motions that we all go through in order to not feel awkward around people we do not know well or at all. But in our well-mannered politeness, I think we lose some of the richness of the more archaic salutation: "Well met, Stranger!" To say that a person is "well met" is to approve of the particular set of circumstances that led this specific person to be with you at this specific time. It suggests that it is well or good that this person has come to you and come to be together with you. Someone who is "well met" is, to continue with another archaic form of expression, "well come." The etymology of the word "welcome" refers to the fact that a person's arrival suits the desires and wishes of the one welcoming them. Well met and well come!

This is where we must begin—with being welcoming. But also with thinking carefully about the words we use and what we mean by them. I have given a lot of thought to the words, categories, chapter headings, and themes I use in this text. I slowly developed them over two decades as I have worked, thought, lived, listened, learned, tried, succeeded, and failed, in the company of others. Words matter, not because they (as "signifiers") are somehow ontologically or intrinsically connected to the things they represent (the "signified"), but because they help us to make sense of the everything in which we live and from which we distinguish (or cut out) ourselves and others. The everything (or "the world," if we want to call it that) is not made up of words, but words are ways of intervening into everything

---

1. In what follows, when I discuss the roots and origins of various words, I am especially indebted to the Online Etymology Dictionary, which is available here: https://www.etymonline.com/.

and, just as making observations in the realm of quantum physics causes the "observer effect" to occur (i.e., the act of observing things changes what those things are, where they are, and how they act), so also using words creates a "worder effect." Words change what things are. They change where things are. They change how things act. And, most of all, they change us, the makers, givers, and takers of words. By saying this, I don't mean to suggest that words have as much power as those who are paid to study, manipulate, and play with them frequently assert. In fact, after many years spent trying to invite academics and members of dominant classes to reevaluate their participation in our death-dealing culture, years spent trying to invite outsiders to taste the richness of life that is to be found in the company of the left-for-dead, I came to the conclusion that, when it comes to effecting change, words are very weak. Other things—greed, fear, busy-ness, loneliness, selfishness, (but also!) love, wonder, kindness, and intra- and interconnectedness—are much stronger.

In light of these conclusions, one might say that words matter in the same way that glasses matter. They shape our foci, influence what things we see, how we understand those things, and, as a result, how we engage with them. Different people will be drawn to different styles of glasses with different foci, and my prescription will probably be different than yours. In such a context, with people viewing things through very different lenses, words become simultaneously more fragile and more important for, as we communicate with one another, we learn that we use the same words for very different things and for very different reasons. Take the word "love" as an example. It is hard to find another word that produces such different and contradictory actions as love. White Supremacists claim love as the foundation of their actions (the infamous fourteen words—"we must secure the existence of our people and a future for white children"—are a declaration of love), as do anti-racist organizers ("Black Lives Matter!" is also a declaration of love), as do Evangelical Christian parents who beat their children ("spare the rod, spoil the child," and so the loving patriarch, with his belt held aloft declares, "this is going to hurt me a lot more than it hurts you"), as do revolutionaries (to quote Che Guevara: "At the risk of seeming ridiculous, let me say that the true revolutionary is guided by a great feeling of love"), as do social workers (Brené Brown: "Daring to set boundaries is about having the courage to love ourselves"), politicians (Trump: "We will make America loving again. Love it. Love it"), abusive men ("I killed her because I loved her too much"), and even parents who suicide ("my kids would be better off without me," they think as they kick the stool away).[2] Therefore, while you could make

---

2. See Guevara, "Socialism and Man in Cuba"; Brown, "3 Ways to Set Boundaries";

the case that "love" or "loving well" or "loving in ways that people who have been abandoned and left for dead experience as loving" is the subject of this book, I deliberately avoid the language of love until the latter parts because I do not think we are anywhere close to having any kind of consensus when it comes to "what we talk about when we talk about love."[3] By the end of this book, it will be clear what I am talking about when I talk about love. And clarity, when communicating about such muddled, obfuscated, and dangerous things as love, is (in my opinion) a very good thing.

Here, then, to return to my first comment about words ("signifiers") and their connection or lack thereof to what we experience as reality (the "signified"), I wholeheartedly agree with Robert MacFarlane's observation that there should be "no opposition between precision and mystery, or between naming and not-knowing."[4] We speak, not because we think we can aptly summarize, capture, or dispense with everything through words. In fact, having come close to much that is wondrous in the everything, in the world, in others, and in ourselves, I know that *silence* is one important way of *honoring* the wonder; but I have also learned that *speaking*—and speaking very carefully—can be one way of *caring for* the wonder, not only as it exists as a fundamental component of the everything but as it exists in us and in others, in you and in me. Speaking, then, should not be done to exhaust, explain, categorize, and do-away-with the wonder. Rather, speaking should be done to both honor and deepen the wonder. The wonder tends to us and we, in turn, tend to the wonder. But to get to the wonder, in our thoroughly desacralized, and disenchanted world, we need to open ourselves up to texts, images, names, and ways of talking, thinking, listening, and engaging, that may initially strike us as quite strange. To borrow from Mark Fisher's exploration of "the weird and the eerie," we need to return to that which seems all-too-familiar or taken-for-granted, and experience a form of "cognitive estrangement" that leads to a process of "unworlding," precisely so that we can discover that entirely new and wondrous worlds are possible and, in fact, already pushing up from below.[5]

This leads us back around to welcoming. Being welcoming means recognizing the wonder that is in others not as some generic thing that is

---

and the line from Trump comes from a speech he delivered in North Dakota in June, 2018 (see Cillizza, "Donald Trump's 54").

3. See Carver, *What We Talk About When We Talk About Love*.

4. MacFarlane, *Landmarks*, 10.

5. See Fisher, *Weird and the Eerie*. Here, Fisher quotes Darko Suvin's definition of science fiction as the art of "cognitive estrangement" in his examination of "unworlding" as it occurs in Rainer Werner Fassbinder's *World on a Wire* and Philip K. Dick's *Time Out of Joint*.

in the everything (although I also believe this to be true). More than that, welcoming means recognizing this specific other person as the *distinct and uniquely wonder-full person they are*. In this way, being welcoming takes us well beyond the social norms of politeness or the codes of "respect" that tend to govern how social service workers, healthcare workers, and other so-called "caring professionals," interact with people.

Politeness is one way of presenting as though one is friendly while actually maintaining a carefully guarded distance from others. Well-intentioned polite people may not be aware that this is often the case but it only takes one person's refusal to comply with standard protocols of politeness to make this apparent. Mostly, when people ask, "how are you doing?" they don't want an honest answer—they are engaging in a formality and the expectation is that others will reciprocate that formality with an equally disengaged response like, "oh, you know, keeping busy but doing okay!" Politeness then establishes a "friendly" form of contact that is essentially a bridge to completing some kind of purposive transaction (or to end that interaction after the formalities have been exchanged). As such, politeness is a way of meeting people in order to attain a specific result or outcome—it is utilitarian and pragmatic. This is useful in terms of getting things done (and especially useful when we are engaging with strangers to get those things done), but, when it becomes an all-encompassing way of governing our relationships with others, it objectifies people and limits how open we are to and with them, as well as limiting what it is permissible to expect from one another. Essentially, due to its inherent pragmatism, politeness tends towards reducing people to measurable outcomes and, as such, to their ability to attain those outcomes. In programs like social services and government-funded hospitals, where funding and the very existence of the programs are premised upon the production of metrics, stats, and data that demonstrate the relevance and success of the programs, such objectification then becomes not only a requirement but the gold standard of success. Therefore, over time, the objectification of people goes from being viewed as "a necessary evil" to something that is celebrated and rewarded as a "best practice."

Thus, within our society, politeness fulfills a role analogous to the good manners for which slave-owners in the American-occupied South were renowned. As Northerners became increasingly critical of the most explicit and violent forms of racism in the South, Southerners appealed to "Southern hospitality," and their way of being well-mannered and chivalrous, to justify and defend their lifestyle, values, and moral codes (including the valorization of slavery). Hence, politeness was utilized in the Antebellum South to maintain a system that was violent, oppressive, and abusive and, I think, it plays a similar role in the world of social services and healthcare today. Performing politeness demonstrates that you are not looking for a connection or a way of being in relationship with others that exceeds or violates the boundaries established by the utilitarian pragmatism that works to ensure all of our relationships are producing desirable outcomes. Consequently, those who violate the codes of politeness are refused assistance and labeled ("non-compliant," "dangerous," "needy," "attention-seeking," oppositional defiance disorder," and "borderline personality disorder," are all common labels) in order to justify the imposition of multiple disciplinary, exclusionary, or punitive measures. Politeness, then, is far removed from the notion of welcoming I am pursuing here.

I believe that similar criticisms apply to notions of "respect" that govern many of our relationships. Here, it seems to me that various agencies and organizations engage in a particularly insidious form of bait-and-switch: those who access the agencies for help are expected to respect *the rules and regulations* of the agencies. When this takes place, the people working at the agencies will respond by respecting *the people* who access their services. In other words, while workers at agencies will deploy the language of mutual respect, they make their respect of those who access their services conditional upon whether or not those accessing their services follow whatever rules (no matter how arbitrary, unreasonable, ignorant, or death-dealing) the agency has established for the space. There is no genuine mutuality here. More simply, this boils down to the following: "Do what we tell you to do and, in our interpersonal engagements with you, we will try to avoid mistreating you or deliberately disrespecting you. But if you do not obey us, there is nothing we will not do to you." And this is why friends of mine have literally died on the concrete steps of homeless shelters that kicked them out and refused to provide them with any other support. There is no difference between this approach and what greedy bosses have always told exploited workers, what abusive adults have always told abused children, what White plantation owners have always told Black slaves, what guards have always told those whose existence has been criminalized, and what colonizers have always told the colonized: "If you obey and accept the lot we have assigned to you in life, we will not violate you above and beyond the ways in which the status quo is premised upon your violation; but if you do not obey and do not accept the lot we have assigned to you in life, then we will not recognize your membership within the company of the living and will, instead, feel justified in abusing you, abandoning you, and leaving you for dead."

Therefore, to be genuinely welcoming means not only exceeding the standards of politeness and respect that govern social services and healthcare organizations, it also means violating those standards because politeness and respect are connected to broader structures of oppression and abuse. Such oppressive moral codes are barriers to seeing each person in their own uniquely awe-inspiring way. They make the kind of welcoming that is premised upon the understanding that a person is "well come," nearly impossible to believe let alone practice. For almost all services see the people who come to them seeking good company as *victims* of tragedy, as personal *moral failures*, as community *public health concerns*, as intransigent *deviants*, as substance *abusers*, as *criminals*, or as *transients* fated to die or disappear. Consequently, the undergirding assumption behind their approach is that the people who come to them for help or support are most definitely *not* well come. Given everything that is assumed, how can it be possible to say that a person's arrival suits the desires of wishes of the ones to whom they have come seeking good company? Thus, being welcoming also challenges these undergirding assumptions and makes us consider the agency people have, the power that they have to choose, the ways in which they participate in their own life trajectories, all the goodness, beauty, wisdom, strength and experience each person brings, and how—even in the midst of adverse circumstances, even while suffering under the most brutal forms of oppression—people can still be well met and well come.

And, dear reader, if you have come this far and I have already made you uncomfortable or angry but you choose to press on then you are, indeed, well come!

A. Inviting

When I was in my mid-twenties, three friends and I moved into the ground-level apartment of a house in Vancouver's downtown eastside. The downtown eastside (the DTES) has long been labeled as "the poorest urban postal code in Canada" and, while I was already familiar with impoverished communities from time I spent living in Toronto's Parkdale neighborhood (prior to gentrification) and working with abandoned youth on Yonge St. and men deprived of housing on Jarvis St. (while also kicking it in Regent Park before the projects were "redeveloped"), the level and concentration of impoverishment, pain, and suffering in the DTES caught me by surprise. I had not yet learned that, just below the surface of what attracts the attention of outsiders, the DTES was actually the most community-focused and caring neighborhood in which I would ever live. I had not learned to see well, I did not know my neighbors well, and it was the concentration of pain, impoverishment, and folx living in close proximity to Death that I saw.

I started a job working at a residential program for youth deprived of housing or fleeing other forms of abuse who ended up in the neighborhood (approximately 75 percent of youth who are "on the street" are there because of violence in their parents' or caregivers' homes; a high percentage of these youth, roughly 40 percent of all youth who are deprived of housing, have also been deprived of housing because their bio-families rejected them due to their sexual orientation or gender identity and a good many of these kids are innocent, do-gooders from Conservative Christian homes who never did anything to rebel—in other words, kids who are not at all well-prepared to survive "street life"). However, I quickly found that I disagreed with many of the abusive policies of that program and, when youth were kicked out of the program for periods of time (for doing such forbidden things as being twenty-one, sad and traumatized, and daring to return to their apartment under the influence of alcohol or some other self-soothing medication), I would take them home and let them sleep on my couch or, when I worked overnight shifts, in my bed, until they could return to the program. These teens had nowhere else to go and when the program punished them and told them they were bad, that they no longer deserved to be cared for, and threw them onto the streets, there were no other shelter options available to them. They were left isolated, alone, and vulnerable, sleeping in alleyways, trading sex for a place to stay, or trying to find a safe space within flophouses, SROs (bedbug-infested Single Room Occupancy hotels run by millionaire slumlords), or in makeshift camps tucked away within the trees at Stanley Park. So, of course I took them home. I still remember one morning, meeting a young man in the park after I had finished my nightshift and he was huddled under a blanket completely soaked through by the rain because he had been kicked out for smoking a joint while in the shelter program. How could I not take him home? I knew that it would probably cost me my job if the bosses ever found out, but nobody ever ratted me out. I took a risk on trusting the teens and they took a risk on trusting me (because, of course, there are no end to the creeps and predators who prey on homeless youth on the street but also within social services), and, time after time, we discovered that each one of us was trustworthy. I regularly found this to be the case and never once had my trust betrayed by the teens and young adults. For example, on another occasion, I was accompanying a youth to the corner store late one Halloween night and a party bus full of drunken university students drove by slowly. A young White man leaned out the window and yelled, "Go back to East Hastings you fucking bums!" and threw a can of party spray at us. I picked up the can, blessed it with a "fuck you!" and threw it back. By the grace of God, it went through the now barely-opened bus window, hit that young man squarely between the eyes, and knocked him flat on his back. Only then did I recall that I was working, and knocking out abusive and entitled White bros was not in my job description. While the youth I was escorting told other youth in the program about this David-and-Goliath moment, nobody ever ratted me out. And this is what solidarity as complicity (the kind of thing captured in the saying, "accomplices not allies") actually looks like. Taking risks premised upon our commitment to care for one another, which then allows us to understand one another as trustworthy is, in my opinion, a much more accurate illustration of what genuinely *mutual* respect looks like.

As I became more and more aware of the ways in which award-winning social services actually mistreat, abuse, and cause considerable harm to many of those who come to them seeking help, I began to look for alternative ways of being in life-giving and life-affirming relationships with those who were seeking good company. Over against the hierarchical

A. INVITING

and status quo supporting "non-profit industrial complex" (a useful term that I learned from the always-brilliant group, INCITE! Women, Gender Non-Conforming and Trans People of Color Against Violence), I wanted to explore mutually shared, mutually liberating ways of going about celebrating life together.[1] Already in Toronto, I had started seeking more just and caring ways of being together with people who were abandoned, oppressed, and left for dead (taking street friends on family vacations with me, having people crash on my couch, chilling in parks and alleyways with whoever happened to be around). Over and against the abusive power dynamics inherent to social services, I wanted to find better ways to be a *friend* and a *neighbor* to and with others. This is what led myself, my friends Jenna and Bob, and my then-partner to create our "community house" in the DTES. We wanted to be friends with people, we wanted to be part of the community, we wanted to find ways of being in loving relationships with others who were our peers, our equals, our neighbors. Looking back on that time now, I have mixed feelings. I think well-intentioned do-gooders like we were often end up being the shock troops of gentrification in a manner similar to the ways in which occasionally well-intentioned priests were the shock troops of colonization. But I stop to mention this now because we learned an important lesson about being welcoming when we started that community house. That lesson was this: it is not enough to have a welcoming space, you also have to find ways to make people aware of this, you have to find ways to *invite people in*.

The origins of the word "invitation" contain references to being pleasant towards someone, but they also contain the notion of a challenge, and the suggestion of pursuit (even vigorous pursuit!). I like this combination of concepts. Furthermore, "being pleasant towards" also implies being *alluring*, and so "being inviting" means *being pleasant towards others in a way that appeals to them*, that attracts them, that makes them want to accept the invitation. However, because we live in an environment premised upon mutual *mistrust*, wherein it is often easier to exploit and take advantage of others (while sincerely believing that one is doing nothing wrong by acting in that way), both issuing and accepting invitations to and from strangers is challenging. Invitations require courage and risk-taking from all parties involved and there are also the challenges we face, and the awkwardness we experience, when we try to work towards community-oriented relationships of mutuality in a culture that is adverse to such things. However, as I mentioned, I learned that the culture of the DTES had a far more natural

---

1. For more on the non-profit industrial complex, see INCITE!, *Revolution Will Not Be Funded*. For how this plays out within a Foucauldian rubric of neoliberal governmentality, see Willse, *Value of Homelessness* and Eubanks, *Automating Inequality*.

and immediate understanding of community and mutuality than any other neighborhood in which I had lived so, in this regard, my friends and I made the mistake of thinking we came as teachers when, really, we should have come as students.

Thus, for example, when we first started our community house we wanted to do "community meals" in our home twice a week. Especially influenced by the writings of Henri Nouwen regarding L'Arche, as well as various monastic communities, base ecclesial communities formed by liberation theologians in Latin America, anarchist collectives, squats, and post-hippie communes, we felt that sharing meals together was an especially important element of community formation and relationship building.[2] We went out into the neighborhood and invited whomever we happened to meet to come and have dinner with us. It didn't matter who they were or what they were doing, if we met them, we invited them over for dinner. But it turns out that people tend to think strangers who invite them over for dinner are weirdos and maybe serial killers (and, in fact, there was at least one serial killer hunting women in the DTES at this time). It also turns out that people are busy and, as I have seen over the years, people who have been impoverished, dispossessed, targeted by various forces of state-based violence, and cast-out by various charities, are the busiest of all. Just safely surviving a day, getting the meds one needs, keeping one's few belongings safe, getting decent food to eat, finding a toilet and maybe even a shower, and finding a safe place to sleep for the night can take many hours of hard labor. As a result, we learned that just because we were there and just because we thought our intentions were good, did not mean that people were going to come to us. And this is as it should be. Oppressed communities are frequently flooded by people who claim to have good intentions and who genuinely believe they do have good intentions—from poverty porn tourists to social workers to missionaries to bylaw enforcement officers to philanthrocapitalists—who then go on to do considerable, long-lasting, and frequently irrevocable harm. (I still vividly remember the day when I was literally giving the clothes off my back to a sex worker who had been stripped completely naked and kicked out onto a busy street in broad daylight by a bad date and, while I was doing this, a group of teenage boys and their male leaders from a church youth group doing a poverty porn tour were standing idly by, staring, pointing, and laughing.)

---

2. Jean Vanier's work was also a big influence on me at this time but, having since learned that Vanier was continually, regularly, and unrepentantly exploiting his position of power to sexually abuse and assault those who trusted him to care for them (at least 25 adult women without disabilities who came to him for spiritual guidance over a thirty-year period), I no longer have any interest in citing him in a positive way.

A. INVITING

Therefore, in order to distinguish ourselves from the non-profit industrial complex and other death-dealing do-gooders, in order to be alluring, in order to overcome the challenges we faced to getting together in ways not prescribed by neoliberal economics, charity, commodification, and consumerism, we had to vigorously pursue—i.e., go out to seek and find—those whom we wished to welcome. But this pursuit must always be done gently, cautiously, and with the utmost respect for the desires, well-being, and self-expressed needs of those whom one pursues. It is done *invitingly* rather than *forcefully*. One goes out to issue invitations, not to coerce or compel. Furthermore, one does not go out as if on an excursion, mission, or adventure—one goes out to *develop friendships*, to *integrate into the community*, to *introduce oneself*, and to *give others the opportunity to witness* what kind of person one is. In the DTES, we learned to do this in various ways. One of us took to gardening beside the house which led to conversations with many of the folx who traveled down the fairly high-traffic alleyway behind our house. Another of us began to volunteer at an all-women's program that ran a few evenings during the week. I took to doing my schoolwork in Oppenheimer Park—a central hub for people to meet, visit, hang-out, engage in various economic transactions, take medicines, sleep, and, also at times, settle debts or resolve conflicts. A couple of us took to regularly traveling via the alleyways instead of the streets in order to allow the folx who spent time there to become familiar with us and learn that we were not snitches or narcs or, for that matter, individuals interested in taking over the block and serving as the local pharmacists (and I still remember when a friend and I had that conversation with a young Honduran man and his coworkers in an alleyway one morning around 3:00 a.m.—we were checking out the property of one of the millionaire slumlords, but they were concerned that we were scoping out their business; once we figured out what everyone was concerned about, they were more than happy to make friends and give us some solid advice about the security measures that existed around that slumlord's property). I also regularly walked those alleyways at night looking to connect with youth (or others) whom I knew and, to be honest, I always felt safer in those alleyways then I ever felt on Granville St. at 2:00 a.m. when all the clubs were closing and the drunk, misogynistic, self-entitled frat boys with anxious relationships to their own masculinity, were spilling out onto the street (I saw more random violence on Granville at those times then I ever saw in any DTES alley at night, and I remain convinced that there is no more dangerous gang on the street at night than a group of drunk, university-educated, well-to-do, young White cis-men). Only once was I ever in serious danger in an alleyway and that was due to my own ignorance. I was about to find my way into what I thought was an abandoned building because a group of us were considering organizing a squat there in order to try and make a stand against the gentrification that was rapidly accelerating in the neighborhood thanks to the 2010 Olympics. Unbeknownst to me, a rather large and not totally legal organization was using that property to store medicines that they distributed to local street-level pharmacists. My life was possibly saved by an old bank robber whom I knew and who had crashed at our place for awhile after he finished serving a life sentence. I happened to run into him in that alleyway that night and, thankfully, he let me know what was up before I did anything hasty.

Essentially, then, we made ourselves known *as members of the community* and we made it known that we were not a threat to anyone in the community. We found ways to engage that worked with the community—we realized that being inviting to others required us to first *be integrated with others*. And when our pursuit of that integration led us into situations that challenged our pre-existing understanding of what constituted moral, healthy or good living, we reevaluated our values (if we want our invitations to be infectious then we, ourselves, must become infected). Thus, for example, we carried lighters even if we did not smoke because many people in the neighborhood smoked. Answering, "Yes," to the question, "Do you have a light?" was often the best way to casually and unobtrusively begin a conversation. As a smoker at that time, I took to carrying a cigarette behind one of my ears when walking through the neighborhood. Because of this, people would regularly initiate conversation with me ("Do you have a smoke?" or "Can I buy a cigarette off of you?") and I found that this fundamentally altered the dynamics of our engagement. For example, there were cis- and trans-women who worked as "low track" sex workers in the neighborhood. As a stranger and a somewhat sketchy looking male, were I to approach these women, I would be instantly viewed as a potential business transaction or a potential threat (given the level of violence experienced by sex workers and given that sex-working women had been disappeared for many years in that neighborhood). However, if I was passing by with a cigarette behind my ear and if they chose to initiate conversation with me by asking for a cigarette and I stopped to sell or give them one (if they asked to buy one, I sold one; if they asked for a free one, I gave one if I had one to give—because refusing to sell things to others, out of some sense of one's own nobility and generosity is an act that all too easily dehumanizes the recipient of the gift and undercuts the agency which they wish to express and use by purchasing their smoke). While providing the smoke, they might quickly feel me out to see if I wanted anything ("looking for any company tonight, honey?") but when I declined, the conversation would quickly move on and we would share a few words as locals within a community do. Over time, then, these

A. INVITING

relationships developed and, eventually, our home became a space where some sex workers would go to visit, or to check their emails, or to have a meal, or to have a safe place to recover from a bad date.

Therefore, one becomes inviting not by putting a welcome mat in front of the door or by hanging up a "positive space" poster on the office wall (although, in and of themselves, these are not bad things), but by going out to meet people where they are at and by being consistently present, reliable, safe, and open to constantly reevaluate, not others and their values, but you and your own values. As such, being invitational is a particular way of existing in a community and in relationships with others. And you will know when you attain it because others will start issuing invitations on your behalf. They will describe you as inviting, they will suggest that others seek you out, they will listen to their friends discuss their lives or challenges they are facing and they will say, "hey, look, I know this person . . . " Here, you can say not so much that your *reputation* precedes you but that your *invitation* precedes you. When that is the case, you will know you are on the right track.

Furthermore, when that is the case, you will know you have been welcomed into a community. And this is one of the critical lessons to learn about being welcoming: it only works if it is reciprocated and, as much as you may desire to be welcoming, *it is essential that others welcome you*. Here, again, the theme of mutuality comes to the fore in ways that are often missed by institutional services. There is an imbalance of power and a latent paternalism in relationships where one party is always doing the welcoming and the other party is always being welcomed. It requires a certain leveling of the playing field and a certain shared vulnerability and risk to also put oneself forward as a person who, although desiring to be welcoming, also needs to be welcomed. It places you before the critical gaze of others, whereas, in institutional positions of power, you are accustomed to holding a monopoly on that gaze (and having the power to discipline and punish those who try to gaze back at you in anything close to an equally critical manner). Therefore, as much as invitations go out to others, *those who wish to be inviting must also be invited in*.

i. Making Safe Space

Over the years, I have heard innumerable academics, city planners, business and neighborhood associations, and poverty pimps, propose all kinds of "creative solutions" to "our social problems." In all of these solutions, there are inevitably two irredeemable flaws. First, their analysis of the source of the problem is incorrect and so they will never arrive at the solution they claim to desire. Take, for example, the fact that some people in our cities are deprived of housing and, although there are many empty condos, houses, buildings, or even other public spaces that could be used as camp sites, these people are forcibly prevented from living in any of those places and so they are classified as "homeless." However, lest we dehumanize those who have no housing, we do not call them "the homeless" or "homeless people" (as if the state of being homeless is somehow fundamental to their identity or personhood or being). Instead, we refer to them as "people *experiencing* homelessness." But this seemingly sensitive language is misleading. To illustrate this consider some of the pushback that has arisen amongst disabled people. The same language game has been employed by well-meaning, temporarily able-bodied people who try to speak well about disability. They speak about "people with disabilities" rather than "disabled people." However, many disability activists who actually are disabled, prefer to speak of "disabled people." They do this, as Amanda Leduc explains, because they view their "disabled identity" as a fundamental part of who they are and because they feel that speaking of "a person with a disability" separates disability from identity in a way that continues to "malign disability and perpetuate the idea that it is a negative thing."[3] It may be the case that something similar (but not identical) is taking place when people deploy the language of "people experiencing homelessness." Specifically, we may find that this is still a way to malign those who have that experience.

3. Leduc, *Disfigured*, 14–15.

I. MAKING SAFE SPACE

Because how is homelessness experienced? As a *disease*. Thus, municipalities have transitioned from speaking about "ending homelessness" to "*curing* homelessness." Biopsychosocial health indicators then provide the lenses through which we view things like "people experiencing poverty" or "people experiencing homelessness." As a result, the ability to track outcomes that are reported to improve a person's or a community's *health* now drives funding models and program evaluations. What all of this entirely neglects is the fact that "homelessness" and "poverty" are not simply "things that exist out there." This discourse makes it appear as though we can experience or "catch" homelessness or poverty like we catch the influenza virus (the "less fortunate" or "more vulnerable" catch it, the "more fortunate" or "less vulnerable" do not). Furthermore, while we do what we can to protect ourselves from it, the flu, like poverty and homelessness, is always going to be around. What this language game misses—and all too often deliberately masks—is that "homelessness" is not a naturally occurring virus that already exists out there in the world. Rather, *people are actively deprived of housing* and are subsequently just as actively prevented from accessing possible housing or shelter options by laws, cops, security guards, moral codes, property owners, neighborhood associations, and other purportedly "concerned citizens." Like homelessness, poverty is not a natural state. *People are actively impoverished*. Hence, the discourse of public or communal health fails to lead us to the solution to housing-deprivation-framed-as-the-experience-of-homelessness because what is needed is an analysis that prioritizes *oppression*. People don't sometimes randomly catch "The Poverty Virus" and get sick with homelessness as a result. People are systematically oppressed, forcibly dispossessed, actively impoverished, and deliberately left to die by others who have other priorities.

Now, okay, I know, the disease model of poverty resonates today, in part, because well-intentioned liberals want to push back against conservatives who see poverty as reflective of the personal moral failings of "the poor" (i.e., according to conservatives, "the poor" are lazy, they are criminals, they choose vices like sex, drugs, and rock'n'roll over being responsible people, and so on) but this corrective measure is only half correct. Poverty *is* the result of personal moral failures—but it is the result of the personal moral failures of *the rich*. In other words, it only makes sense to view poverty from a health-based perspective if we also view the rich (i.e., those who hoard wealth at the expense of others, those who exploit labor to extract every possible bit of profit they can from people who are treated as disposable bodies, those who accumulate properties and leave buildings empty while people are freezing to death outside, and those who advance legal, political, economic, and communal structures that do more to protect their wealth than they do to protect the lives of others or the well-being of a community), not as paragons of health but as *the disease itself*.

The second critical component missing in the innumerable "creative solutions" that have been brought forward to address "our social problems," is that in almost all of the solutions that are brought forward by those who are trying to "*manage* homelessness" or "*cure* poverty," the agencies and organizations pitching the new idea lack the self-awareness needed to realize that they are not failing because they have tried everything and now need to try something else (a new solution, a more creative idea or something based on collecting more and more and more data about every component of the people whose lives they claim to manage and cure). They are failing because *they never did even the most basic things well to begin with*. It is this observation that leads me to the critical importance of making or holding space for others and of ensuring that, first and foremost and before all else, this space is *safe*.

Over the years, I have learned that it is impossible to develop community spaces premised upon mutual aid, mutual respect, mutual care, and open and honest communication, or spaces that work towards meeting the self-identified needs of community members and of the community as a whole, if the space, itself, is not safe. However, almost every agency—from hospitals to homeless shelters to drop-in centers—takes the wrong approach to safety. They try to create environments where their doctors, nurses, social workers, case managers, community support workers, mental health workers, outreach workers, supervisors, occupational therapists, counselors, psychiatrists, security guards, administrators, social service workers, volunteer coordinators, and nurse practitioners, do not feel uncomfortable. Stated succinctly, safety is understood *as the absence of discomfort in those who are paid to be present*. As a result, when those who are paid to be present experience fear in response to the actions or presence of a certain person or demographic of people, this fear makes them feel uncomfortable. Their institutional solution is almost always to remove that person or that demographic of people from their space. Anything or anyone that provokes discomfort-experienced-as-fear is to be excised, immediately terminated, or shut down, so that those who are paid to be present can go back to feeling comfortable. This, then, leads to people being banned, barred, suspended, restricted, or otherwise prevented from accessing spaces that offer critical supports to them (although the oh-so-sensitive healthcare workers don't like to think of themselves harming people in this way—after all, they like to think of themselves as non-judgmental, empathetic, and inclusive—so instead of using the language of banning or barring, they issue "step aways" ... only these "step aways" last a month and result in the police being called

I. MAKING SAFE SPACE

and trespassing orders being given if the person doesn't "step away" for that long). This approach to safety then *actually endangers and harms those for whom the space is said to exist*. Placating the comfort-based fears of those who are paid to be present creates an environment that is *unsafe* for those who are present because they are seeking help, support, or good company (i.e., it makes the environment unsafe for those who don't have to be financially coerced to be there in the first place!).

This is especially harmful because with the increasing professionalization of social work and healthcare—wherein staff members in various agencies are paid to be present not because they come from impoverished or oppressed communities or because they have meaningful "lived experience" and have worked through similar challenges, but because they had enough money and personal supports to complete multiple levels of post-secondary education—many of those who are paid to be present bring in fears that are rooted in stigma, biases, and ignorance. Fears, in other words, that are associated with the comforts afforded by fenced-in and well-protected privilege rather than fears that are actually rooted in genuine threats to one's self or others. Many have their feeling of safety shaped by the racism that still undergirds settler colonialism, or by White privilege and White fragility, or by the stigmatizing, inaccurate and harmful presentations of people like crystal meth users, people who see or hear things others don't, Muslims, or members of racialized populations, that are all over social media and in the news.

Therefore, if spaces are to be made genuinely safe for those who are not paid to be present there, but who choose to be present (and who perhaps feel they have literally nowhere else they can go), those who are paid to be present must be asked to re-examine their privileges and their concomitant comfort levels and fears. Instead of rushing to terminate anything that causes them to feel discomfort-as-fear, they must ask themselves: *why do I feel afraid right now?* Here, the critical question is this: *Do I feel afraid because what is happening is unfamiliar to me, or do I feel afraid because this situation is genuinely unsafe?* What I have learned over the last twenty plus years—including six years spent facilitating a community space for people who were kicked out of every other social service and public space in the city because they were considered too violent, too psychotic, too non-compliant, or too sick (in all the wrong ways), to be able to be around others—is that in the overwhelming majority of cases, I feel afraid because something is unfamiliar. Over and over again, I have learned that situations I was taught or encouraged to interpret as unsafe actually were not.[4]

4. In fact, as a life-long pedestrian, motor vehicles have been and remain a far greater threat to my personal safety than the people I have journeyed with for the last twenty-plus years.

Social workers or mental health workers who work with people who are "emotionally dysregulated" sometimes talk about helping people to "expand their window of tolerance." By encouraging this practice, they are trying to assist people who feel large amounts of pain and discomfort—and who then might engage in activities that *temporarily* sooth their pain or ease their discomfort while also contributing to the entrenchment of their suffering over the long-term (like self-harming via cutting or seeking comfort via an abusive partner)—to explore ways to feel more okay even in the midst of higher levels of pain or discomfort than they would previously find tolerable. This can actually be pretty solid advice. More and more, I have realized that people—myself included—have suffered *irreparable* harm and *irreplaceable* losses and so, rather than trying to make it so that this harm and loss no longer exist, we need to actually find ways to be okay with those harms and losses *still existing* within us in some capacity (more on this below, in the sections on "Grieving" and "Commemorating"). However, agencies need to apply this same insight back onto the fears felt by those who are paid to be present—especially given that the vast majority of these fears end up being unfounded, false, and arising from stigma and biases that have not yet been uprooted (sadly, uprooting these things takes some time and care, mostly because people involved in so-called caring professions are very attached to viewing themselves as welcoming, inclusive, non-discriminatory, and unbiased people and so this makes it hard for them to admit when their actions reveal that this is not always the case).

The first step to making genuinely safe space, then, is this: *prioritizing the safety felt by those who choose to attend to space, over the comfort felt by those who are paid to attend*. In fact, given that many aggressive and violent acts in community and healthcare agencies result from people feeling unsafe—i.e., aggression and violence are almost always a *defensive* reaction premised upon the perception of threats to oneself—prioritizing the safety of those who choose to attend actually ends up producing an environment that is genuinely safer (if not always more comfortable) for those who are paid to attend. This means re-orienting one's comfort level around various activities—from raised voices to waving limbs to passionate disagreements—so that they match the community of people one is trying to serve. On this point, the enforcement of bourgeois standards around manners, what it means to be polite, well-behaved, and well-spoken, should never be correlated with whether or not a space is safe. As already stated above, such things are all too often used to justify violence against oppressed groups and, when these measures are related to safety, we can be sure that it is not the safety of those who choose to access the space that is being prioritized.

Take, for example, the community space my friend Mechele and I helped to create and hold for people who had been kicked out of all other services and communal spaces. Many people attended this space because they saw and heard things that other people did not see or hear and what they saw and heard was sometimes very upsetting to them (psychiatrists use terms like "psychosis" and "paranoid delusions" to describe this but people in the Mad Pride movement or in other cultural contexts push back against these terms). As a result, these people frequently yelled, groaned, and cursed in ways that those who were not familiar with them might view as scary or aggressive. Because paid staff members felt uncomfortable with behaviors like these, and had no desire to become familiar with the people who were experiencing these things, these folx were now kicked out of shelters, drop-ins, hospitals, libraries, and shopping malls, and the cops regularly chased them out of city parks or away from other places where pedestrians were present. Having nowhere to go, and hearing that we were welcoming (our invitation preceded us), they came to us. While with us, they would continue to yell, groan, and curse, but they were familiar members of the community, other people who came to us knew them from the street, knew that they were not violent, knew that they had nowhere else to go, and—themselves knowing what it is like to have nowhere else to go—they showed considerable compassion, patience, and care towards these members of the community. Nobody felt unsafe just because there was a fellow sitting in the corner of the room grunting and occasionally yelling "FUUUUCK!!" or "Fuck off, asshole!" at someone or something we could not see or hear. And, if someone new came and did feel uncomfortable, community members would take the time to explain to that person that everything was okay.

This is just one example, but prioritizing the safety and well-being of those who come seeking assistance also challenges our comfortable notions of safety in other ways. Almost all agencies and organizations resort to *force* to address the discomforts felt by those who are paid to be present and to terminate the supposedly unsafe situation and restore the equilibrium they desire. For legal reasons (which are also ideological reasons, given how "caring professionals" don't like to think of themselves as those who use physical force—i.e., *violence*—in order to compel oppressed people to do what they, the rule-enforcers, want them to do), this means involving the police. Police are called very quickly, they are called very often, and they are not only viewed as critical supports but as valued allies and, in many ways, *experts* on who or what is safe or unsafe. This occurs despite the fact that the police have been regularly called-out for providing false and misleading information about both individuals ("look out for that guy, he's really dangerous," they said to me as I tried to stop them from ticketing some of my close friends for drinking by the railroad tracks) and various substances ("you can overdose and die if you get even the smallest amount of fentanyl on your skin," they lied and said to a group of social service providers who were gathered for a presentation on street drugs).[5] However, if you spend any amount of time actually listening to or living with any community of oppressed people, it becomes obvious that the police are actually one of the greatest threats to their safety. For members of the middle- or upper-classes, or other privileged groups who are accustomed to police treating them with dignity and respect, while protecting their property and their sense of safety, this can be a very difficult and unsettling truth to accept. And yet, over and over again, in every city I have known in Canadian-occupied territories, I have witnessed the absolutely brutal, death-dealing force that police officers have directed at oppressed people—even as police have rebranded themselves as "police services" rather than "police forces," in efforts to blur the lines between healthcare and policing. I have known many teenage girls who had been deprived of housing who were raped by police officers, many teenage boys who were deprived of housing who were beaten just for fun by police officers, many Indigenous people taken on the "Cherry Beach express" in Toronto (where cops took people to beat them, pepper spray them, and then put them cuffed and choking in the trunk of a squad car where they would leave them to feel like they were dying—in fact, I have sometimes wondered if part of the reason why cops ignore people who say "I can't breathe" is because they are so accustomed to almost killing people all the time that they don't realize when they actually cross the line from very-nearly-killing to actually killing), others taken on "Starlight tours" in the prairies (i.e., dumped outside the city without a coat or shoes on a winter night when the temperature is negative forty degrees), others beaten viciously then put on a bus to another town and told to never come back, countless broken bones, missing teeth, sexual assaults, mockings, stalkings, acts of bullying and, in the massage parlor where underaged girls were being sexually trafficked in downtown Vancouver, any member of the police who wanted to fuck a child received free perks—two for the price of one, that kind of thing—and in exchange, the client-cops would give advance notice to the traffickers if a raid was being planned.

Consequently, when I was helping to facilitate the community space for those who were not welcomed anywhere else, I learned that while community members were fine with people acting in some unusual ways,

---

5. In fact, police at all levels lie so frequently that they, themselves, have an in-house term for what they do in court rooms—"testilying" (see Stern, "Police Lie"; Stern highlights not only the ubiquity of lying in policing but the fact that policing, as we know it, would not be possible if cops did not lie all the time to everyone).

they did want us to do something about the police who came around the property, who tried to intimidate people there and who, generally, made people feel unsafe in the space. The program that had previously existed at our location operated within an informal, buddy-buddy type of relationship with the police. Although people who attended that program were supposed to be protected by confidentiality laws and protocols, the police regularly received information from staff members there. Staff members would call-in people whom the police had reported as breached, they would provide information from client files to the police, and they would help with investigations, always taking the police at their word. In return, when staff members at that program felt unsafe, the police would respond quickly to their calls. While not actually legal or ethical, this kind of "you scratch my back, I scratch yours" relationship is very common between social services and healthcare providers and police ~~forces~~ services (from what I have observed, agencies that do not act this way are actually a very small minority). Therefore, in order to help create a space where oppressed people felt safe, Mechele and I had to address this. Here, we were able to use the law against itself. Given that our space was officially classified as a community mental health program, the standard of confidentiality was higher than usual (rather than falling under the regular laws around privacy, i.e., Ontario's Freedom of Information and Protection of Privacy Act, the program actually fell under the Personal Health Information Protection Act). This means that, unless subpoenaed, no information about any person in the space was to be given out without the free and informed prior consent of that person. Furthermore, given that we operated on private property, we had the right to tell the police to leave unless we had invited them in, unless they had a warrant, or unless they were in "fresh pursuit" (i.e., were literally chasing after someone whom they had solid grounds to believe had committed a crime and this person ran into our space to try and escape from them). Consequently, we immediately stopped providing information to the police and, when police showed up on our property, we politely but firmly told them they had to leave (although we did offer to let people know—if we happened to see them—that the police were looking for them).

The police were unhappy with this and, because I was usually the one to speak with them, they began to bully and target me. Some days, I had six different cruisers show up in our parking lot and, when I went out to speak with the officers, they said things like, "So you're the guy who doesn't want the cops coming around, eh? We just wanted to see what you look like. We'll remember you. And we'll remember this if you ever call us looking for help." They acted quite aggressive with me (although always in ways where they could deny their actions and say that, oh, I must have just misunderstood).

One day, when walking home from work at this time, a cruiser slowly followed along behind me for several blocks. Having been personally assaulted by cops more often than I have ever been physically harmed by any person from an oppressed group, this was a very scary experience for me. I found inspiration in Maggie Kuhn's words: "Leave safety behind. Put your body on the line. Stand before the people you fear and speak your mind—even if your voice shakes." And so I did and I faced into my fears, and sometimes my voice *did* shake when I told the cops they had to leave, but I still told them they had to leave, because I was committed to helping to create a space that was safe for people who were regularly harmed by the police.

As a result, over the years, I learned to understand courage in the following way. Courage is not the absence of fear but *the refusal to allow fear to make us act in ways that betray our most deeply-held values*. If some people now view me as courageous, it is not because I do not feel fear—in fact, as a survivor of sexual, physical, and emotional violence as a child (and as an adult), as an introvert, and as a "naturally" shy and gentle person, I think that I am more easily frightened than most people. If people view me as courageous, it is because I have learned to not permit my fears to be the sole determinant of how I act when I am afraid. Because my fear of the police was well-founded. As their bullying behavior towards me and our space continued to escalate, there was a stabbing close to our location. Police were attending to that situation when a "mentally ill" (but essentially harmless) man passed by and yelled some curse words at them, and accused them of spying on him and following him to London from the east coast of Turtle Island, before entering into our space. One of the young male police officers took great offence to this and, rolling up his sleeves, began yelling at the man and walking towards our space. I managed to reach the officer before he was able to enter the door and I explained to him that the man was unwell, that he meant no harm, that he was now in a place where he was safe, and would be well cared for. However, the officer was enraged and was emphatic that he was going to go into the space to "get that guy." I explained that, in fact, our program was private property, that no crime had been committed, and that the officer was not permitted to enter. I stood in front of our door while explaining this as calmly, gently, and as non-threateningly as possible. In response, the officer picked me up and threw me into a wall. Originally, the cops involved (the incident was witnessed by the officer's young male partner and their older male staff sergeant) tried to fabricate a story to suggest I was at fault and lucky to not be charged for assaulting a police officer, but after we showed them the video we had of the event, their story (and tone!) very quickly changed. Because of this, we were finally able to get the police to leave our space alone.

1. MAKING SAFE SPACE

Accomplishing this made the space far safer for people who experienced oppression because community members saw how we were dedicated to make the space safe, first and foremost, in *ways that they identified as safe*, and because they also saw that we sometimes put ourselves in scary situations to accomplish this. Many of them had also experienced the hands and boots of cops on their own bodies, and I still remember one cop laughing about how he always used his boots and never his hands when he beat people so that there was no evidence to prove what he had done (a boot is easily polished, skinned knuckles take time to heal). Consequently, a wonderful and genuine spirit of mutual care and respect came to define the space. This was not respect as it is usually practiced in social services (i.e., you respect the rules and we will not be total assholes to you); rather, it was more like the kind of respect that people who have gone into battle together, fought valiantly, and survived, feel for one another.

This was of critical importance because, given that many people who chose to spend time in that space were suffering a great deal, given that many of them had become accustomed to the violence of other institutional environments, given that many of them felt as though they were carrying more than they could bear, given that many were sad, angry, frustrated, overwhelmed, and coping with everything that one copes with when one is treated unjustly, and given that our space was very small and the number of people who chose to be there was constantly increasing, it was inevitable that conflicts would occur. It was also important because, once it became obvious that Mechele and I would not break confidentiality laws, violate professional and personal ethics, or betray the people we desired to serve, the police made it abundantly clear to us that they would be in no hurry to come to our aid if we called them for help—they wanted us to understand that receiving their help was a privilege not a right, and one that we forfeited by no longer breaking the law for them (they said this like it was a bad thing, but all I could think of was Brendan Behan's observation: "I have never seen a situation so dismal that a policeman [sic] could not make it worse"). But this did mean that, precisely because we were dedicated to making and holding safe space, we sometimes needed to be the ones to help people through conflict.

Conflict, of course, is part of any relationship, any family, and any community and what matters is not if conflict is or is not present (although high levels of conflict are disconcerting and worth exploring), what matters is how people mediate and resolve conflict. Unfortunately, social services and healthcare agencies *do not permit conflict* and, instead of trying to mediate or resolve conflicts, they rush to terminate them, penalize those involved, and restore the well-ordered "peace" desired by fearful or uncomfortable staff members. This response harms oppressed people and further endangers them. Instead of rushing to terminate conflicts or have conflicts moved "off property," those who are invested with the responsibility of holding space for others (especially those paid to do this), need to know when to not intervene as conflicts work themselves out, and when to intervene in order to try and encourage people who are hurt, scared, angry, or upset to stay safe while working through conflict and seeking some kind of mutually acceptable resolution. Sometimes this means helping to clarify confusion. Sometimes this means helping people to remember the values of the community space in which they are in, sometimes this means helping people know when they are at an impasse and providing people with ways out of the conflict that do not make people feel like they will lose the respect of others for walking away (this is especially true in conflicts involving weapons—almost nobody actually wants to be in a knife fight but many people do not know how to get away from the fight, once the knives are drawn, without losing face; having a third party intervene can make that possible for all the other parties involved even though, I confess, jumping into the middle of knife fights, or possible knife fights, is one of the things that scares me the most). Furthermore, given that people involved in conflict experience heightened vulnerability, they also experience heightened sensitivity, so any intervention and mediation must avoid being aggressive, authoritarian, or shame-based. However, if those who are paid to be present in these spaces have demonstrated that they have the safety of the community and its members foremost in their minds—in other words, if they have demonstrated that they intervene not in order to police people or enforce norms that are rejected by the community, but because they actually care about the community and all its members—then they will have earned the right and respect necessary to intervene and be heard in moments when emotions are running high. People will listen to them and, even if people are new to a community and do not know those who try to intervene or mediate conflicts, their peers will assist and vouch for the mediators.

This is why, for example, I had the ability to ask the most respected street-level pharmacist in the neighborhood to respect the boundaries around our community space—especially when it came to transacting business or settling debts at our location in ways that conflicted with our shared values—and he would grant my requests. He knew that I wasn't asking because of my commitment to policing, prohibition, or "law and order." Quite the opposite. He knew that I was actually letting him know when the people who worked for him were becoming heatscores[6] and so whenever I asked

---

6. A "heatscore" is someone who behaves in a way that draws unwanted attention to

him to pull his people back, he did, and whenever I spoke about our values, he agreed those were his values as well. Not so tangentially, it also helped that, once I knew my program was moving onto turf that he felt was his, I bought a bike from him in order to begin to intentionally build a certain kind of rapport with him.

Over time, what this commitment to providing a safe space where conflicts can be resolved establishes is a culture of safety that all members of the community buy into and do what they can to develop and support. People who feel unsafe almost everywhere else they go—at risk of being robbed in a shelter, at risk of being kicked out of the shelter by staff members, at risk of being fined for taking their medication in public washrooms, at risk of being arrested for trying to earn some money so that they have gifts to give their kids when they see them next, at risk of being assaulted by drunken university students, at risk of being raped, beaten, and robbed by cops, at risk of being sold the wrong medicines or given a hot-shot, at risk of catching pneumonia, at risk of completely breaking down in the never-coming-back-again kind of way, at risk of freezing to death, at risk of being disappeared without anyone knowing, or noticing, or caring, or looking for them ever again—are keen to promote the safety of a space once they are assured that it is safe. As a result, when people get upset, friends frequently step-up to comfort them. When disagreements occur, companions help to resolve them. When other ways of being in relationship with people that violate the safety of the space are brought into the space (for example, if someone tries to collect on a debt), people are reminded by others who live by that code that this place is not intended to be used for that purpose. Debts can be collected elsewhere. Not here.

In other words, if all the organizations, agencies, and do-gooders would actually do the necessary work required to establish the most basic and fundamental elements of what constitutes a life-giving and -affirming community, then these elements become *self-propagating*. This requires those who make and hold space to be *proactive* in culture-building rather than simply being *reactive* to other cultures that are permitted to dominate the space (be that the culture of policing or the culture of the prison—cultures which are remarkably similar, largely because prison culture is established by the guards who take their lead from the cops). If the collective who views the space as theirs—their home, their community, their place to go for help, their last resort—are not actively and proactively working towards building a particular culture that is mutually agreed upon, then others will build a

---

their activity. Frequently, this would be someone who engages in a criminalized activity in a way that draws the attention of the public, security guards, or the police (who are the real "heat").

different culture. A much more violent, fearful, selfish, and distrustful culture will become self-propagating (since that is the default culture of the neoliberalism that dominates public life today, and it is especially forcefully imposed upon those whom neoliberalism polices most heavily). When that occurs, unless the trajectory of the culture can be changed, those who try to do things like make safe space will find themselves fighting a losing battle, going from crisis to crisis, conflict to conflict, until either the authoritarian violence of the police or the lateral violence of gang-bangers becomes the means of restoring some simulacrum of "safety" to the community. But, of course, truly marvelous things can occur if the opposite trajectory is pursued and falls into its own self-reinforcing feedback loop and that is why, for example, for every year that we worked at building the community space for people who were branded as too dangerous to go elsewhere, I can count on one hand the number of times we actually had to call-out for support. For example, in one year, we called the police three times (three near-death situations involving weapons and people with a willingness to use them in fatal ways), whereas a program that saw many of the same people in the same building during different hours called the police more than *one hundred and twenty-five times*—in other words, we called once every four months and they called a little more than once every three days (although, that being said, I personally view those four calls as times when we failed our community and as a community, even though the calls were made because there was a very real chance of someone being very seriously hurt or killed); I have a shirt that says, "NICE PEOPLE DON'T CALL COPS," and this is a good way of reminding myself that I was not a very nice person on those three occasions, and my inability to imagine someway of being nice in those situations does not, somehow, take away from the fact that what I did was not nice (sadly, sometimes we have to do "not nice" things, as I will explore in more detail in the section on "Exiling"). Therefore, although we have all been indoctrinated into cultures premised upon violence, fear, selfishness, and distrust, we can still carve out spaces that are truly welcoming and that demonstrate this by being safe.

B. Acknowledging

In recent years, community and other public gatherings in Canadian-occupied territories have started incorporating "land acknowledgments" into their introductory welcoming remarks. It's an interesting development that demonstrates the hybridity, mimicry, and ambivalence that exists in colonized spaces and how grassroots resistance movements can push institutional authorities towards more liberative practices, while institutional authorities simultaneously try to co-opt liberative practices and grassroots movements in order to make them contribute to the smooth functioning of an oppressive status quo.

Land acknowledgments are rooted in the political practices of the sovereign Indigenous nations that were colonized, dispossessed, and occupied by European settlers and then by the Canadian state. However, despite Canada's best (and ongoing) efforts to annihilate or assimilate those who have claims to territorial sovereignty, these nations and practices persist in Canadian-occupied territories. One of the results of this is that, for several decades, grassroots movements that participated in struggles for decolonization (whether because they were Indigenous-led, had Indigenous members, or were acting as friends, allies, or accomplices to and with Indigenous groups) have used land acknowledgments within their own gatherings as a way of recognizing various Indigenous sovereignties, as a way of recognizing the ways in which all Canadians are complicit in colonization, and as a way of affirming and making themselves accountable to their commitment to decolonization.

However, most of these movements and their practices were small and little-known to the broader Canadian public. Then, between 2008 and 2015, media and public attention focused increasingly on Canada's so-called "Truth and Reconciliation Commission" (one of the responses to the "Indian Residential School Settlement Agreement" struck in 2006 between the government of Canada and approximately 86,000 living survivors of

Canada's genocidal "Indian Residential Schools").[1] The government was hoping that this would absolve Canada of the guilt related to its past (and supposedly not present) treatment of Indigenous peoples and chart a way forward to "reconciliation" and "harmony." Justin Trudeau and the Liberal Party of Canada adopted much of this rhetoric in their successful 2015 federal election campaign (although it was entirely and markedly absent in their successful re-election campaign in 2019, when it had become apparent that the current Liberals, like their Conservative and Liberal predecessors, would do anything to ensure that oil pipelines, mines, tar sands, and so-called "natural resource" extraction corporations would always have their desires met, regardless of what that meant for Indigenous peoples or lands). Justin Trudeau's assertion that fulfilling the federal "duty to consult" Indigenous peoples prior to destroying their land and poisoning their water was, in no way, a "duty to attain consent," exemplifies the Liberal approach to these things. Essentially, to pick a closely related point of comparison when it comes to relations between the Canadian state and law and Indigenous peoples, this is like a rapist saying that rape is legal as long as the rapist asks first ("she said 'no,' but I asked first so I raped her anyway and that's okay according to the laws us rapists have made" is essentially the Liberal approach to Canadian/Indigenous relationships—the Conservative approach, of course, is to skip asking and go straight to the raping). "Reconciliation," Canadian-style, means nothing more or less than forcing Indigenous peoples to assimilate or die. Reconciliation, then, is a more up-to-date tool in the ongoing process of genocidal colonization.

However, even after the completion of the Truth and Reconciliation Commission, attention to Canadian/Indigenous relations continued to be brought before the public eye, notably through a multi-year campaign that arose from grassroots movements led by Indigenous women which brought attention to the extremely high number of unsolved cases of missing and murdered Indigenous women and girls in Canadian-occupied territories. This led to another (highly controversial) federal inquiry that ran between 2016 and 2019, and forced the government of Canada and Canadians in general to reckon more deeply with the ongoing history of settler colonialism in the territories that they claim as their homeland.[2]

Partially in response to this, land acknowledgments have become a way in which Canadians have tried to demonstrate that they are not like

---

1. National Centre for Truth and Reconciliation, "Final Report." For more, see Government of Canada, "Indian Residential Schools Settlement Agreement."

2. The Final Report of this inquiry is available in National Inquiry into Missing and Murdered Indigenous Women and Girls, "Reclaiming Power and Place."

B. ACKNOWLEDGING

their violent and death-dealing forebearers, that they are sensitive and woke, and that they are committed to reconciliation and harmony. A standard acknowledgment—whether being offered by a politician, CEO, poverty pimp, academic, gallery owner, or event coordinator—tends to run something like this:

> We would like to begin by acknowledging that we are gathered together on the traditional territories of the X, Y, and Z peoples. We recognize the long history these peoples have not only with this land but also with our City and Region [usually mentioned by their Canadian names and any relevant treaties can also be mentioned at this point—if people are especially woke they may also mention the watershed that feeds their territory and use a local Indigenous name for that watershed]. We recognize that X, Y, and Z peoples were the caretakers of this land for many generations before Europeans arrived here and that they continue to care for it today. We thank them for this and for the ways in which they have welcomed us here.

There are a few things worth highlighting about this. First, this recitation—wherein the speaker has almost always never bothered to learn how to properly pronounce the various Indigenous names mentioned—has become something of an inane formality that is rushed through in order tick the "good ally" box and then get on to the stuff that people think *actually* matters. Second, the way in which this is phrased suggests that the "territories" are now the legal property of Canada even if they are also, and simultaneously the *traditional territories* of *peoples* or *caretakers*. All of this language is cleansed of any obvious political overtones. Territories, not nations, are mentioned. Peoples are named but, again, not as subjects or citizens of sovereign Indigenous nations. This bias towards Canadian title or ownership of the land (that Indigenous peoples took care of so well before we got here, thank you very much), is only furthered when land acknowledgments contain references to peoples who are no longer living today (at least not in ways that Eurocentric ontologies and epistemologies recognize as living—more on that in a moment). It is almost as if a succession of ownership is postulated. Thus, in the territories where I reside, European histories move sequentially from the Attawandaron (who are no longer living in a way recognized by Europeans), to the Anishinaabe (who came here thousands of years ago), then the Haudenosaunee and the Lenape (who came here more recently), and finally to the Europeans (who have only existed, as Canadians, since 1867).

Consequently, land acknowledgments (a political act that was originally part of Indigenous political practices, adopted by others seeking to affirm Indigenous sovereignty over colonized territories and stolen land), have been exploited and partially transformed into a gesture that is used to support *Canadian* sovereignty and the ongoing existence of the *Canadian* state. Hence, the hybridity, mimicry, and ambivalence that marks the colonial context. The Canadian state has been forced to acknowledge what it has tried to deny since its origin—that, in fact, this land is the traditional territories of Indigenous peoples who were here before us and who continue to live alongside of us—but the state, its agents, beneficiaries, and well-intentioned citizens alter this acknowledgment so that, rather than displacing the Canadian state and exposing it for what it is (i.e., an illegitimate, immoral, and illegal occupation), it *displaces Indigenous sovereignties in order to provide comfort to Canadians and affirm Canada's claim to the land*. In this way, the Canadian adaptation of land acknowledgments offers what ends up being the simulacrum of welcome—it is essentially welcoming (and reassuring) to *Canadians* but only welcoming to Indigenous peoples if they choose to view themselves, not as subjects of sovereign nations but as culturally distinct (and marketable) minorities within the mosaic of Canadian multiculturalism.

The welcome that is contained in a proper land acknowledgment, as they have been taught to me, is very different than this. At the heart of a land acknowledgment is *the land itself*. However, the notions of "the land" that are indigenous to the epistemologies of Great Turtle Island are very different than Eurocentric and capitalist notions of land. According to local Indigenous knowledge, the land is not simply the soil or the earth; the land is much more than that. The land includes earth and water and air, stone and sun and moon. Because of this, the land is also at the core of *all that is*. So the plant nations, and fish nations, the four-leggeds and various other animal or insect nations, are all *a part of the land*. Not only this but Indigenous understandings of the land extend backwards and forwards in time—one's ancestors are a living part of the living land (which is why, to return to the example above, it makes sense to acknowledge those like the Attawandaron when speaking about the land not only in the past but in the present) and one relates to the land in ways that take the next seven generations into consideration. Thus, *acknowledging the land is a way of acknowledging the inter- and intra-connectedness of all the constituent elements of the land*. It acknowledges that each sovereign manifestation of life *belongs*. Furthermore, this is an egalitarian form of belonging. Recognizing plants, fish, animals, and others, as *nations*, acknowledges the sovereignty of these

B. ACKNOWLEDGING

various constituents of the land and affirms that all constituents are equal members and co-participants in the formation of our collective life together.

This is also why it makes sense to draw special attention to people who are Indigenous to the land when acknowledging the land (and why it also makes no sense whatsoever to engage in land acknowledgments without also calling for and working towards decolonization and the recognition of Indigenous sovereignties)—these are the people *of* this land. And this, too, reverses another Eurocentric epistemological expectation. Because indigenous people are of the land, it is not so much that the land belongs to them, as that *they belong to the land* (as such, it demonstrates why the notion of people owning land is nonsensical and unethical within Indigenous knowledge systems and why the transformation of land into property is at the core of colonization and theft). My people—settlers, colonizers, occupiers, and thieves from Europe—are not of this land. Consequently, acknowledging the land means allowing the sovereign peoples and nations of this land to determine how or where we belong. This is a critical component of belonging—belonging is something one does together with others. One belongs in certain relationships and these relationships have certain obligations and expectations. To belong together with others means that one is accountable to some others, responsible to and for some others, and expected to participate in ways that contribute to the greater thriving of all others. Belonging is an experience that assigns great value to people—"you have a home here with us and a critical part to play in this with all of us"—but it is also a thing that assigns responsibilities to people and, in doing so, recognizes their agency, powers, and abilities to fulfill those responsibilities.

All of this has a great deal of significance for those who desire to be welcoming. First, is shows that welcoming is always local, contextual, and specific to one's place. Paying attention to these factors is important because—like a politician murdering the pronunciation of an Indigenous nation's name (usually accompanied with some kind of joking apology, which elicits a lot of laughs from other White people who are thinking, "yeah, I wouldn't want to try and pronounce that in public either!")—it shows how people can think they are being welcoming when, in fact, they are being unwelcoming, abusive, and contributing to the broader dynamics of oppression.

Second, it shows that being welcoming means acknowledging that *people belong here*, in this space, with us. Furthermore, because they belong here, in this space, with us, they actually play a critical role in accomplishing the well-being of everyone else who is connected to this space. They are essential to us, collectively, thriving. This actually goes back to the origins of the word "acknowledge" which communicates the idea of "admitting or showing one's knowledge of" someone and which also contains the idea of *recognizing what is due to others*. Therefore, we welcome people by showing that we know that they fit in this space with us, and by recognizing their place therein. This means that we both expect people to do what they can to fulfill their role in the community, and we also expect that people have a great deal of ability to accomplish this. In this regard, a lot of the stigma, discrimination, and oppressive dynamics (sometimes referred to as "burn-out," "jadedness," "real talk," or "compassion fatigue") in social services and healthcare must be exposed, counter-acted, and overcome. That "caring professionals" refuse to acknowledge the people whom they claim to care for, says more about how these professionals go about structuring life together with others than it says about what people are or are not capable of. I have seen the proof of this—despite all the ways in which nay-sayers who were "experts in the field" told me our "overly idealistic" efforts were doomed to failure—time after time after time.

Third acknowledging belonging also means that, if people are absent or lost, the community itself is deeply wounded and the ecosystem balance is thrown-off and needs to be attended to. I will spend more time on this point in Section Four ("Parting"), below.

Fourth, welcoming others by acknowledging them means not only attending to the specificity of place but also attending to the specificity of each person. It means recognizing, honoring, celebrating and caring for that which is distinct about each individual. It means acknowledging their pain, acknowledging their fears, acknowledging their strengths, acknowledging their intentions, acknowledging their efforts, acknowledging their dreams, acknowledging their despair, acknowledging their needs, and also acknowledging their unique location and where they are situated in relation to others. There are four ways of doing this that I think are especially important when it comes to being welcoming. These are: greeting, prioritizing (wasting time together with), listening, and remembering. I will attend to each in more detail.

i. Greeting

We demonstrate our awareness of others and welcome them by greeting them upon their arrival. This is not simply a meaningless formality—*the way in which we greet others establishes the kind of relationship we are seeking to have with them*. For example, when I go to the social assistance office for information regarding the subsidy I receive for child support, I am "welcomed" by a sign that tells me to take a number and then sit and wait for my number to appear on a video screen before I can approach the workers at the front desk so that those workers can grant me access through the locked metal door with reinforced glass so that I can access my case worker who is on the other side. Until that happens, I sit and wait with others, including a uniformed security guard who regularly passes through the space and who helps ensure that everyone is "behaving themselves." This is one way of greeting people and it says a lot about relational expectations, how the workers view themselves, and how people (like me) who receive social assistance are viewed. Similarly, if a large man in a cop uniform approaches me with his hand lingering close to his gun or taser and the first statement he makes is a demand that I perform a certain task (provide my name, provide my driver's license and vehicle registration, keep my hands where he can see them), this is also a greeting that establishes a certain kind of relationship, certain roles to be performed, and certain power dynamics to be respected. Or, for that matter, if I am cold and hungry and have nowhere to sleep and I enter into a building (a homeless shelter) that looks similar to a jail, and has similar security structures to a jail, and am made to wait between locked doors in a standing-room-only space like in a jail, until a worker who sits behind a cinderblock wall with reinforced glass finishes what they are doing on a computer (or a conversation they are having with another worker), before my presence is even acknowledged, this, too, is a form of greeting that tells me a lot about myself, about those who are going to be offering me shelter, and about the kind of relationship we are going to have.

All three of these forms of greeting are treated as normal and not that different from how most of us are greeted in medical, institutional, or corporate environments where the fear of others—especially those who are impoverished, deprived of housing, viewed as deviant, or labeled as mentally ill—creates ever-increasing markets for security technologies, for the presence of people with weapons (from tactical gloves and tasers to guns) and armor (from steel-toed boots to bullet proof vests), and for people to close in upon themselves so as not to attract unwanted attention. To make matters worse, these fearful security-focused dynamics are being added to a business culture that is driven by efficiency, productivity, and extracting every possible ounce of profit or performance from ever smaller margins of time. Taken together, these dynamics produce environments that are both profoundly demoralizing and profoundly unwelcoming. Furthermore, as with any ecosystem or biosphere, these dynamics create their own feedback loops—fear begets more fear which begets increasing levels of security which begets more fear, just as a push for increased profits and productivity creates ever-shifting targets and ever-increasing worker surveillance which increases profits and productivity, which shifts the targets once again, which, well, you get the idea. This is the critical point: *environments that are demoralizing and unwelcoming incline towards becoming ever more demoralizing and unwelcoming over time.*

However, if you look into the origins of the word "greeting" you will find that it carries overtones of *seeking people out*, of *approaching*, of *coming into contact*, of *wishing good health*, and of doing all of this *gladly* and with *respect*. Consequently, while most of our contemporary ways of greeting others are actually about establishing barriers, clear boundaries, lines not to be crossed, expectations linked to the promise of reward or the threat of punishment, and the establishment of strictly enforced disparities of power, greeting is actually intended to do the opposite of these things. Greeting, properly done, annihilates the barriers that exist between people, and brings people closer together (so close that they come into contact!). Furthermore, those who wish to welcome others in this way are to be proactive in seeking out others, approaching them, drawing near to them—especially others who have been subjected to all kinds of disciplinary environments and who, as a result, have internalized a sense of "their place" based upon the force that has been brought to bear upon their bodies—and doing so with a genuine sense of joy and enthusiasm that proclaims: "You are welcome here, it's *so good* to see you!" And this is communicated, not only with words, but with some kind of physical contact—a handshake, a hug, a fist bump, or whatever kind of physical greeting is culturally relevant for communicating affection, camaraderie, respect, joy, and welcome.

Greeting, then, begins with drawing near to another person with a joyful declaration that lets a person know that they are seen, heard, and well come. This declaration establishes a commitment—we commit to be welcoming in ways that others experience as welcoming—and, like any commitment, if it is to be meaningful, those who make it must have structured their relationships with others in ways that permit others to hold them accountable to it (I will have more to say about this below in the chapter about Inter- and Intra-Connectedness). But, even prior to making any kind of intentional declaration of welcome, the very act of seeing another person (and being seen by the person while you are seeing them) makes contact and has the potential to foster intimacy and reciprocity. Seeing does not just mean visually recording that a person is now present in a certain space—seeing is also a way of acknowledging what people have experienced, what they bring along with them, and who, in their heart, they long to be and are. There are many different ways of seeing and being seen by others (think, for example, about the experiences of being seeing by surveillance cameras, or in a meeting on a virtual platform, or by a loved one after a long absence). We all long to be seen in a way that acknowledges us as we are and as we long to be. This is why, in some circles, when someone shares something especially vulnerable or dear to them—or, conversely, if an established authority says a lot of nice things but then acts in a lot of not nice ways—others might respond by saying, "we *see* you."

Seeing, then, is a way of knowing not only what seems to be apparent on the surface, but also what lies beneath. As such, seeing is related to knowing a person *by name*. Generic greetings only go so far. We establish a much more welcoming environment when we see and know not some mass group called "clients" or "consumers" or "participants" or "patients" (or, for that matter, "the impoverished," or "the dispossessed," or "those deprived of housing"), but when we see and know this person—Cindy, Tamir, Neil, Georgina, Sammy, Eric, Tina. Welcoming in a manner that is caring and respectful means welcoming each specific person in all their specificity: "Welcome, Cindy, it's good to see you again. Come on in and grab a coffee. How are your daughters? How are you?" In other words, while program funders may require us to keep statistics related to how many people access the program that I help to facilitate, and while the documentation where those statistics are recorded makes people anonymous (i.e., transforms people into individual client numbers) so that this data can be used for research or funding proposals, we must find ways to push back against the feedback loop this creates in terms of how we relate to and understand others. More than this, we must also try to create alternative feedback loops that pro-actively create a welcoming culture wherein each person is seen, known, greeted, and celebrated for who they truly are—in all their individuality, uniqueness, and specific place of intra- and inter-connectedness with others.

This also means that, if we are to greet others well, we must have the time, attentiveness, and ability to do so. Greeting must be a priority. Spaces must be structured in such a way that people can be properly greeted, and workers cannot be so overwhelmed with data entry, stat collection, or the completion of "tools," that they are pinned-down in offices behind computer screens (or, alternatively, greeters must not be treated as second-class workers who are just not as smart, educated, or capable as workers who have registered with various professional bodies and who, all too often, treat those who work as greeters in a paternalistic, condescending and abusive manner). Greeting, in other words, is not simply a box we check (like a Canadian politician doing a land acknowledgment) so that we can get it out of the way and get down to doing the stuff that "really matters" (i.e., that which we can actually track with measurable outcomes in order to ensure we maintain our funding). Greeting, itself, is one of the things that really matters and, just as with making safe space, it is one of the fundamental things that most places have not done well although they tend to assume that they have.

ii. Prioritizing
(Wasting Time Together With)

I was born in Baketigweyaang (At the Side-Flow, known by its colonial name, London, Ontario) and raised by the forks of the Deshkan Ziibiing—the Antlered River (which the French first renamed La Tranche and the English later renamed the Thames)—in the land of the Anishinaabe, Haudenosaunee, Lenape, and Attawandaron. After spending time in Tkaronto and then in unceded Coast Salish territory, I returned to Baketigweyaang and the Deshkan Ziibiing watershed in my early thirties. Having worked to develop community spaces in some of the most oppressed neighborhoods in both Toronto and Vancouver, I thought living and working in London would be relatively easy. I was wrong. If considered on a per capita basis, London may well be the crystal meth capital of Canadian-occupied territories (although I believe Sudbury now offers some solid competition for this oh-so-coveted title). Different cities develop different cultures around the medicines that people purchase from street pharmacists—in Tkaronto in the late 1990s and early 2000s (when I was there) the culture was centered on crack, in Vancouver the culture was centered on heroin (and had been for many decades), and in London, prior to my return, the culture was heavily focused on prescription opiates like OxyContin or Hydromorphone and its interest in amphetamines goes back several more decades (in the early '70s London was nicknamed "Speed City" because of this). A lot of this had to do with London's geopolitical location and the fact that much of its workforce was composed of blue-collar factory workers (given London's proximity to Detroit and the auto industry that was centered there). For years, large pharmaceutical companies had aggressively marketed opioids to doctors (leading to nationwide lawsuits—like one recently settled in American-occupied territories against Purdue Pharma and the Sackler family—wherein the state tries to recover millions of dollars in financial costs incurred by the so-called "opioid crisis") and factory workers were especially susceptible to experiencing some kind of physical injury or some kind of ongoing pain due to their jobs. As a result, large numbers of opioids went out into factories. If you did not have your own script, it was always easy to find someone who did and who would be willing to share if you shared a little something in return. Opioids then quickly moved from parents into the hands of their (curious, entrepreneurial, or also injured) teenage children and, especially in small towns where kids don't always have much to do other than raid the med or liquor cabinets of their parents before going off to bush parties, pills also became prominent as a recreational medicine self-prescribed for things like loneliness, boredom, insecurity, and childhood trauma. In addition to these medications, "speedy" drugs (stimulants) fit well with factory work providing much needed energy for long shifts in demanding jobs that frequently required people to work mandatory overtime. As with opioids, these drugs also trickled down from adults to children and teenagers.

But, for the most part, people were able to manage this and were able to take their meds, go to work, pay their mortgages, go to school, and so on. However, when the Detroit-based auto industry collapsed in the market crash of 2008, and as neoliberal corporations continued to off-shore labor jobs, many blue-collar workers found themselves unemployed with "few transferable job skills." Widespread and sustained unemployment impoverished many people. In order to survive, some people began to fill and then sell their prescriptions. Other people, facing high levels of stress, uncertainty, and hopelessness, mixed with feelings of failure and shame, began to take much higher doses of their medicine than they took before (unfortunately, as studies show, opioids actually make people progressively *more* sensitive to any kind of emotional or physical pain). While providing momentary respite, as a long-term strategy this tended to produce further impoverishment—which, of course, produced further suffering, which, of course, produced a further reliance upon their medication, and so a self-reinforcing feedback loop emerges.

A final aggravating factor in all of this is that, predominantly White working-class communities on Turtle Island tend to be politically and religiously conservative and, as a result, tend to lack the socioeconomic and political lenses to help themselves understand how global neoliberalism and austerity work to impoverish communities. Consequently, they tend to view poverty as related to personal moral failure, as evidence that there is something wrong with someone, and as something that can be altogether avoided if one does all the right things—works hard, avoids indulging in costly vices, pulls one's self up by one's bootstraps, and so on. However, this means that many communities impoverished after 2008—communities like London

II. PRIORITIZING (WASTING TIME TOGETHER WITH)

and several other regional small towns of predominantly conservative blue-collars families—are full of people who are mystified as to what went wrong, who are sure that they are not like "those other people" at the shelter or in the Social Assistance office, who have no sense of class solidarity, and who are just as quick to continue to shit on other people who have been dispossessed or deprived of housing. After all, while they themselves are where they are simply due to some kind of unfair stroke of bad luck, those "other people" (especially if they are not White) probably don't deserve any help (and here the imperialist and racist Christian tradition of distinguishing between the "deserving poor" and the "undeserving poor" still plays an ongoing role in the social imaginary).

For me, this element of London's "street culture" (and the backstabbing, lying, and box-thieving that goes with it) was especially striking given the strong movements dedicated to solidarity, liberation, and resistance that have been organizing for decades in Tkaronto or in unceded Coast Salish territories (from the Ontario Coalition Against Poverty, to the Downtown Eastside Women's Centre and the Power of Women group, to the Vancouver Area Network of Drug Users, to the Red Braid Alliance, to the Drug Users Liberation Front, and many, many others). In London, people who have been forcibly deprived of housing are acting towards others who have been forcibly deprived of housing in the same way that bougie assholes from the 'burbs act towards them. In other words, many people who have been impoverished in London since 2008 are still identifying with the oppressive classes even though they, themselves, have fallen down into the company of the oppressed-to-the-point-of-abandonment.

Opioid sale, exchange, and use, which the state and medical authorities deemed "illicit" and criminalized then rapidly increased from 2008 until 2013, at which point the federal government began to "crack sdown" on opiate prescriptions (threatening to suspend the licenses of doctors who "over-prescribe") and began to push back against pharmaceutical companies (leading to the withdrawal of the much-loved Oxy 80s and the production of OxyNEO pills, which are harder to snort or shoot—a change which has not made a discernible difference in terms of the harms associated with criminalizing how some people attain or take their medications). Two things then happened simultaneously: opioids became less readily available in street markets, and many of the people who had avoided the full effect of impoverishment in 2008 or subsequent years were now tapped-out of their savings or had no other supports to whom they could turn. Thus, as more and more people began to feel the effects of sustained unemployment, more and more people also ended up being deprived of housing (causing so-called municipally funded and monitored "homeless counts" in London to produce higher and higher numbers every year up until homeless counts were stopped). Opioids are "downers"—they make you feel sleepy, peaceful, relaxed, pain-free, and euphoric. But if you have no home, if you do not trust the people around you, and if you are afraid of being raped, robbed, or of literally freezing to death if you fall asleep, you may want to take a different medication. Thus, the path is cleared for crystal meth—an "upper" (i.e., a stimulant) that is chemically nearly identical to Adderall (so much so that regular crystal meth users cannot tell when they are given Adderall and regular Adderall users cannot tell when they are given crystal meth).[1] Crystal meth helps you stay alert, stay warm, and feel more confident, less anxious, and less afraid (unless one uses meth for days without sleeping, then the reverse occurs). Thus, in London you end up with a community of people who have been impoverished and deprived of housing and whose medication of choice is an opiate but whose medication of convenience is crystal meth.

Two ways in which London responded to this are worth noting. First, a considerable amount of stigma was produced and reinforced both in relation to crystal meth and in relation to people who medicate with crystal meth. Meth was taken to be *the* worst thing ever, something nobody in their right mind would *ever* even consider doing ("Crystal Meth: Not Even Once" is a common slogan). Meth, apparently, turns people into rotting, violent, out of control, psychotic, paranoid, sexually aroused, criminal-monster-zombies (even though, as mentioned before, meth is indistinguishable from Adderall, which is prescribed to millions of people every year). Of course, such drug scares are nothing new and, if you look at the history of drug scares—from "reefer madness" in the thirties, to LSD in the seventies, to "crackheads" in the eighties and nineties, to "bath salts" and flakka, "the zombie drug," in 2013 and 2015 respectively—you find that drug scares are usually encouraged by the propertied classes in order to further their dispossession of racialized and impoverished groups (thus, for example, the criminalization of cannabis, along with arguments that it turned people into criminal-monster-zombies in the 1930s were tied to racism directed at Mexican and Asian people in order to try and make impoverished Whites blame the racialized Other for the harms impoverished White communities were experiencing, and, of course, we all know that the crack scares of the 80s and 90s were used to dispossess impoverished Black communities of urban neighborhoods that were designated as prime locations for gentrification). However, it is worth emphasizing the way in which the fearmongering related to crystal meth use is currently cloaked in the language of science,

---

1. The work of Dr. Carl Hart is especially important here. See *High Price*.

medicine, and healthcare. Thus, for example, I once attended a workshop hosted by a "City Manager of Homeless Populations" (although this position has been rebranded in more recent years) and at this workshop two very concerned social workers talked about neurochemistry and the various adverse psychological, biological, and communal health affects of sustained crystal meth use. They then put forward such "evidence-based" suggestions as (I kid you not!) keeping a distance of seven to ten feet from a person on meth when talking to them (as "[c]oming too close can be perceived as threatening"), not shining a bright light on the person (because "[t]he meth user is already paranoid and if blinded by a bright light he [sic] is likely to run or become violent"), lowering the pitch of your voice and slowing your speech (although no comment is made as to how the "meth user" will then hear you as you are presumably speaking from a distance of seven to ten feet away), and encouraging the person to keep talking (because "[a] meth user who falls silent can be extremely dangerous"). Of course, this is almost all total nonsense and is basically designed to make people feel afraid while further stigmatizing an already marginalized and oppressed group of people. Recalling that *only 10 to a maximum of 25 percent* of people who use crystal meth ever end up becoming addicted to it (and then, even of those, only a minority end up being deprived of housing and used as horror stories to scare schoolchildren), one could easily make a similarly scientific, medical, and caring-while-terrifying presentation about any number of prescription medicines. All of these medicines have many pages of possible negative health outcomes up to and including death. To pick a few examples, Effexor has been especially associated with rapid and dramatic weight loss; Paxil has been especially connected to life- and non-life-threatening birth defects; Prozac and psychotropic medications more generally have been frequently connected with mass shooters; and Venlafaxine has been especially connected to suicide. Or, to pick even more mundane activities, one could present equally scientific and medically-concerning presentations about the sustained negative physical and mental health outcomes of commuting to work daily or spending hours sitting under neon lights at an office desk. Why, then, do we focus on a small number of the most extreme worst-case scenarios, that only occur in a small minority of people who use a certain medicine, and then universalize that experience to all people who take that medicine, when we clearly do not do the same with other medicines or activities? Because people who medicate with crystal meth, many of whom do so because they can no longer access other stimulants their doctors prescribed for their ADHD, are *in the way*. Specifically, while sensitive healthcare officials identify them as a community health concern (which is not that far from the ways some European societies up to the mid-twentieth century identified Roma, Jews, Slavs, Queers, disabled people, militant Leftists, some religious minorities, and many "social deviants," as a "disease" or "plague"), the real issue is that the businesses and property owners identify the very presence of people who medicate with meth as *an obstacle that interferes with their ability to maximize their profits*.

This connects with my second point. The neoliberal transformation of the city, from being a community with shared spaces, neighborhoods, and housing accessible to all people, to being the private property of a few transnational corporations and even fewer extremely wealthy individuals, was already well on its way in London (and elsewhere) by the time the "meth scare" and so-called "opioid crisis" began to gather a lot of attention in the media. However, the supposedly devastating and demonic effects of crystal meth became the *moral justification for deploying new levels of force upon impoverished communities and individuals*, in order to forcibly transfer them to peripheral neighborhoods where investments in properties, businesses, and commercial transactions were less obviously profitable. Much of this was accomplished via a bastardized "Housing First" approach.

"Housing First" is a model that claims to "cure" or "solve" "homelessness" by granting people access to housing before they are required to do things like go to a residential drug treatment program, or stabilize on mental health medications or get a job, and it has had some success around the world if all the key pillars of the program model are respected and implemented. In actual practice, the first pillar (that which allows individuals to choose the neighborhood in which they want to live) is almost never respected and people are made to move away from core urban communities that are being gentrified and privatized. They are also deliberately moved far away from lifelong friends or supports because social workers determine that "those people" are a "negative influence." Furthermore, the fifth pillar (which is about community integration and providing people with their desired level of support once they are in housing), is almost always significantly disregarded or entirely neglected due to inadequate budgets forcing massive caseloads onto housing workers. This displacement process and forced migration isn't quite loading people into boxcars on trains, but the intent and outcomes are uncomfortably similar (and, in this regard, it's worth noting that a disturbingly high number of people I have know died within the first year of being placed into this kind of housing—a trend also observed in other cities—although the Housing First program that had assigned them to apartments on the periphery of the city initially counted those who died in their stats as "successfully housed long-term").

However, people are often deeply rooted in their communities and in relationships they have developed there. When speaking with people

II. PRIORITIZING (WASTING TIME TOGETHER WITH)

living in tents in certain neighborhoods, many of the residents said they did not want to leave those neighborhoods because those were the neighborhoods where they used to have homes. Workers ask them to leave, tell them why other options are "better," but people like to be where they feel most at home. Consequently, if people cannot be convinced to leave their community, steps are taken to force them to migrate elsewhere. And, again, the fearmongering around crystal meth plays a critical role here. Meth users are frequently labeled as too violent, too psychotic, too oppositional, too non-compliant, or simply too "high acuity," to be able to access the services or spaces that they used to access. As a result, a "service drought" occurs. People are barred from shelters, drop-ins, community health centers, or other community spaces (libraries, malls, parks, etc.). At the same time, government-based funding priorities are changed and programs that emphasize performativity, measurable outcomes, and successfully moving people into either housing or job markets become dominant. This is an oft-neglected element of neoliberalism's assault upon the commons. Spaces that were once shared in common with some of the most oppressed people in the city are transformed and made into inaccessible outcome-and-stat-driven program spaces. These spaces are not designed to meet the needs of people who are actively using crystal meth and others who have been expelled from the commons, and so more and more doors are closed to them as barriers to service—justified by the discourse of "health and safety"—climb higher and higher. "Drop-ins" and "Resource Centers" vanish. Housing outreach workers proliferate. Money used to fund *spaces for the impoverished* becomes money used to fund *jobs for those who are not impoverished* within the expansion of the social service field.

This, then, provides the context for what I want to say in this section about prioritizing others as being a critical and fundamental component of what it means to be welcoming and acknowledging others. Always in my work, I have looked not just for those who are "falling through the cracks in society" (although that's a lie—people aren't "falling through cracks," they are *being pushed down through cracks* and *forced back down* when they try to climb out). I have also looked for those who are "falling through the cracks" in the support networks that are supposed to catch people falling through the cracks of society (although this, too, is a lie—people are also pushed-out and kicked back down by those who claim to support them and who receive funding based upon that claim).

As my friend and my coworker, Mechele, and I became increasingly aware of these local dynamics, we became deeply concerned. We knew that people who medicate with crystal meth were valuable members of our community, we knew that people who medicate with crystal meth were full of the wonderfulness that we acknowledged when we welcomed them into the space we facilitated (as they also welcomed us into their company), and so we also knew that losing these folx from our communities and from our shared spaces was a loss not only to them but to *all of us*. And so we knew that we had to prioritize their needs and ensure that, first and foremost, we were creating a space that was safe and welcoming to them. Consequently, we pushed back against neoliberalism's enclosure of the commons to ensure that the common space we held was open and available to them (and did not have high barriers in place—like a requirement to participate in workshops or a requirement to fill out various forms or complete various "tools" in order to access the space).

Furthermore, we knew that we wanted to prioritize the self-identified needs of our community members rather than prioritizing outcomes identified by funders (although finding creative ways to talk about what we were doing when drafting reports to satisfy funders was also an important skill to develop). In order to do this, we knew we had to actually spend *undirected* time with those whom we were claiming to prioritize. And so we spent a great deal of time chatting with people, visiting with people, sitting together drinking coffee, playing a game of cards, or making art. We spent time with people with no agenda other than that of getting to know them and doing what we could to affirm that we were glad to see them, doing what we could to affirm that they mattered, doing what we could to affirm that it was good to be together with them. While we were doing this, workers from other programs would sometimes pass through the space and they would make comments suggesting that they thought what we were doing didn't count as *real* work—"I wish I had a job where I just drink coffee and play cards," they would say sneeringly—as if "real work" required sitting in an office or filling out forms or taking people to appointments (where other "real workers" sat in real offices and filled out real forms). They sometimes referred to our work as "glorified baby-sitting," as if adults in need of a space where they would be seen, known, and welcomed—adults who had been excluded from all other spaces and who came seeking good company—were nothing more than needy, entitled, or spoiled infants (which is doubly offensive for it asserts that those who have been dispossessed are spoiled and that those who are adults are children). And that's the thing—stats-driven, outcome-focused funding and program models are often antithetical to true community building. If we really want to welcome, get to know, and acknowledge others for who they are, then, from the perspective of philanthrocapitalists, government agents, and poverty pimps, we have to be willing to *waste time together with them*. But here's the difference: we do not consider time spent developing relationships with others, time spent just being with others whom almost everyone else has rejected (from family members, to members of the general public, to other social services), to be a waste of time—our priority is *the person*, not *the predetermined outcomes we can record and feed back to funders*. The irony, of course, is that if more people and programs were willing to "waste time" in this way, they would actually be able to better attain the outcomes they desire. To pick just one example, people are becoming increasingly aware that the solution to "addiction" is not some kind of sobriety-focused programming but is, instead, *connection*—people are much less likely to self-soothe and self-medicate in ways that can make other areas of their life more difficult, in fact they are much less likely to need *any* kind of chemical intervention, if they feel meaningfully connected to others in a community. This is why, paradoxically to outsiders, programs like safe injection or safer consumption sites actually produce better outcomes in relation to *abstinence* and quality of life than residential treatment programs which consistently fail no less than six out of seven times.

In other words, being good company means spending time with people with no other agenda other than that of spending time with them. We do this, of course, with any other relationship in our lives that is meaningful to us. I do not ensure that all my interactions with my partner, my children, my friends, or my brothers, are focused on attaining some kind of outcome that can be tracked, measured, and then replicated with others—I simply spend time with them because I love them and they love me and we love to be together. And, if we are to be good company to and with other people, then we should also spend time with them in this way. If poverty pimps, government agents, spiritual-but-not-religious do-gooders, and philanthrocapitalists consider this a waste of time, then I suggest we joyfully and extravagantly waste time together in this way.

iii. Listening

One of the losses that has occurred in our communities, as oppressed groups of people have been deprived of spaces that they used to hold in common, is that it is harder and harder for people who are oppressed to go somewhere *where they can be heard*. As program spaces raise barriers and require people to participate in scheduled groups and workshops that are geared towards measuring outcomes and tracking stats, there are fewer and fewer places where people can go to *talk*—to talk about the *things they care about*, to talk about the things they have experienced in their day-to-day lives, to talk about their hopes and dreams, to talk about their fears and losses, or to banter, joke, shoot the shit, and make small talk as people are wont to do with other people. As a result, people must sit silently or only participate as desired by the employment counselors, addiction support workers, nurses, housing support workers, HIV or HCV outreach workers, doctors, chaplains, nurses, social workers, child protection workers, financial advisors, job coaches, cognitive behavioral therapists, occupational therapists, dialectical behavioral therapists, practicum students from social services programs, practicum students from social work programs, practicum students from nursing programs, practicum students from women's studies programs, practicum students from occupational therapy programs, or god-knows-who-else, who talk at them during this or that focus group, support group, recovery group, anger management group, life skills workshop, resume building workshop, budgeting workshop, interview skills workshop, making healthy meals on a budget workshop, systems navigation workshop, or an interview for research on this project for school, this project for a professor, this project for the city, this project for an independent research body which won a provincial grant, and so on, until you want to fucking die even more than you already wanted to die. Furthermore, as financial aid for talk therapy has been clawed-back by governments who have reduced funding for low-to-no income people in order to enforce expanding austerity, police budgets and corporate tax breaks, and as the few "geared-to-income" therapists, or counseling services provided free by community mental health agencies, are overwhelmed by the ever-increasing number of people who need their support, *brief* counseling sessions focused on teaching *coping* skills (whether via cognitive behavioral therapy or dialectical behavioral therapy or whatever will trend next because it promises to make people more functional—i.e., more able to go to work and pay their bills—in less time) have become hegemonic. As a result, talk therapy as traditionally understood has become, almost exclusively, the private property of those who are wealthy enough (in both time and money) to be able to afford it. As with other program models, brief counseling permits the kind of stat-production (seeing more clients in less time and demonstrating changes in the core areas that funders care about, rather than areas that those seeking support may have identified as their top priorities) that has become necessary for ensuring the survival of programs in an increasingly cutthroat market where the government is always eager to take money from those who they think are doing less and give it to those who they proclaim are doing more. Long-term counseling simply isn't fiscally responsible. People need to get their shit together in three to five sessions and if they can't, well, that's their fucking problem. Because we have studies that prove the brief counseling model is effective—so if it doesn't work for you, you're the problem.

But the fact of the matter is that people need to have other people in their lives who listen to them. And they need to have other people in their lives who allow them to set the agenda for the conversation instead of always having people listen to them with some kind of ulterior motive. And if this is true of people who are not oppressed or suffering greatly, if, in other words, it is true of all of us (and I think that it is) then it is doubly true for those who are oppressed, abandoned, and left for dead. Here, again, the importance of prioritizing others comes to the fore and requires concrete practices of listening to demonstrate that it is taking place.

This kind of open-ended listening takes time and, from the perspective of most institutions and funding bodies, *wastes time*. But this is a lie. Being able to listen to people—without talking over them, without being distracted by screens, without ensuring you are accomplishing certain outcomes along the way, without just looking for a chance to say the clever thing you heard in school or in a workshop—is *never* a waste of time. In fact, over the last twenty years, more often than not, I have found that almost all the situations where people who came seeking help but ended up escalating and acting in a violent way, resulted because *the people who were supposed to help them never actually took the time to really listen to them*. So much of the crisis de-escalation work I have done, and so much of the work I generally do with people who are in crises, comes down to being willing to listen to people whom others have refused to hear. This means being willing to open myself to what they are saying and feeling. It means being willing to allow *them* to set the agenda for what *they* want from the conversation. And it means being willing to spend the time that it takes to see if we can get *where they want to go*.

Remember, we are still at the introductory stage of being together with others. Listening in this way is critical to being welcoming and, if we fail here, we fail at being welcoming and the whole thing falls apart before we even get going. We have to begin by listening in this way because it is by listening that we become attuned to and with others. Listening, in other words, is very similar to learning to sing in a choir. If I am tuned to C major and you are tuned to C sharp minor, and we both begin to sing, we are going to clash very soon and we will likely want to either sing so loud we can't hear the other person or stop singing altogether. Either way, the opportunity to connect is lost.

Here, I am reminded of Barry Lopez's reflections on how various Inuit peoples relate to the land. In his beautiful book *Artic Dreams*, Lopez observes the following:

> Hunting in my experience—and by hunting I simply mean being out on the land—is a state of mind. All of one's faculties are brought to bear in an effort to become fully incorporated into the landscape. It is more than listening for animals or watching for hoofprints or a shift in the weather. It is more than an analysis of what one *senses*. To hunt means to have the land around you like clothing. To engage in a wordless dialogue with it, one so absorbing that you cease to talk with your human companions. It means to release yourself from rational images of what something "means" and to be concerned only that it "is." And then to recognize that things exist only insofar as they can be related to other things. These relationships—fresh drops of moisture on top of rocks at a river crossing and a raven's distant voice—become patterns. The patterns are always in motion ...
>
> The focus of a hunter in a hunting society was not killing animals but attending to the myriad relationships he understood bound him into the world he occupied with them.[1]

We listen to others, then, to try and understand "the myriad relationships" in which they and we exist and by which we are "bound" to one

---

1. Lopez, *Arctic Dreams*, 199–200.

another and the world more broadly. We listen to others, not to slot them into already established systems of meaning or sense-making that we possess and wield like weapons or maps in community spaces, but in order to be incorporated into them. We listen in order to let go of what we think others mean so that we can understand who they actually are and what they are actually saying. Thus, if we dig up the roots of the verb "to hear," we learn that it actually carries overtones of "acceding to, following, and obeying." To listen well means that we will have to do all three of those things much more than we have been taught. Once again, this requires a complete reversal of the power dynamics that operate within institutions. If I truly listen to the people who come to me seeking good company, I end up acceding to them, following their lead, and doing what they ask.

Lopez then goes on to say the following about the Inuit approach to attunement with the land:

> Whatever evaluation we finally make of a stretch of land, however, no matter how profound or accurate, we will find it inadequate. The land retains an identity of its own, still deeper and more subtle than we can know. Our obligation toward it then becomes simple: to approach with an uncalculating mind, with an attitude of regard ... To intend from the beginning to preserve some of the mystery within it as a kind of wisdom to be experienced, not questioned. And to be alert for its openings, for that moment when something sacred reveals itself within the mundane, and you know the land knows you are there.[2]

So, too, in our relationships with others. Even after listening, or, better yet, *especially because we have listened*, people retain a depth of mystery, sacredness, wisdom, and identity that we can never fully know or put into words but that we can, at times, *experience* as we share life together with them. Because we learn to hear and recognize this in others, it is true that we also learn that we are *obligated* to approach them with what Carl Rogers refers to as "unconditional positive regard" and with an uncalculating mind—with, that is to say, precisely the opposite frame of mind and perception than that which is enforced and normalized within social and healthcare services today.[3] Here, then, it is worth concluding with a story Lopez tells:

> A man in Anaktuvuk Pass, in response to a question about what he did when he visited a new place, said to me, "I listen." That's all. I listen, he meant, to what the land is saying. I walk around it

---

2. Lopez, *Arctic Dreams*, 228.

3. A recurring theme in Rogers's work but see, for example, "The Characteristics of a Helping Relationship" in *On Becoming a Person*, 39–58.

and strain my senses in appreciation of it for a long time before I, myself, ever speak a word.[4]

The man in Anaktuvuk Pass listens not just once, not just briefly, but continually and "for a long time" before he speaks. May we go and do likewise.

---

4. Lopez, *Arctic Dreams*, 257.

iv. Remembering

Finally, if we are welcoming people by acknowledging them, we must also remember them. Etymologically, the verb "to remember" refers to the idea of "keeping someone or something in mind" and "being mindful of someone or something." To be mindful of someone, in turn, implies not only thinking of them. It also means *being heedful of them*—showing them care, thinking of them in a way that is careful or *considerate* (and consideration, here, carries tones of both deliberation and feelings related to tenderness or kindness). In other words, being welcoming and inviting others into a safe space is not simply something that is done in our shared communal space, it is also something that we do within ourselves. When we welcome others, we welcome them into ourselves—into our hearts and into our minds.

Some medieval rabbis, struggling with similar ideas to those of early Christian scholastics, but from a much more esoteric and mystical perspective, asked themselves how it was possible for God to be everywhere but not be everything—essentially, they faced the problem of resolving monotheism with a belief in divine omnipresence (i.e., they did not want to limit the ubiquitous presence of the divine but they also wanted the divine to be a singularity). Rabbi Isaac Luria Ashkenazi proposed the following solution: it was possible for God to be all-present and for things that are not-God to exist at the same time because, at the moment of creation, God withdraws God's self in such a way as to create an empty space within God's self where it is possible for those who are not-God to exist. This kenosis, this act of self-emptying for the sake of the other (known as Tzimtzum within the Kabbalistic tradition), is thus a fundamental element of the character of the divine. It is also what we do, I think, when we welcome others into ourselves in the ways in which I have tried to describe above. If we are to listen well to others, we must empty ourselves to make space for them in all of their uniqueness, so that we can actually hear what they are saying and become attuned to them, instead of thinking about what we are going to say or hearing what we want to hear in what they're saying. If we are to prioritize others, we must empty ourselves of other pressures and priorities. If we are to greet others well—seeking them out, acknowledging them, coming into contact with them, and doing so joyfully—we must have a home prepared for them within ourselves. If we are to acknowledge others, we must ensure that we have room enough within ourselves so that they can be who they truly are in all their expansive mess and glory. If we are to create safe spaces, we must have made ourselves a safe space. And if we are to be inviting to others, so much so that they are inviting to us, then we must open ourselves to them, not in order to spill all our priorities, beliefs, needs, and desires onto them, but in order to invite them—and their priorities, beliefs, needs, and desires—into ourselves.

A critical proof that we are doing this well is the way in which we remember people. When we carry other people in our minds and hearts and bodies, in our communities, and in the physical environments where we gather, we inevitably remember them. This occurs in at least two ways. First, we remember them by thinking of them—perhaps a passing car reminds us of a story they told us, perhaps an empty chair in the room reminds us of where they always sit and the conversations we had while they were sitting there, perhaps certain dates make us think of them—and so, when we see them again, we recognize them, we call them by name, we pick up where we left off (as we do with all old friends). Second, we also remember them by remembering them in our own bodies. If we invite others into ourselves, we begin to see things through their eyes, hear things through their ears, feel things in our bodies (fear, hope, sorrow, joy, anger, persistence, playfulness, and so on) that they have felt in theirs. For example, it was only after a dear friend told me about the experience of being raped and the flashbacks that would occur, that I became attuned to the ubiquity of rape jokes and sexual violence in our culture (I vividly remember a radio DJ making a rape joke one day shortly after I awakened to this and there, in the back seat of the car, I felt waves of discomfort, grief, anxiety, anger, and despair wash over me). Thus, as we learn to be good company to and with others, we learn that being together with others means that the lines between who I am and who someone else is begin to blur and some (but not all) boundaries that used to be firmly established become porous or are swept away altogether.

Welcoming, then, is an act that, when done well, produces intimacy. It is both an intimate act and it is an intimacy-forming act. As such, welcoming produces a self-reinforcing feedback loop wherein people are increasingly seen, heard, acknowledged, celebrated, and welcomed in ever more genuine, natural-feeling, and intimate ways. This feedback loop produces

IV. REMEMBERING

a true counter-culture—one that develops in opposition to the feedback loop of isolation, dehumanization, performance, pragmatism, and wealth accumulation, that currently structures our collective life together. This culture-forming element of welcoming, when done well, cannot be over-emphasized. It is by establishing this kind of self-affirming, self-reinforcing, self-perpetuating, and self-strengthening culture that we make the kind of world where it is easier to be good company to and with others. It is here, and not with figuring out how we are going to track and measure our ability to meet the outcomes required by funders or government agencies, that we must begin. If we do not begin here, I suspect we will not get to the kind of world where we all desire to live. Instead, we will end up with statistics, people-as-numbers or populations-to-be-managed, increased levels of surveillance, increased dehumanization, and an increased reliance on data-driven disciplinary technologies, to which we are all increasingly subjected and wherein those who are already abandoned and left for dead exist both as a warning and as a grim vision of our collective future. We already know where this trajectory leads—it leads to programs that can claim to have staggering successes, even as we all become ever-more impoverished.

Here, however, our remembering of the abandoned and left-for-dead, now, already, in our bodies, brings us into a critical solidarity which paves the way forward to a different future. For, by remembering one another in this way, we demonstrate that we will not abandon one another, we will not forsake one another, we will not leave one another to die but will, instead, make homes for one another within ourselves as we learn not only how to stave off the death and dying that is being forced upon us but also learn how to share life—life in all of its abundance, joy, and goodness—together with one another. Welcoming one another in all the ways described above (and surely in more ways as well!) is a first critical step towards this. Remembering is a critical part of this welcoming but it is also important to parting. I will return to this topic again in Part Four when I discuss "Commemorating."

2. Honoring

If we begin relationships through a mutual and shared process of welcoming, then we continue and deepen them through an equally reciprocal process of honoring. However, the ways in which we currently structure our communal spaces (from businesses, to social venues, to social services and healthcare organizations—all of which, along with our cities and nations, are increasingly run like transactional, profit-oriented, capital-building, risk-adverse, outcome-oriented businesses), make this very difficult to accomplish. This is so for a number of reasons.

First of all, as I already began to explore in Part One, the notion of "fiscal responsibility" wherein money is given in exchange for the production of certain outcomes—outcomes that are prioritized and enforced, not by members of impoverished and oppressed communities but by those who control access to the money—continually undermines our ability to meet people where they are, welcome them, and honor them for who they are (right here, right now). Instead, we are encouraged to view people as populations to be managed, outcomes to be measured, and statistics to be collected. This is a rather insidious process and it tends to create a certain trajectory, regardless of the good intentions of many of those who contribute to it.[1] To use Martin Heidegger's language, this focus on "fiscal responsibility" is a type of *enframing*.[2] Heidegger used this term to describe the ways in which technological advances fundamentally reorient the ways in which we perceive, relate to, and engage with the so-called "natural world." Instead of viewing things like forests, rivers, and mountains as entities with their own dignity and sacredness, entities that both require care and contribute to the broader well-being of the interconnected whole (i.e., the world

---

1. The old saying that "hell is paved with good intentions" is, in my opinion, one of the most apt ways of summarizing a lot of our so-called humanitarian and charitable activity in this neoliberal age. For more on this, see Jay and Barry-Shaw, *Paved With Good Intentions*.

2. See, especially, Heidegger, *Question Concerning Technology*.

itself, of which humans are but one part), Heidegger argues that technology transforms "nature" into a "standing reserve" of "resources" that can be extracted and used for tool-making which, in turn, furthers technological development and makes its enframing ever more all-encompassing (hence, again, a self-reinforcing feedback loop). Thus, instead of a forest we see a standing reserve of lumber; instead of a river we see a standing reserve of hydroelectric power; and instead of a mountain we see a standing reserve of ore. However, as is now obvious to us, this enframing paved the way for the annihilation of the earth and has resulted in catastrophic climate change and the sixth mass extinction (what some have referred to as the *Necrocene*—the Epoch of Death).[3]

However, with his focus on technology, Heidegger pays insufficient attention to the ways in which capitalism, itself, is not only complicit in this but is at the center of technological development moving in this direction (furthermore, as a devout Christian and an equally devout Nazi, Heidegger also neglected other theopolitical elements that were critical to the advance of this kind of enframing). Technology is not simply driven to transform *nature* into *natural resources*; technology is driven by a *profit motive*, and standing reserves of lumber, hydroelectric power, and ore are sought out, privatized, and extracted because they are so highly profitable. It is this search for ever greater profit margins, and the desire to get the very best possible financial outcomes for the very least amount of financial investment that has produced the kind of enframing that Heidegger highlights and which we now know produces death on scales we find hard to imagine (even though that death is playing itself out every day in the world around us). However, and this is the critical point for what we are exploring here, it is this same enframing that philanthrocapitalists, government agents, and corporations bring to bear upon the ways in which they fund social services and healthcare. There is more to this than simply observing that those who have money, and who choose to give some away, want to ensure that the money is put to "good use" (i.e., that they get the "best bang for their buck") and so continue to live according to the fiscally conservative *moral* code (because this is, indeed, a moral code for those who live within it). Today, within capitalism's enframing, few things are considered so immoral as wasting money. In fact, governments and businesses are in general agreement that it is *more virtuous to waste lives than it is to waste money*. This is

---

3. On the "Necrocene" and where one might look for hope in such a time, see Clark, *Between Earth and Empire*. Others, like Donna Haraway, have referred to our age as "the Cthulucene" as she seeks hope by exploring how human and nonhuman beings can live and die together in a process of sym-poiesis which could produce a more desirable future (see Haraway, *Staying With the Trouble*).

so, in part, because *the making of money is premised upon the wasting of lives* (and so those who love money and who hoard it are horrified by the suggestion that the making of life—abundant life, life for all and everyone—may also be premised upon the wasting of money—and they aren't wrong about that).

However, this fiscally conservative approach is mostly a defensive measure. It is a reaction to pressures that are brought to bear upon the rich (i.e., those who have dispossessed others) and the governments that work hand-in-glove with them in order to facilitate the enriching of a very few and the impoverishment of very many. Historically, even this outcomes-focused form of "charity" had to be forced out of dispossessors against their will because they feared for their so-called property (or their so-called lives) if they refused to act charitably in some way. As a result, where and when this fear is absent, this kind of charity also tends to disappear just as quickly—which, of course, is what we see now in this age of austerity, where tax dollars are increasingly diverted to fund the militarization of the police and the barricading of borders in mainland Europe and The Five Eyes (Canada, the US, the UK, New Zealand, and Australia, with Japan now poised to become the Sixth Eye). Rather than pretending to care for most of those whom they impoverish, the dispossessors are increasingly focused on raising barriers between them and the human waste (the refugees, the *refusees*), produced by neoliberalism.

However, as any strategist knows, always being on the defensive is something of a losing battle as the trajectory tends to push more and more in the direction of those who are on the offensive and who are being proactive rather than reactive (the ways in which Conservatives have continually "moved the goalposts" or "shifted the Overton Window" around what counts as "centrism" in contemporary global politics is a good example of this). In terms of this proactive work, few things are more powerful in this regard than shaping the ways in which people view themselves, others, the world in which they live, and the ways in which all of these things are or are not connected. By framing people who are impoverished, dispossessed, oppressed, and left for dead as populations to be managed, as statistics to be gathered, as outcomes to be measured, and, more generally (in language that is taken to be more caring and more neutral but which, in actual fact, is usually neither), as "community health concerns," people are de-sacralized in the same process that Max Weber describes (and that Charles Taylor develops) in order to be "dis-enchanted" and then put to use or subordinated to profit-making.[4] In other words, the current paradigm that exerts

---

4. Weber explores this in several places, but see, especially, "Science as Vocation," in *Sociological Writings*, 276–303; Taylor, *Secular Age*.

a hegemonic influence (an "iron cage" in Weber's language) on how we pursue life together and that shapes our social imaginaries is one that is premised upon *dis-honoring* the vast majority of people in order to enrich a very, very few people.

The ways in which capitalism maintains a *standing reserve* of the utterly impoverished and dispossessed in order to depress wages, claw back labor rights, withdraw benefits, and wring every drop of productivity from the working poor is a good example of this (although the term "working poor" is a misnomer given how hard the "non-working" poor have to work just to get through each day). Charity is an important element of this. On the one hand, charity is essential to the smooth running of the trajectory of the status quo. As Raphael, a friend of mine from El Salvador, once taught me, if the poor are literally starving to death they will be more inclined to revolt and use whatever level of violence is necessary in order to not have their loved ones starved to death. Thus, social assistance becomes a tool not so much of care for the impoverished as a means of disciplining the impoverished while they remain impoverished. On the other hand, being "too charitable" (presumably this is a thing?) may incline some folx to walk away from the brutal and death-dealing types of labor that are required to maximize profits. Therefore, charity is provided but it is usually provided at well below the levels required to maintain any kind of decent or adequate, let alone stress-free or enjoyable, standard of living. This is why social assistance rates in Canadian-occupied territories are well below the poverty line, why "discretionary benefits" (like having a healthy diet or receiving money to help move out of an apartment with an abuser, or receiving funds to purchase clothes for a job interview) are continually being cut back, and why we are constantly bombarded with messages about the "deserving poor" versus the "undeserving poor." In this way, people are encouraged to actually fight to have the kinds of jobs that workers a century ago were fighting not to have! This produces the kind of "race to the bottom" that we have seen with the development of transnational capital flows and the rise of global neoliberalism. It is a deeply and inextricably dehumanizing trajectory (although a tiny number of people are making billions of dollars off of it) and those who *refuse* to go along with it end up being labeled "undeserving" or "noncompliant" or "too dangerous" or "too sick" and discarded as *refuse* (hence, therefore, the double entendre within the neologism *refusee* that I used a moment ago).

The second monumental obstacle we face when trying to organize our life together in a way that honors everyone is the fact that almost all areas of our lives are under the influence of strictly enforced, maintained, and naturalized hierarchies of power. This is so ubiquitous and has become so normalized to us that we have trouble even imagining things could be another way. But human societies have often been structured in other ways (as anarchist anthropologists and scientists, from Peter Kropotkin to James C. Scott have reminded us), and when disasters cause state-based power structures to collapse, people often go back to practicing mutual aid in some wonderful ways (as both Rebecca Solnit and scott crow demonstrate).[5] Furthermore, it turns out that Darwin's original thesis about evolution as "survival of the fittest" neglected the multitude of ways in which various organisms—both among their own kind and with others—work *collaboratively* to not only survive but to help life itself thrive in all of its great diversity and abundance (here, I find work in evolutionary developmental biology, niche construction, immunology, bacteriology, epigenetics, environmental evolution, and even virology to be especially useful, fascinating, and wonderful).[6] It turns out that life is less about survival of the fittest as it is about *finding and then reveling within one's fit* in the midst of the great many relationships and connections (connections that run as deep as our DNA and the composition of our cells) that make up who we are both as individuals and as communities.

Ecological developmental biologists have a term for species that they regard as playing an especially essential role in this process—they refer to them as *ecosystem engineers* because of the ways in which they transform the environment to contribute to the flourishing of a greater variety of life than would otherwise be possible. The beaver is a widely cited example of an animal that fulfills this role. By building dams, the beaver transforms an environment from being a place that can only host some kinds of life to being a place that hosts many more lifeforms. However, what has become increasingly clear is the way in which *all* organisms within an ecosystem actually contribute in this way. This is as true of predatory starfish in tidal pools (starfish who help prevent certain non-predatory species from annihilating other non-predatory species, because the former are more successful at getting to food faster and more efficiently than the latter) as it is of wolves (who, as we saw in Yellowstone, not only create a better balance between animal species but also, as a result, allow a greater flourishing of

---

5. See Kropotkin, *Mutual Aid*; Scott, *Art of Not Being Governed*; Solnit, *Paradise Built in Hell*; and crow, *Black Flags and Windmills*.

6. There are all kinds of fascinating source materials to draw from here. See, for example, Bosch and Miller, *Holobiont Imperative*; Cordingley, *Viruses*; Demas and Nelson (eds.), *Ecoimmunology*; DeSalle and Perkins, *Welcome to the Microbiome*; Jablonka and Lamb, *Evolution in Four Dimensions*; McFall-Ngai et al., *Influence of Cooperative Bacteria on Animal Host Biology*; Odling-Smee et al., *Niche Construction*; Sultan, *Organism and Environment*; Turner, *Extended Organism*; and Yong, *I Contain Multitudes*.

2. HONORING

plant life and, in fact, a healthier *river* to flow through the region), as it is of many, many species of bacteria (without whom humans could not develop a healthy immune system and without whom life as we know it on earth would never have occurred, as cyanobacteria were terraforming our planet billions of years before eukaryotic life even existed). It is even true of our own cells and the ways in which our immune systems engage with the multitude of other life forms who live within us and make us who we are (with cytotoxic "killer" T cells and macrophages fulfilling roles similar to that of predatory starfish or wolves). It is also true of fungal networks (which redistribute food between trees in a forest in order to try and ensure there is enough for all the trees instead of spruces just sharing with spruces, maples just sharing with maples, and so on) and, as we are only just learning, it is even true of viruses who, amongst other things, have contributed to our own genetic development (for example, the incorporation of viral DNA into the genome provided pre-mammals with the ability to have a placenta and thus give birth to babies instead of eggs—mammals exist because pre-mammals and viruses merged to create an entirely new form of life!). Consequently, over against Darwinian (or neo-Darwinian) notions of evolution that posit hierarchies of power, wherein the fittest are those who *come out on top*, what we have increasingly learned from the world around us is not so much that some are above and others are below but that we are both *interconnected with others and intra-connected with others*, and so it is within these networks that we discover what it means to meaningfully interact (and intra-act!) and what the effects of our actions are. In other words, the hierarchies of power that we assume are simply part of "the way things are" may actually be a lot more unnatural, harmful, and detrimental to both our evolution and our long-term survival, than we have been led to believe.

It is important to emphasize this, in relation to what we are thinking about here, because hierarchies of *power* create hierarchies of *honor*. Those with more power are given more honor and those with little or no power are given little or no honor. We listen to, esteem, respect, or, at the very least, put up with, contextualize, give the benefit of the doubt to, or excuse, people whom we consider powerful, much more than we listen to, esteem, respect, or put up with, contextualize, give the benefit of the doubt to, or excuse, people whom we consider to be powerless. We praise the powerful for the hard work they must have done to get to where they have gotten (although studies show that the "working poor" or the absolutely destitute actually work harder than the average person and work much harder than the very rich), we praise them for the wisdom they must have demonstrated to be able to make such important decisions (although studies also show that people who have power tend to be there because of *who* they know, not *what* they know, just as the rich tend to inherit wealth their ancestors stole from others rather than having "earned" it), and we praise the nobility of their character (for, as highly-praised and much-awarded philanthropists and advocates for various charities, the wealthy are those who have the capacity to hoard *both goods and goodness*—unlike the supposedly lazy, deliberately stupid, immoral and undeserving poor whom, we are told, simply leech off of the goodness of others).

Hierarchies of power also facilitate the dishonoring of people through the systematic abuses that become possible due to imbalances of power between people. John Dalberg-Acton's aphorism that "power tends to corrupt and absolute power corrupts absolutely" is, perhaps, one of the most well-known and little-heeded sayings of our time. Everyone, it seems, views themselves as the exception to this rule. "Precisely because power corrupts," they think to themselves, "precisely because power is so dangerous, it should be held by someone incorruptible—someone like *me!*—who will actually use it for good. The more power *I* have, the better it will be for *everyone!*" And, in this way, those of us suffering within the ever-expanding empires of such paragons of virtue are reminded, time after time, of the truth in Dalberg-Acton's words.

Hierarchies of power incline towards abuse. Consequently, while we are seeking the kind of world where it is easier to be good company to and with others, *hierarchies of power create the kind of world where it is easier to abuse and be abused by others*. As with most things, this all-too-quickly and all-too-easily becomes a self-reinforcing feedback loop. Thus, for example, one of the ways in which hierarchies of power operate, and one of the tools they use to reinforce their power, is by establishing control over who has access to what information, who is considered an authoritative source of information, and what counts as legitimate information in the first place (because of these dynamics, Foucault sometimes speaks of power and knowledge as a singular thing: power/knowledge, wherein he reverses the truism that "knowledge is power" to assert that "power is knowledge" given, for example, the ways in which those with power are able to set the standards for what gets to count as "true knowledge" and what ends up being "uninformed opinion" or less reliable hearsay).[7] This control of information then becomes a tool that can be weaponized against others who threaten the trajectories or outcomes desired by powerful people. For example, a person may bring forward a grievance that challenges the vision of a particular program or its commitment to the values it claims to hold, but properly addressing that grievance may be costly for the organization

---

7. On Foucault, see *Power/Knowledge*.

2. HONORING

and so, rather than addressing it well, the person who brings the grievance forward is made to feel as though there is something wrong with them, as if everything is working just fine for everyone except them, when, in fact and unbeknownst to them, several other people have brought forward the same grievance and been treated in the same way (I did not pick this example randomly—I have seen this exact scenario play out many times, especially with grievances related to so-called homeless shelters and other social services). Thus, in this instance, power is used to facilitate gaslighting and then, because those who wield power generally know that this is a form of abuse, further abuses of power are required to cover this up—the person gaslit by shelter staff members on Monday is the person kicked out by shelter staff members on Tuesday—and the feedback loop continues to reinforce itself.

Not only this but powerful positions within hierarchies are attractive to people who have less pure motives than those who go into them thinking they can "change the [abusive] system from within" (or some such thing). Some people want power for the sake of power. Or they want power because they are lazy, or violent, or selfish, or vainglorious. Furthermore, because their goal is the possession of power, they are willing to do whatever they feel is necessary in order to attain it. They will manipulate, lie, bootlick, backstab, or bullshit their way into positions that others who are harder-working but more focused on caring for community members will not attain because more altruistic workers are focused on actually doing the work rather than on working the system to their own personal advantage. Hierarchical power dynamics incline towards rewarding people who act selfishly and neglecting those who act otherwise. As a result, all too often, people in positions of leadership (in hospitals, in non-profits, in social services) are actually *the worst people possible* to be in those positions. Here, I am reminded of Jacques Rancière's comment in *Hatred of Democracy* regarding how the ancient Greek city-states elected their representatives through the process of a random lottery (although, *nota bene*, this lottery was open only to free-born, male citizens, so we needn't romanticize the ancient polis overly much). Rancière concludes that this is actually a wise way to elect representatives, for "the drawing of lots was the remedy to an evil at once more serious and much more probable than a government full of incompetents: government comprised of a certain competence, that of individuals skilled at taking power through cunning."[8] This further fits with another observation made by Rancière (and with which I also agree): far more often than not, "good government is the government of those who do not desire

---

8. Rancière, *Hatred of Democracy*, 42.

to govern."⁹ These are lessons that hierarchies of power, top heavy with those who are "skilled at taking power through cunning," urge us to forget. Thus, as with the economic lens imported into so-called caring professions, so also hierarchies of power invalidate, abuse, and *dishonor* the vast majority of people who come seeking good company. As a result, those who take power because they claim to have the best interests of others in mind, just like those who take power because they only have their own interests in mind, end up *staying* in power because they sacrifice those whom they consider most disposable.

The third major obstacle we encounter when trying to organize our life together in a way that honors everyone is the fact that now, in our age of austerity, those who attempt to do the work of building caring communities are continually forced to do more and more with less and less. Not only do major corporations (like Amazon or Google) manipulate the law in order to pay no income taxes on the hundreds of billions of dollars of revenue they bring in every year, they also receive billions of dollars in tax *rebates* every year thanks to income taxes paid by everyday workers and small, local businesses. However, as more and more wealth has become concentrated in the inheritances (which are also taxed less and less) of fewer and fewer people, and as those people and the corporate interests they represent have realized that they can get away with off-shoring their wealth in tax havens (as revealed, for example, in the Panama Papers), the amount of money available to fund things like hospitals, low-income housing, community health clinics, groups homes, and support workers, or any kind of not-profit-generating venture, has been rapidly shrinking. When you combine this with the municipal neoliberal gentrification dynamics I already described in Part One, you end up with a combination of factors that is almost guaranteed to overwhelm, burn-out, exhaust, disillusion, injure, or incapacitate even the most enthusiastic and caring people. The warning issued by Upton Sinclair in *The Jungle*—the story of a Lithuanian immigrant who arrives in Chicago full of life and strength and intent on making a way for himself and his family in the meatpacking plants of the early twentieth-century but who, despite his great fortitude, character, and commitment, is eventually beaten down, broken and destroyed along with everyone he loves (see also, the story of Boxer the horse as told by George Orwell in *Animal Farm*)—is just as relevant for "care providers" today as it was for industrial workers then and now.¹⁰ Over the last twenty years, I have seen most of the very best workers—the most considerate, the most welcoming, the most thoughtful,

---

9. Rancière, *Hatred of Democracy*, 43.
10. See Sinclair, *Jungle*; Orwell, *Animal Farm*.

2. HONORING

the most dedicated, loving, and fair—deeply wounded, destroyed, or driven from the work (more on that in Section Four below). And I have seen those who are not the very best workers become some of the very worst and most cruel, violent, and dehumanizing abusers. This is so, not only because of the first two barriers I described above, it is also so because those who cannot do a lot are given too much to do, and those who show an ability to do a lot are given more and more to do (there is, simply put, ever more to be done), until nobody can stand up under the weight that is piled on them. And so, people are used up and then discarded and the next young, hard-working, starry-eyed, do-gooder, or the next opportunistic power-hungry abuser, is hired and the cycle repeats and further entrenches itself.

Furthermore, as some workers are broken down by the unreasonable expectations of their employers, the misguided demands of their funders, and the grief, loss, and lateral violence they witness in the lives of those whom they desire to serve, they begin to treat others less well. They become impatient, they become afraid, they become insecure, they become frustrated, they become overwhelmed and they close off, withdraw, or lash out. Their work starts to slip, they stop following through on things they said they would do, they spend more time in offices or behind screens where those who come to them for help assume that they are busy working (when, in fact, they are often just gapping-out on social media because they feel they cannot take it anymore). Then they become short-tempered with people who they previously treated with respect and kindness. They betray their own values, which only worsens the way they feel and strengthens the feeling that they are dealing with more than they can bear, and, all too often in these and other ways, *they become abusers*. From seeking to honor that which is special within each person, they regress to dishonoring both their own values and others because they are overwhelmed, done in, defeated.

Thus, environments that are supposed to be places of nurturing, recovery, safety, attentiveness, and care (is that, for example, not what one would want to find at a hospital or a homeless shelter?) frequently end up being even more harmful than what one finds in many more purely profit-oriented workplaces (because some businesses have learned the lesson that happy employees do better work and, in a competitive market where people can earn high incomes—some domains of the infotech industry, for example—the workers are not likely to stick around with an employer or in an environment that is super abusive when they have the option of going elsewhere and being paid the same but treated better).

At this point, it is worth observing that abusive bosses and ruthless capitalists derive a certain smug satisfaction from watching this kind of breakdown occur. "Looks like you're not so noble or patient now," they are quick to point out. "Looks like you can be petty and angry and hurtful, too," they add. In this way, they seek to discredit any way of being in the world that prioritizes people over property or community over self-interest, and they seek to present the Necrocene (i.e., the age of global capitalism) as "not perfect but the best of all possible options." And this, too, is part of the feedback loop that reinforces and normalizes all the ways in which we are taught to dishonor ourselves and one another.

This dominant perspective moves us from the domain of mutually shared honor to honor's opposite—*disgrace*. Etymologically, the word "disgrace" carries connotations not only of shame but also of mutilating someone. When we disgrace others, we *deface* them, we refuse to acknowledge who they are (and, in fact, force them into becoming something other than themselves) and so we, quite literally, *deprive them of grace*. Here, grace should not be considered an unmerited gift that we give to others (as in imperialistic Christian understandings of divine grace, rooted as they are in the notion that grace is the almost exclusive domain of the emperor). Rather, grace should be understood as *the gift that others give us simply by being present with us* and sharing in life together with us. Thus, for example, the old saying that a person has "graced us with their presence." Therefore, to disgrace a person is to go from seeing their presence as a gift to be honored and celebrated to seeing their presence as a burden to be borne, a cost to be calculated, an outcome to be attained, or as a thing to be used, abused, ignored, cast out, or discarded.

Therefore, if we are to create the kind of world where it is easier to be good company to and with others, honoring is something we must learn to do. It is something we must think about carefully and something to which we must regularly attend, so that we can confirm that we are doing it and that we are doing it well. Because, although we face great challenges—a whole world that is structured so as to normalize and enforce disgrace—if we fail here, chances are we will not get to where we wish to go together. In what follows, I will explore honoring others in four main ways: trusting, working together with (collaborating), affirming, and celebrating. As with most of my section headings, these are verbs. Honoring others, just like welcoming others, being together with others, or loving others, is a thing that we *do*. The four ways I explore below are not the only ways to honor others, but they are good places to start.

A. Trusting

Honor will never be fully experienced as real if trust is absent. Trust refers to a "reliance on the veracity, integrity, and other virtues" of the person or people with whom we are interacting. Tracing back the origins of the word, we also find notions of comfort, consolation, strengthening, and making safe. Trust means believing that people have understandable reasons for saying the things that they say to us, believing that people have understandable reasons for feeling the ways that they do, and believing that people have understandable reasons for acting the ways that they do. Trust means knowing that the overwhelming majority of people—regardless of their background, labels, past experiences, or diagnoses—desire to be good, desire to love and be loved, desire to find a place of connection and belonging, and have some kind of moral code that they live by. Trust means affirming that all people have unique strengths, experiences, perspectives, wisdom, and virtues. And trust, especially when it exists in relationships with people whom others have treated as untrustworthy, can be a great balm on wounds, broken-heartedness, isolation, and self-doubt or self-loathing. Time after time, in situations where people are very upset, angry, or volatile, I have seen the ways in which expressions of trust (whether verbal, paraverbal, or nonverbal), are experienced as a form of comfort and consolation and, as a result, restore everyone's sense of safety. Trust truly is a thing that strengthens those who receive it.

One of the most consistent and brutal ways in which oppressed, abandoned, dispossessed and otherwise marginalized or othered people are abused is by the ways in which social service workers, healthcare providers, police officers, security guards, or members of dominant populations treat them as scary and dangerous animals—as those who are somehow less-than-human, whose very presence in a space jeopardizes the safety and well-being of anyone else who is there. This is a relentless process of dehumanization that almost always has devastating consequences when experienced over a sustained period of time. It is a process that, at its core, is an expression of distrust. It communicates to people that they are untrustworthy. But it is critically important to understand that this distrust is an element of oppression and is one of the ways in which oppressors help themselves to "sleep the sleep of the just" (to quote the words of Erik Prince, the founder of the world's largest mercenary army). Just as White cops distrust Black youth, just as controlling and abusive men distrust their intimate partners (or, for the most part, women more generally), just as Canadian settlers distrust Indigenous peoples, so also the dispossessors (i.e., "the rich") distrust the dispossessed (i.e., "the poor"), real estate developers distrust those who can't afford to pay rents, governments distrust those who don't pay taxes, social assistance workers distrust the unemployed, and those who are trying to get ahead by playing along distrust anyone who appears to be deviant.

If we do not trust people, if we do not operate from the initial assumption that those who come to us are trustworthy, then regardless of whatever rhetoric we deploy regarding "respect" or "client-centeredness" or "unconditional positive regard," or even "empathy," we will not actually honor people with our actions and with the security measures we deploy to try and feel less afraid of those whom we say we exist to serve. People come to us seeking help, they come to us seeking good company, and when we respond by treating them as untrustworthy, we actually *betray the trust they put in us*. More often than not, it is this betrayal of trust on our part that leads to an escalation of aggressive, angry, or threatening behaviors on the part of those who came to us. Thus, our lack of trust creates a feedback loop that produces what is known as the Pygmalion Effect (or, more colloquially, a "self-fulfilling prophecy"). Time after time, studies reveal that our expectations of how a person will be in a certain environment have a very serious effect upon how that person actually then is within that environment. If we have high expectations, people tend to meet them. If we have low expectations, people also tend to meet those. The same applies to trust. If we treat people as trustworthy, they trend towards acting in trustworthy ways. Conversely, if we treat people as untrustworthy, they trend towards acting in untrustworthy ways. Time after time, I have seen the evidence of this as people who are poorly treated, respond to this treatment with hurt, anger, and some kind of escalated behavior, and who are then "red flagged" as "too dangerous" to be able to access support. These people then came to spaces I was helping to facilitate and never once harmed or threatened to harm another person. As one man who was kicked out of every other service in the city of London, and whom the cops would only approach once four officers were present, said to me: "Other people are nice to me here, and that makes me want to be nice to other people." In the space where we spent

A. TRUSTING

time with that man, we only ever saw him as a nice man and he never gave us any reason to regret or reevaluate that perspective (and, while this man never once laid hands on me, I did have a cop lay his hands on me and throw me into a wall when I tried to prevent the cop from violently and illegally abusing this man).

Consequently, when violence regularly occurs in one environment (but almost never occurs in other environments), I always ask the following questions: what is it about this environment that makes violence seem like an appropriate, reasonable, or obvious course of action here? If we are trying to create the kind of world where violence is less likely and it is easier for people to be peaceable, then what is it about the ways in which this environment is structured that makes it easier for people to be violent? For example, have we structured our physical space in a way that reminds people of other environments where violence is more normalized and is actually a very useful survival strategy? Have we heightened our building security to such an extent that we remind people of prison (and I have lost track of the number of times that people staying in shelters have said they were reminded of being in prison—an accurate observation despite the ways in which it offends the managers of those shelters)? If so, we can expect people to deploy the same survival skills in that environment that they deploy in prison. Furthermore, what are we doing when we engage with others that makes violence a more likely outcome? We need to ask this question very carefully—it is *not* okay to blame victims of violence for the harmful actions of their assailants, and people who act violently need to learn to be responsible for their own actions (a point emphasized repeatedly by Alan Jenkins in his work with violent and abusive men).[1] However, it is worth asking if we are interacting with people in unkind ways, and if we are posturing or communicating in ways that remind them of other abusers (like cops or prison guards). Do we expect people to behave violently? If so, we are contributing to the Pygmalion Effect and, while we are not responsible for the actions other people choose to take, we do make certain actions *more or less plausible, likely, natural-feeling, or appealing* to them by the expectations we bring into our interactions with them.

That said, given that people are constantly moving between environments, and given that people may spend considerable amounts of time around people (like cops) or environments (like prison) where things like violence are normalized and taken-for-granted, we can never fully prevent violence or threats of violence from occurring in some spaces. This is why, for example, Shawna Potter avoids talking about "making safe space" and,

---

1. See Jenkins, *Invitation to Responsibility* and also Jenkins, *Becoming Ethical*.

instead, talks about making spaces *safer*. Total safety is not something that can be guaranteed all the time in most community spaces—but moving towards higher likelihoods of safety is usually possible.[2] Therefore, *precisely because of this*, building relationships of mutual trust is absolutely critical. Working to immediately demonstrate and build mutual trust with people who have had violence normalized to them, makes a world of difference when the time comes to intervene into a violent or potentially violent situation in a way that permits you to be heard and respected. Because I have built this mutual trust with people, I have been able to physically use my body as a barrier in innumerable situations (many of which involved weapons like knives or steel pipes—and, on at least two occasions, a handgun), and this barrier was respected and nobody was physically harmed. Always, when intervening into this kind of situation my desire is to communicate the following—*I trust you not to hurt me, and you can trust me not to hurt you* (alternatively: I am not afraid of you acting like a mindless monster, not because I am going to try and posture and be more macho, tough, or intimidating than you, but because I *see you* and *acknowledge you* and *trust you*, and *you don't have to be afraid of me* either because I am coming from a place of care and concern, not just for others involved in this situation, but also and especially for you). Both sides of this equation are essential, especially when we remember that in the majority of situations where people threaten violence or act violently in community spaces, they are doing this because they are afraid.

Of course, when things get violent and especially when weapons come out, I do feel fear—this is a natural reaction to this kind of situation and I don't want people to imagine that I have some kind of superhuman (or delusional or sociopathic?) courage. In fact, as I mentioned already, as an introvert who experienced some trauma and abuse as a child (and then again as an adult), I have a very strong aversion to conflict. Generally, four categories are used to describe how people respond to trauma, abuse, violence, or the threat thereof. These are the fight, flight, freeze, and fawn responses.[3]

---

2. See Potter, *Making Spaces Safer*. She makes a good point and a lot of mainstream agencies have started adopting this language—in part to demonstrate their wokeness, in part to protect themselves from lawsuits—but I still think we have to fundamentally commit ourselves to making safe space (not just "safer" space, especially given that "safer" is such a vague term—safer than prison? safer than being locked in a house with an abuser? safer than what exactly?—which, of course, is part of why those seeking to avoid lawsuits use it so much). We commit to creating a *safe* space and, by making this commitment and wording it in this way, we make ourselves accountable to those to whom we make this commitment and *open ourselves up to being help responsible by them*.

3. My friend, Jemma Tosh (author of the highly recommended *Body and Consent*

A. TRUSTING

Physiologically, thanks to my experiences and how I have developed, I incline towards freezing and fawning. However, I have learned that my fear-response does not need to determine the course of action I take or how I choose to engage with others. That is to say, while my body may feel fear, I have learned how to sit with that feeling in my body and still talk, think, and act based on my commitments to other values that I hold more strongly than my fear—values like a commitment to the safety and well-being of others, a commitment to acknowledging the sacredness of all people, a commitment to not jeopardizing everyone's safety further by calling the police, and a commitment to being good company to and with others. Therefore, I frequently deploy a tactic that I call "strategic vulnerability." This means using my body language (how I stand, what I do with my hands, how open my posture is and, significantly, avoiding posturing or taking stances that are favored by cops or guards who make people feel unsafe) and using how I position myself (where I stand or, if I am talking with someone who is seated, whether I loom over that person by standing or whether I sit by them so that we are on the same level, or whether I take a knee beside their chair so that they are actually looking down on me) to communicate openness, trust, and respect so that people in a volatile situation are presented with a real alternative to a violent outcome. Having used this tactic for many years, it is worth repeating what I said above: I have been physically assaulted and more seriously injured by police officers *while doing my job*, more often than I have been physically harmed by anyone labeled "psychotic," "dangerous," "high-risk," "noncompliant," or whatever else.

Furthermore, when relationships of mutual trust and respect are established, it becomes more possible to *mediate* conflicts rather than simply terminating or relocating them (i.e., what standard tactics of "conflict de-escalation" entail). When conflicts occur, the ideal goal is to resolve them in a way that is, at the very least, momentarily acceptable to all the parties involved. Conflict mediations take time and require people to be able to remain in a situation that is escalated or uncomfortable in order to get to the resolution. This means finding the space for this rather than simply rushing to restore the peaceful equilibrium that social workers or healthcare providers think they need to feel comfortable. Trust finds a way to create this space. After all, trust is not something we have to think about much unless we are in situations that challenge us—it is precisely in uncomfortable, unsettling, escalated, and volatile situations that we get the opportunity to demonstrate

---

in *Psychology, Psychiatry, and Medicine*), points out that there is actually a fifth trauma response that is often neglected. The five responses are fight, flight, freeze, fawn, and *fuck*. This explains why many people who have experienced sexual traumas can experience physical arousal in distressing situations.

that all our talk about "respect," "unconditional positive regard," "empathy," and "client-centeredness" *actually means something*. It is precisely here that we see how much we live out our values or how much we simply claim to hold those values in order to feel good about ourselves even as we go on to harm, cast out, and reject others at critical times.

Building trust, then, requires us to operate with two presuppositions: first, that those who come to us are trustworthy; second, that *those who come to us have legitimate reasons to question our trustworthiness*. These presuppositions are a direct reversal of the presuppositions that are operative in almost all social services and healthcare organizations: i.e., that those paid to be present are trustworthy and that those paid to be present have good reasons to question the trustworthiness of those who come to them for help or companionship. In other words, against standard practices, *we are actually the ones who must prove our trustworthiness* to the oppressed, dispossessed, and abandoned folx who come to us—not the other way around.

Spiritual-but-not-religious do-gooders might be inclined to use the language of humility or of walking humbly in this context, but I think that would be a misapplication of that concept (and practice). This reversal of presuppositions is not about some kind of modesty or noble condescension. Far from it. It is actually about recognizing and being honest about the pervasive reality of oppression and the ways in which oppression operates even in institutions, agencies, and community spaces that are branded as safe, welcoming, therapeutic, and caring. In other words, it is about *genuinely and actively honoring others* and not simply just posturing or speaking as if that is the case.

B. Working Together With (Collaborating)

Trusting others as we actively demonstrate that we are serious about honoring them requires us to recognize that genuine community is only built if *all* members of that community are invited into the work of community building. Ultimately, the kind of world where it is easier to be good company to and with others is not the kind of thing that can be enforced from the top down—although, as I explore throughout this work, we certainly can collectively agree to structure and frame our communities in such a way as to make that kind of world more probable and, as a part of this, we can designate certain people to help hold us accountable to this. We must collectively work together with others in order to move towards creating the kind of world we desire to live and participate within. And, if we genuinely honor others, this will not be something burdensome or a frustratingly difficult necessity (as if we actually believe things would be so much better and easier if everyone did what we told them to do); rather, it will be something we genuinely desire to do because we know that everyone who comes into our shared space brings their own wisdom, experiences, strengths, perspectives, and sensitivities, and we know that finding ways for all people to contribute to our mutually agreed upon trajectory will bring us to a far better place, and engage us in a far richer journey, than if we, alone, were leading the way or controlling every step thereon.

Here, it is impossible to lay claim to terms like "mutuality" and "reciprocity" (terms which both refer to a back-and-forth process of give-and-receive between equals so that at some points a person gives and at other points that same person is given to by others and, in all of this, no one is posited as superior to anyone else but each person is granted the equivalent level of status as every other person) without coming to the conclusion that, actively pursuing mutuality and reciprocity means ensuring that everyone is also actively contributing to building the cultural and political trajectory that those who seek help and good company desire to find and participate within. This does not mean that people will all have the same roles within a community—different people will come with different skills, passions, and desires, not to mention different levels of time and energy that they can commit to forming the space—but it does mean being very careful to not allow a *demarcation of roles* to become a *demarcation of status* (so that, for example, those with certain roles end up having more status than those with other roles). This is not to say that some voices will not carry more influence than others—that will inevitably happen in any group—but it is to emphasize that the nature of that influence should be *charismatic* rather than *institutional*. By that (and following Weber), I mean that influential voices should be influential because when they speak the other members of the community respond by saying, "yes, that is what I also think; you have managed to put words to the feelings I carry in my heart and haven't known how to express." These voices, then, only have the level of influence they have because they speak what the group feels. If they begin to speak in other ways—and no longer speak in a way that is representative of the feelings of the group—their influence is rescinded and given to another voice that the group feels continues to speak what is in everyone's heart. This is the antithesis of the kind of institutional influence (or authority) we are accustomed to governing our shared spaces. Hierarchies of power are firmly implemented, institutionalized, and enforced, in part, so that so-called leaders can do what they want, and take the community where they want it to go, regardless of what other members of the community desire.

Therefore, honoring others means preventing the institutionalization of unequal power divides within a community and developing practices that contribute to *meaningful* collaborations developing between all community members.

Here, it is absolutely essential that shared spaces avoid the paternalistic, tokenistic, and condescending approach to "peer support work" that has been trending in social services and healthcare institutions. Recently, this has become a popular approach although, like the land acknowledgments explored above, how things have actually played out well illustrates the complexities related to systems-level changes within the context of colonization and how hybridization moves in multiple directions simultaneously (producing some more liberative elements while simultaneously producing the co-optation of that which has the potential to be liberative.)

People who have direct, personal experience of being targeted by oppressive practices (from the war on people criminalized for how they obtain or take their medicines, to the pathologization of victims of abuse, to the

B. WORKING TOGETHER WITH (COLLABORATING)

disciplining of deviants, to the criminalization of survival in the context of oppression) have long expressed frustration with the fact that they are systematically excluded from meaningful participation in the formation of the programs that target them and the decisions that are made that have very real, substantial, and long-lasting effects on their lives, what things are possible to them, and what things are denied to them. "Nothing about us without us" is a rallying cry in many of these communities and, in fact, as researchers have made strides to catch up with "people with lived experience" (as they are commonly called), it has become increasingly clear that people who are actually suffering the consequences of something (dispossession, housing deprivation, criminalized medication use, racism, sexism, heteronormativity, trans-antagonism, ableism, settler colonialism, and so on) are also usually the people who are most aware of the best solutions to that situation—solutions that would remove or adequately manage their suffering and create environments that would transition from being death-dealing to being life-giving and life-affirming. Perhaps the most obvious example of this is the ways in which "harm reduction" (i.e., providing unused needles, unused pipes, safe supply, protected consumption sites, and other things to people who take medicines that the state tells them they are not allowed to take) was practiced among those criminalized *for decades* before it was adopted as an internationally recognized, evidence-based best practice— "Oh, having a safe place to inject reduces harm? Well, fuck, we've known that since the very first person injected."

Because of this recognition, there is increasing pressure (especially from liberal funders) on agencies to demonstrate that they are incorporating the feedback and participation of "people with lived experiences" into their programs. This, too, is now considered a "best practice." However, given the rigid hierarchies that exist in most organization (and the elitism that exists not around "lived experience" but around things like degrees, certifications, and registrations with certified professional associations), and given the continual pressure to do more and more work with less and less money, the ways in which "peer supports" are actually integrated into organizations are frequently exploitative and abusive. Generally, peer supports are hired to do the same work as other workers but for much less money and with much less of a say into how programs develop. Other workers—those with all the right degrees and certifications—tend to then look down on the peer supports (and paying people who are doing roughly the same work very different wages is a very good way to encourage this). Following in the footsteps of their bosses, these more highly paid staff members treat peer supports in a disrespectful and condescending manner (often giving peer supports the work that they, the registered social workers or registered healthcare professionals, feel too important to do). Further, "peer supports" are almost always trapped at the frontline level, lacking the certificates and level of education required to even qualify to be interviewed for a position that grants them higher-level decision-making authority.

Acknowledging the wisdom, strengths, and profound insights of "people with lived experience" has the potential to be a genuinely disruptive move forward—disruptive in that it has the potential to shift who has the power to make decisions, who is considered a leading authority on any given subject, whose voices are given priority and whose voices are "deliberately silenced, or preferably unheard" (to use Arundhati Roy's term for those whom others refer to as "the voiceless").[1] Consequently, agencies and organizations, invested as they and their leaders are in hierarchical power structures, gesture towards recognizing and incorporating "people with lived experience" into their decision-making and other practices, while doing their utmost to ensure that this incorporation does not disrupt, threaten, or displace their power and priorities. Of course, so-called "people with lived experience" are not powerless and utterly incapacitated by any of this and so there is constant pushback, flanking and counter-flanking, and renegotiations of all of these dynamics—it's just that those who already have power and who desire to hold onto their power are playing with the deck fully stacked to their advantage for as long as we understand such hierarchies to be necessary, natural, desirable, and enforceable.

It is the recognition of how all of this tends to play out in practice that has led many who are organizing themselves to create more life-affirming and life-giving worlds to criticize the language of "allyship" as it is deployed by liberal do-gooders and so-called caring professionals. As more and more potentially liberating analyses, discourses, and practices are incorporated into organizations that actually have no interest in significantly disrupting the oppressive trajectory of our status quo in any meaningful way (in part, we have realized, because these organizations actually benefit from the continuation of that oppressive trajectory), it is increasingly common to observe that talking about being allies has become a form of virtue-signaling that is more about making the self-proclaimed "allies" feel good about themselves than it is about actually making any kind of meaningful difference in the lives of those with whom people claim to be allied. For this reason, those who are oppressed, criminalized, and left for dead, more frequently desire *accomplices not allies* (and *Taking Sides*, a volume put together by Cindy Milstein, is a useful entry point into this conversation).[2] Accomplices go

1. Roy, "2004 Sydney Peace Prize Lecture."
2. See Milstein, *Taking Sides*.

B. WORKING TOGETHER WITH (COLLABORATING)   75

beyond the posturing of allies and actually become complicit in the kind of justice that refuses to be bound by (imperialistic, capitalistic, settler colonial) laws that consistently prioritize profits or "fiscal responsibility" over peoples. An accomplice is a person who assists in the completion of activities that, although often necessary for both survival and one's ability to also participate in the glorious abundance of life, are considered crimes under the regimes of carceral states. An ally will say they have your back; an accomplice will actually keep six for you when you need to liberate some Christmas presents for your kids at the local big-box store. An ally will say they support what you are trying to do, even if they don't always support how you go about doing it; an accomplice will mask up with you and, even if they don't smash the windows of a bank with you or help de-arrest those assaulted by riot cops, they will still help provide the critical mass needed to ensure the safety and anonymity of those who will do those things. An ally will cheer from the sidelines; an accomplice will place themselves between you and the weapons deployed by the state when called upon to do so. An ally will agree that, theoretically, legality should never be correlated with morality or justice on a one-to-one basis (after all, everything the Nazis did was legal); an accomplice will go on to break unjust and immoral laws, rules, or regulations with you.

Take something as simple as regulations regarding how bathrooms are used in drop-in centers. When my friend Mechele and I began to hold space for people who had been kicked out of all other social services and community spaces, the other programs and workers who also participated in that space were adamant that only one person at a time was allowed in each bathroom (as per the written policies and procedures). They claimed that this was for the safety of the people who used the bathroom but, in actual fact, the policy was part of a "war on drugs" mentality that punished people for finding their own ways to attain and take medicines they experienced as helpful. Mechele and I urged the higher-ups to change this policy but they declined to do so. Consequently, we refused to enforce it and made it known (to those who came to us seeking good company, not to the bosses!) that we would not enforce it. We made this decision for a number of reasons. First of all, our community was experiencing a sky-rocketing number of overdose deaths due to the so-called "opioid crisis" and the mass distribution of fentanyl (although this is really a "criminalization crisis" not an opioid crisis). Given this, and given that people were far more likely to die while using alone (and Mechele and I both prevented multiple overdoses from occurring in those bathrooms when people did use alone in them), we encouraged people who would be injecting their medication to not do so alone. Furthermore, and this is the second point, people with more experience injecting were able to assist those who had trouble handling needles due to being disabled or differently-abled, having had a stroke, having shaky hands, or whatever else, and this then prevented abscesses and other infections from occurring. But these were not our only reason for violating this policy. Many couples who are deprived of housing face incredible challenges to being able to have private moments together. Given the inability of couples to stay together in local shelters (a practice that has shifted to a certain extent in larger cities like Toronto but which persists in smaller cities like London), and given the lack of access to showers for those who are "sleeping rough," permitting couples to use bathrooms together so that they could have some private time to engage in an intimate act like showering together, was one way of recognizing their humanity. Other times, and this is now the fourth point, people had wounds or abscesses in areas that were not easy for them to reach, clean, or change their dressings on and so, of course, a friend should be allowed in the bathroom with them to assist with that. Finally, for those involved in sex work, being able to turn a quick trick in a shower at a drop-in center—while very, very far from ideal (we will remain very far from any ideal for as long as sex work is criminalized)—may still be a much better option than tricking in a public place or somewhere more remote and dangerous. Thus, while Mechele and I left the bosses with the impression that we would follow the rules and regulations they imposed upon the space (i.e., we lied to their faces), we informally chose to follow life-giving and life-affirming practices related to harm-reduction, genuinely listening to the self-expressed needs of community members, and trying to just be caring people in the company of other caring people. We did this knowing that we faced the possibility of punishment (up to and including the loss of our jobs which, in my case, would have jeopardized my ability to care for my own children), and we accepted this as a possible outcome, and then did our damnedest to get away with being genuinely good company (and here the words of that Jesus guy from Nazareth come to mind: recognizing that we sometimes work "as sheep amongst wolves" we must be "be innocent as doves and wise as serpents"—fuck yeah, you got that right, Jesus; it's just that the Christians always tend to think it is the dispossessed who are the wolves when really it is the dispossessors).

This, then, is one example of what it looks like to move from the rhetoric of allyship to the practices of accomplices. It illustrates what it means to work together with others (to be *collaborators*—to co-labor with others in traitorous ways for, here, we are acting as race and class traitors and are betraying the expectations imposed upon us by our bosses) in ways that permit all members to determine what the community needs to do and what each person needs to do as a part of that. Thus, years before so-called London,

Ontario, had an official "supervised consumption site," we quietly had one running in our bathrooms. How could we not? People were overdosing and dying en masse. In 2017, for example, at least *eleven people died every single day* in Canadian-occupied territories due to this criminalization crisis. This was (and continues to be) a crisis manufactured by oppressive laws that target those who are dispossessed and left for dead. It is less like people dying of natural causes and more like people being murdered by the state and its agents—and even when the state created "Good Samaritan" laws to allow people to call 911 if a friend was overdosing without the person making the call having to worry that they would then be arrested on a breach or for simple possession of an illicit substance, the cops responded by arresting everyone on scene as potential *murder suspects*, thereby circumnavigating the intent of the Good Samaritan laws and ensuring that people would never feel safe calling 911 for help. So, we opened our bathrooms not only to those who had need of private, shared space, but also so that our loved ones would not die. And, while we ran the bathrooms in this way, we had multiple close calls but we *never once* had a single person die in the space we helped to hold.

i. Meeting

Working together with others requires us to finds ways to come together to meet in order to make this form of collaboration possible. However, doing this well can be a tricky thing. Much of that trickiness is found in the etymology of the word "meeting." As I mentioned in the opening of Part One, the word "meeting" contains connotations of coming into physical contact with others and of uniting or joining together with others. Sometimes this occurs in order to come to an agreement together, but sometimes this occurs in the context of competition or combat (and, in fact, the English word "joust" is from the Old French, *joster*, which traces back to the Latin, *iuxtare*, which means "to approach" and "to meet"). Thus, for example, we say that people "met in battle" or that they competed at a "track meet." Additionally, the word "meeting" also has overtones related to provision ("this budget meets our needs"), of settlement ("I can meet that payment deadline"), of conjunction ("the lines met at this point"), and of conformity ("this meets all the requirements"). Meeting, then, is something we have all done in many different ways and we all bring our experiences of these previous meetings forward into future meetings. Consequently, if we are hoping to meet in ways that contribute to a certain kind of outcome (i.e., a world where it is easier to be good company to and with others), then we need to arrange meetings that contribute to this and that make it less natural-feeling or likely for us to meet with one another in a manner that contributes to other kinds of worlds.

Given the diverse histories people bring into community spaces, some kind of regular and formalized meeting times are necessary. If we do not have regular, formal meetings with and as community members, then people will default to other ways of being in relationships with others, people will import behaviors that are useful in other environments (but which aren't necessarily useful for developing a space where it is easier to be good

I. MEETING

company to and with others), and other environments will end up establishing the default or dominant culture of the space.

Given the ways in which anarchist modalities and philosophies have resonated with me personally, and given the rampant abuse of authority that I have witnessed in any hierarchical environment, I spent many years pushing back against formalizing community structures. I wanted things to occur more "organically." Rather than imposing structures onto people, I wanted people to be liberated from the structures that oppressed them, and I wanted things to emerge "naturally" from within the group rather than being imposed onto the group. What I failed to realize, in earlier days, was that it is impossible to have a space that is neutral where people can "emerge" or simply "be" themselves. Other environments place *enormous* pressures onto people and as people are socialized, subjectified, and subjugated, they will continue to behave in ways that those other environments have taught them to behave unless we take *pro-active, deliberate, and thoughtful action* to counter this.

This means that those of us who are tasked with holding space for others have a responsibility to create formal, structural elements that try to accomplish this. This does not mean we then view ourselves as the sole authorities over the space, or the sole experts on holding space, who then do what we want because "we know best." A very long history of "people who know what is best for others" (from Christian missionaries and Residential School teachers who set out to "kill the Indian in the child" so that "savages" could be saved and civilized, to the International Monetary Fund and its promises to enrich impoverished communities by further impoverishing them, to armies of poverty pimps and the pseudo-salvation they offer to those who are deprived of housing) demonstrates that this is not an approach *any* well-intentioned do-gooder can trust themselves to embody well (i.e., without actually doing considerable and perhaps irreversible harm to those whom they say they want to help). Instead, what this means is that those who are tasked with holding space for others also have the responsibility to create formal, structural elements that invite others into conversation about what kind of community they want to be, what their shared core values will be, what kind of expectations should be had of community members, how they will commit to caring for one another and holding one another accountable, and how responsibilities and duties will be shared throughout the community. In other words, those who have the power or ability to create and enforce structural dynamics within a space, have a responsibility and duty to ensure that they are engaging in this task in a way that genuinely respects the desires and meets the needs of the community members.

Regularly scheduled meetings to discuss these things are, as far as I can tell, an essential part of this. If we are not setting aside time to talk about these things together, I do not know how we can work well towards these goals. Thus, *communities need to take time to meet as community to talk about community*. For those who are unaccustomed to this way of being in relationship with others, this can be very awkward. We are not generally taught this way of collectively reflecting on how we are with others and what we want from ourselves and others within a particular place. Plus, people are frequently tired and, especially if they are oppressed, impoverished, deprived of housing, and surviving within a system that has criminalized their ability to thrive, people may not immediately understand the urgency of this part of community formation work. Furthermore, even if they do feel that meeting is important, they may need time to develop the kind of trust that is necessary to speak with the vulnerability that it takes to build communities in this way. Consequently, learning to have meetings that folx identify as inviting, useful, genuinely participatory, and open, is a lesson that takes some time.

We all have preconceptions related to how a formal meeting should look but often, in this-or-that specific community with this-or-that specific composition and this-or-that set of unique strengths and needs, such preconceptions become barriers to facilitating the kinds of conversations we need to have to advance the goals mentioned above. Those responsible for holding the space, who are likely engaged in other kinds of formal meetings in other environments, must learn to hold their preconceptions especially lightly. Communities are not businesses, are not Board rooms, are not critical incident debriefings, are not presentations for partners or classmates or funders. Communities are living things that grow and change, that suffer and hope and dream; and while it is frequently said that "communities are messy," it's important to immediately add that communities that are well-developed also have the confidence, structures, and transparency needed to deal promptly, tenderly, and well with their own messes.

Meetings, then, are one essential way in which we learn to work together with others. Not only that, but they are also one essential way in which we learn to work together with others in ways that are more welcoming and more kind. How we meet also demonstrates the ways in which we honor one another and trust that each member plays an essential role in the well-being of the whole.

ii. Guiding

We honor people by trusting them. We demonstrate our trust in them by working collaboratively together with them. And we work collaboratively together with others by ensuring that those most affected by the issue on which we are focusing (loneliness, housing deprivation, rape culture, whatever else) are those who are at the forefront of guiding our community in the direction we hope to travel together.

A guide is someone who "shows the way." Guides are those who can see or find the way in places where others cannot. Furthermore, guides are those who are able to identify risks where those unfamiliar with an environment see none. Thus, an experienced guide on a glacier will be able to identify hidden crevasses where inexperienced hikers see only snow and ice; an experienced mountaineer will be able to read the meaning of shifts in the wind and how soon a person must get to shelter given the cumulonimbus clouds amassing on the horizon; an experienced Artic or coastal hiker will know when to travel based on the ebbs and flows of river levels and tides; and so on. Guides know the "theory" (i.e., they can read a topographical map, the can navigate with landmarks, or stars, or compasses) but they also know that the way things look when you are actually present in a place is often very different than what you see when studying a 1:24,000 scale map on your living room coffee table (where one inch on the map is the equivalent of 2,000 feet of multifaceted terrain). As such, guides also know when to follow the scheduled route and when to deviate from it (when not to try and cross a river, when not to try and ascend a summit or traverse a pass, when to shelter in place, when to move around snow bridges that are no longer stable, and so on). Hence, the word "guidance" has meanings related not only to directing people towards a goal but also to being able to change direction when needed in order to accommodate emerging factors while still getting to where one wishes to go. For example, "guided missiles" are "guided" precisely because they can change direction mid-flight. Not surprisingly, given the complexities that come with different kinds of terrain, different weather systems, different climates, and different co-habitants of the land, the best guides tend to be indigenous to the areas where they act as guides. Thus, if I want to hike the Akshayuk Pass, I would seek advice from the local Iglulingmuit, and if I wish to visit Ribo Drugta and Shey Gompa, I would look for guidance from experienced Sherpas.

The same wisdom applies when we are looking to find our way out from our perpetual lostness in the context of ongoing dispossession, impoverishment, housing deprivation, criminalization, colonization, and abandonment. It is those who are local to those experiences—those who are dispossessed, impoverished, deprived of housing, criminalized, colonized, and abandoned—who are best equipped to collectively guide us to a better future, who are best equipped to see dangers that the rest of us might never notice, who are able to quickly respond to sudden shifts in circumstances, and who can see the way when the rest of us are either hopelessly or ignorantly lost. In their hubris, many outsiders do not even realize that they are lost or well on their way to getting themselves and others lost (and this, of course, is fundamental to the experience of being truly lost—by the time you realize you are lost, you do not know how to find yourself again; if you knew you were getting lost, you would not have gotten lost in the first place). If people who have not been dispossessed, impoverished, deprived of housing, criminalized, colonized, or abandoned go to those who have experienced such things and offer themselves as guides to lead others into "the promised land," they are doing something just as foolish, arrogant, and dangerous as going to a group of Sherpas and telling them they are now well equipped to lead the Sherpas and their families through the Himalayas in January because they read *The Snow Leopard*, watched *Seven Years in Tibet*, and studied a YouTube video on how to read a map.[1]

Learning to follow the guidance of community members is especially important in two areas. First, community members are those best equipped to identify what their needs are—what is missing, what is going wrong, what is insufficient, offensive, or harmful about "solutions" that others are putting forward—and, second, community members are those best equipped to identify how to address, respond to, and resolve those needs. This is not to suggest that every person who is oppressed is able to deconstruct how oppression operates and where it is rooted and who benefits from it, who is most harmed by it, and how we can all individually and collectively liberate ourselves from it. Oppression is sustained, in part, because of the ways in which it creates oppressed subjects who view oppression as natural, just,

---

1. See Matthiessen, *Snow Leopard*; and Annaud, *Seven Years in Tibet*.

II. GUIDING

or right and who adopt the perspectives, judgements, and values of their oppressors. Hence the post-Foucauldian and post-colonial domain(s) of theory devoted to explaining how the subject produced by subjectification is doubly subjected—that is to say, oppressed folks can experience and relate to themselves, as their very core, through the lenses and narrative determined by oppressors. An easy-to-understand example of this is so-called "battered partner syndrome," wherein a person who is being serially abused by their partner believes both that they are unable to prevent the abuse and, in fact, that they deserve the abuse. This is precisely what the abuser wishes them to believe and, very likely, is what the abuser needs them to believe so that he (abusers are overwhelmingly but not universally cis-men) can continue to believe the same thing. This sort of abuse plays out in all domains of oppression. As a result, within communities of oppressed people, one regularly finds those who adopt the values, morals, and norms of their oppressors and who subsequently engage in lateral violence, while being all too happy to shit on those who have been dispossessed once they join the company of the dispossessors (or, at least, shit on the more impoverished when they become less impoverished). Equally damaging and equally related to this fracturing and subjectification of oppressed subjects is the discovery that many in oppressed communities also attempt to enforce distinctions between the "deserving" and the "undeserving poor," as well as advocate for the charity model of care, many who continue to brand deviance as immorality, and many who will only work towards healing those who do not overstep what is or is not permitted to those designated as "sick" and who, therefore, must fulfill "the sick role."

"The sick role" is a term that Talcott Parsons used in order to highlight that society only approves of certain ways of being sick—i.e., temporarily, through no fault of your own, all the while doing your utmost to recover and return to being "a contributing member of society" while expressing excessive and never critical gratitude to officially designated care-providers—and that if people are sick in other ways—i.e., permanently, through their own doing, with no desire or effort to improve and "contribute," and being critical of or even hostile towards officially designated care-providers—then support is replaced with punishment).[2]

Observing all this should not lead those who are coming from outside the community of the oppressed to view themselves as visionaries, leaders, educators, saviors, or some kind of enlightened or radical vanguard leading others into the promised land. Black people don't need White saviors, women don't need men to rescue them, Indigenous peoples don't need Settlers

---

2. See Parsons, *Social System*.

to civilize them, dispossessed people don't need dispossessors to teach them how to live an abundant life, and those who have been abandoned by others most certainly do not need those who abandon others to show them the way to build community. Here, leftists can be as oppressive as those on the right, only instead of trying to force those who have been oppressed to adopt some variation of capitalism's work ethic, bourgeois morality, and a true appreciation of law and order, they think that oppressed people just need to understand a little more Marxist-Leninist theory and, voila, the revolution will come.[3]

Consequently, those who come to these communities as outsiders seeking to be safe, welcoming, and useful need to understand that they are *holding space* and helping to *facilitate an environment* wherein members of a community can collectively find their way to more life-affirming and less death-dealing politics.[4] However, as one does this work, another (hopefully obvious) observation becomes apparent. Different people from oppressed groups will have different opinions and, in fact, will even disagree with one another. And this is as true of those who are seeking life-giving change as it is of those who are just trying to survive or of those who are looking to climb up over the backs of others. There is no single monolithic group called "the oppressed" who all think and feel and act the same way. Consequently, and inevitably, those who attempt to hold space and facilitate a space wherein life-affirming and life-giving changes become more possible are bound to take sides. Liberals often struggle with this—they want to be everyone's friends and say they support this or that group of people (Indigenous people, women, members of the queer community, and so on). As a result, liberals become extremely uncomfortable when confronted with the realization that members of those groups not only disagree with each other but flagrantly contradict one another and work against each other. One cannot, for example, equally and actively support both Indigenous land defenders who gather with hereditary chiefs in order to assert territorial sovereignty and oppose oil pipelines, on the one hand, and Indian Act chiefs who are funded by the government of Canada and who work to abolish Indigenous sovereignty and support Canada's resource extraction industries,

---

3. Of this group, Stalinist "tankies" tend to be the very worst, but one finds evangelists in all political ideologies and born-again anarchists can sometimes be just as monotropic and overbearing as a friend who discovers that AA works for them, or a friend who discovers that their sins have been forgiven because they invited Jesus into their heart, or, for that matter, the old White abusive man who *finally* goes to therapy and suddenly thinks he has a diagnosis and cure for everyone he knows.

4. Much of how to do this is very helpfully explored by Watkins and Shulman in *Towards Psychologies of Liberation*.

II. GUIDING

on the other. To assert that you support people on all sides of *any* group, renders you both incoherent and useless. This position only has staying power in liberal circles because their concern is not so much coherence or active involvement in creating change, as it is about the liberal wanting to feel like they are different than the conservative (who, from the perspective of the liberal, delights in actively oppressing others). Thus, the liberal says to themself, "I'm not like that person, I want to get along with everyone and so my conscience is clean and I can sleep the sleep of the just." In other words, most of the time, the liberal pursues the feeling of personal moral purity rather than actually doing the hard work of actively pursuing life-giving and -affirming change. That work requires you to take sides.

A major element of taking sides is choosing which guides to follow. In my own efforts to work through this, I have found that, in any oppressed group, there are always those who are thoughtfully and actively working to care for themselves and others, who are pursuing a more liberating and liberated way of sharing life together, who are rising up against the downpression of Death, and who speak the words that their companions feel in their hearts. Although this group of people is by no means monolithic (and factions and disagreements will be found under this umbrella as much as anywhere else), it is this company I have sought out and prioritized. The work of outsiders who wish to become accomplices, then, is to help create a space where community members like these—community members who are "ecosystem engineers"—can more easily go about creating the kind of culture, relationships, and connections that make more diverse forms of life thrive and that draw others into ecosystem engineering of this sort. Outsiders do not act as guides but they do help *create opportunities for guides to do their guiding* and to train others to be guides (even as they, the outsiders-becoming-insiders, follow the guidance of those guides).

The early days of harm reduction are an excellent example of this. Prior to the institutionalization of harm reduction through internationally-recognized, evidence-based "best practices," it was communities of criminalized medication-takers who were developing, practicing, and advocating for harm-reduction practices. This work went *directly against* the prevailing norms, standards, and wisdom of addiction services, focused as they were on abstinence and fighting a "war on drugs" (i.e., a war on drug users and a war on adequate healthcare for people who are impoverished). It was people on the street who injected their medicines who developed and practiced harm reduction long before anyone else. It was these people who called for adequate, sterile medical supplies and for safe places to take their medicines. They were the ones who knew, long before the academics, municipal officials, and poverty pimps, that this would save lives and contribute, over the long-term, to people being able to live the kinds of lives they wanted to live. The role of outsiders, then, was to find ways to follow this guidance, heed this expertise, respect these experiences, and make safe equipment and safe spaces available. Thus, for example, in the downtown eastside of Vancouver, street nurses risked their jobs by giving out sterile needles in alleyways. And, many years before Vancouver's first legal safe site opened in 2003, friends of mine risked being fined or imprisoned for quietly operating safe injection sites in the backrooms of small shops (in rooms provided by local "mom-and-pop" business owners who were also residents of the neighborhood).

A lot of this is lost in the institutionalization of harm reduction when "peers" move from being acknowledged as *expert guides* to sidelined as *supports* who are mostly used to manage program participants by cashing in their street cred to encourage "red-flagged" clients to become more compliant. In fact, one of the major outcomes of the institutionalization of harm reduction is the wresting of control of that community's trajectory from the members of that community and placing that control firmly (back) in the hands of those who are more invested in profiting from the broader trajectory of the status quo. In fact, delaying changes while organizations and governments gather (ever more) evidence and analyze (ever more) data in order to formulate "best practices" can become a significant component of the death-dealing structural violence experience by oppressed groups, even in services oriented around "harm reduction." Thus, for example, during the so-called "opioid crisis" that began in 2016, when people in Vancouver's downtown eastside began dying in larger numbers than at the peak of the AIDS epidemic in the late eighties and early nineties, and people whose medicines included opiates were calling for a safe supply of their medication, the government responded by demanding more research (even though the DTES was, at that point, arguably the most thoroughly researched neighborhood in Canadian-occupied territories, if not in all of Turtle Island). As a result of this delay, thousands of people died. And they continue to die—just as the researchers continue to research. And this is what happens when we treat the wrong people as guides.

iii. Mutual Caring

In P. T. Anderson's film, *Magnolia* (1999), William H. Macey's character declares: "My name is Donnie Smith and I have lots of love to give." Donnie makes this declaration as a desperately lonely man who has never recovered from the absence of love that defined his childhood. Yet his cri de coeur is not "My name is Donnie Smith and I want you to love me"— his cry expresses *his desire to love others* and *how deeply it hurts him that he cannot*. Donnie's life feels incomplete to him not so much because others do not love him (this is a factor but, ever since he was a small child, he has learned that he can survive loveless situations); rather, Donnie is devastated because, despite never being loved in ways that would have been meaningful to him, Donnie never stopped loving and the void in his life is that *there is nobody with whom he can share this love*. More than wanting someone who will love him, Donnie wants someone who will accept his love.

There are many ways the viewer could interpret and psychoanalyze Donnie's character, his understanding of love, and why his desire to love remains unrequited (and, for that matter, one could also explore uncomfortable overlaps that exist between Donnie's longing to love others and the ways in which violent and abusive men can present themselves as those who are motivated by a great desire *not so much to be loved as to love*). However, there is one especially important observation he has helped me to make. It is this: to feel whole, respected, accepted, and welcomed as human beings with and among other human beings, people need the opportunity to both receive love *and give love*. Over the years I have learned that one of the most brutal and dehumanizing things that social services and other "caring professions" do is force people to always receive love (and other things) and forbid them from ever giving love (and other things). Now, yes, of course, I understand that these environments are structured in this way in order to try and prevent people with power over others (social workers, managers, nurses, doctors, mental health workers, housing support workers, and so on) from exploiting their position and taking advantage of an already oppressed group of people who—when facing such life-and-death circumstances as having someone else decide whether or not they will be permitted to sleep inside when there is a blizzard raging and the temperature has dropped to minus forty degrees—may feel as though they have no other choice but to not fight back when others exploit and abuse them. Furthermore, as we explored above, given that social services and other caring professions are already structured in a way that encourages violence and abuse, it makes sense to have measures in place to try and limit those things (even if some of those measures are just as frequently used to mask and justify fundamentally abusive dynamics by, for example, suggesting that the issue is not the power that social workers wield over the dispossessed but is, instead, *how* they wield that power). However, over the last two decades I have slowly learned that denying a person their ability to share, to give good gifts, and to give and reciprocate love and care, is a dehumanizing act that wounds people very deeply. I am not exaggerating here—this is a debilitating wound and it is one of the most insidious ways in which many well-intentioned and genuinely caring social services and social workers cause harm. Those who are not permitted to share, to give, or to reciprocate love and care, are those who are *ultimately denied membership amongst the community of those whom we consider fully human*. There are few things so harmful to others as persistently communicating to them that they are not permitted to love or care for you or for others. To deny a person's ability to do this is to further contribute to the pathologization, criminalization, and marginalization of those who are oppressed. It is to position such people as those who are "inferior" and "below" while simultaneously positioning yourself as one of those who are "superior" and "above." Over time, as people slowly realize that their love and care is neither welcomed nor appreciated, they become broken down in ways from which it is very hard to recover. Few things are so effective in making a person accept that they are who their oppressors say they are as making them believe that they are so deficient that they are not even capable of loving others.

Therefore, if we are to participate in the formation of genuinely liberated and liberating communities, *we must recover the mutuality that is inherent to caring*. Caution is required here, not only because there are still very real power imbalances in most community spaces that we are trying to liberate (and so the forms of abuse already explored in previous chapters can easily occur), but also because recovering this jeopardizes the job security of those who are paid to be present in the spaces we are trying to co-opt and transform into something more life-affirming. Having been

III. MUTUAL CARING

parts of communities where we have tried different approaches to this over the years, I have learned a few things.

First, I have learned that recovering the mutuality that is inherent to caring means that we shape our environments in ways that respect and encourage all the forms of mutual care that are *already occurring* amongst members of oppressed groups of people. Hence, a number of the scenarios already mentioned—not enforcing rules about bathroom occupancy numbers so that people can care for one another there; not rushing to kick people out of a space simply because they are being noisy because others in that space know what it is like to be kicked out of social services and have nowhere to go and they are willing to care for the noisy person by including them in the space; and so on.

Secondly, I have learned that recovering the mutuality that is inherent to caring means that those who are paid to facilitate or hold space, need to find ways to open themselves up to being cared for by others who are a part of that community space. This can express itself in various ways. To begin with, it means pushing back against expectations related to professionalism and being thoughtful and deliberate in how one goes about showing vulnerability. Thoughtfulness is required here because, all too often, those with power who are going through emotional turmoil or suffering tend to lash out at those who are under their power—whether through being abusive (from more deliberate forms of abuse like verbally berating someone to less deliberate forms of abuse like not being present to attend to the concerns people bring to them) or through requiring those under their power to tend to them emotionally prior to doing their work (here, the feminist insight into the amount of emotional labor that women are required to do for men can be extended to other domains where power imbalances are operative; people deprived of housing are often required to do emotional labor for shelter workers, people deprived of income are required to do emotional labor for financial support workers, frontline workers are required to do massive amounts of emotional labor to tend to their bosses, and so on). Many professional expectations and codes were developed by people who were concerned about these practices and who wished to provide better care.

However, one of the outcomes of this rise of professional services is the loss of community spaces *as community spaces* and the transformation of *relationships of mutual care* to (well-documented) *transactions* between *professionals and clients*. Thus, for example, professionals complete surveys, screeners, and other data-collection or assessment tools in order to gain information about the most intimate details of the lives of their clients. A random selection of questions from commonly used tools includes the following:

Have you ever had an eating disorder? Have you ever had any menstrual difficulties? Have you ever experienced physical or sexual abuse? Do you have any sexually transmitted infections? Do you wish your family or friends were much different? Do you struggle with feeling close to others? Are you realistic about yourself and others? Do you have goals and direction in life? Do you have any difficulty with sexual activity? Are you preoccupied with sex? Do you have difficulty feeling satisfaction with your life?[1]

All of these questions are highly invasive and expect "clients" (or "participants") to be honest and forthcoming about things that they may not have shared with their closest friends. Transparency and full disclosure are conditions that must be met prior to the reception of care. Conversely, clients are forbidden to know even the barest details about the lives of those who profess to care for them. Structuring services in this way produces two main groups of people: those who are required to be perfect providers of care, and those who required to fulfill their "sick role" in the manner mandated by society. And, while I have highlighted issues related to the latter party, it is important to note here that the former party—the perfect, unflappable worker—is just as much a fabrication of the context of oppression as the latter. Working with people is not the same as operating a machine, marketing a brand, managing investments, or selling a product (and, despite the best efforts to transform social work into a business, the observation that the for-profit customer service industry truism regarding how "the customer is always right" is *never* applied and, in fact, strongly discouraged in social services, helps to reveal how different they are). Working with people requires us to *engage as people*. People being people together, people genuinely sharing in life and death together, is a complex and emotional experience. Working through trauma as a community prompts many different feelings. Working through these things, while also living through the multitude of experiences that people have outside of their working hours, is far more an art than a science. People have good and bad days, they struggle with different things at different times, they sometimes feel invulnerable, and they sometimes feel like they can't go on. Communities are built and bonded together when such things are openly acknowledged and shared.

---

1. These selections are drawn from the Ontario Comprehensive Assessment of Need (used by most community services engaging in "case management" type work) and the Admission and Discharge Criteria Assessment Tool (which was used for accessing residential treatment programs, although it is now been replaced by an even more invasive tool). I picked these tools not because they are exceptional but because they are fairly representative of the general lines of questioning pursued by social workers.

III. MUTUAL CARING

Consequently, a movement towards recognizing the shared humanity of *all* members of a community, and a movement towards establishing dynamics of genuinely *mutual* care, means that those who are paid to be present in a space *must* also begin to practice vulnerability with and among others who are present in a space for different reasons.

On this point, what I am suggesting thoroughly aligns with the perspective of Carl Rogers, one of the core founders of the "person-centered therapy" praised (but rarely actually practiced) by contemporary community-based mental health care providers. Rogers observes the following:

> In my relationships with persons I have found that it does not help, in the long run, to act as though I were something that I am not. It does not help to act calm and pleasant when actually I am angry and critical. It does not help to act as though I know the answers when I do not. It does not help to act as though I were a loving person if actually, at the moment, I am hostile. It does not help for me to act as though I were full of assurance, if actually I am frightened and unsure. Even on a very simply level I have found that this statement seems to hold. It does not help for me to act as though I were well when I feel ill.
>
> What I am saying here, put in another way, is that I have not found it to be very helpful or effective in my relationships with other people to try to maintain a façade; to act in one way on the surface when I am experiencing something quite different underneath. It does not, I believe, make me helpful in my attempts to build up constructive relationships with other individuals. . . . In fact, it seems to me that most of the mistakes I make in personal relationships, most of the times in which I fail to be of help to other individuals, can be accounted for in terms of the fact that I have, for some defensive reason, behaved in one way at a surface level, while in reality my feelings run in a contrary direction.[2]

Environments that force workers to act in a way contrary to that which Rogers advises are, in fact, environments that are abusive towards those whom they pay to be present. It is one element of the systematic ways in which services morally injure those whom they employ.

The language of "moral injury" was developed by therapists and researchers working with veterans with post-traumatic stress disorder. Moral injuries can occur when people are forced to perpetrate, fail to prevent, or bear witness to, "acts that transgress deeply held moral beliefs and

---

2. Rogers, *On Becoming a Person*, 16–17.

expectations."[3] When this occurs, people experience long-term harm in the psychological, behavioral, spiritual, and social domains of life. Feelings of guilt, shame, and betrayal are especially common responses to moral injuries. These feelings are ubiquitous in kind-hearted workers (whether they are working in hospitals or homeless shelters) who have been forced to kick out vulnerable people (some of whom will die as a result), who are forced to turn away people who need help (some of whom will go back to abusers as a result), who are forced to punish those who do not need to be punished (and who will not be aided by punishment), and who regularly bear witness to all kinds of harm that they (whether through the limits of their roles or through the general limits of being human) fail to prevent. This moral injury is only deepened when workers who feel this way are simultaneously required to always be professional, to maintain firm boundaries around expressing feelings or engaging in personal disclosures, and who are expected to both engage in person-centered care *and* provide the stats needed to attain the outcomes outlined in Quality Improvement Plans geared at corporate or governmental funding priorities. Frequently, these core priorities—the moral priorities of the individual workers and the priorities established by the corporation to satisfy funders—are at odds with one another. If or when this conflict comes out into the open, the corporation will *always* prioritize corporate priorities. Because of this, it is not surprising to learn that a considerable amount of the vulnerability that is essential to people being in relationships of mutual care is taking place secretly, out of the eyes of the bosses, below the surface. In fact, if you dig a little, you consistently find that this secret rule-breaking is one of the central elements that makes programs successful. Thus, once again, we see the hybridity of resistance and co-optation that occurs within the context of oppression—good workers secretly act in ways forbidden to them but, by doing so, they keep otherwise abusive programs afloat and, in fact, draw others to those programs for help. Hence, good workers also struggle with feelings of guilt related to the ways in which they both subvert and perpetuate harmful systems and structures.

That said, another way in which people who help to hold or facilitate space open themselves up to being cared for by others is by learning the art of receiving and refusing gifts. Another important lesson I have learned over the years is just how much people desire to give gifts to others as expressions of love and care. To deny people the ability to give gifts is, in very real ways, to deny them the ability to love (conversely, those who always put themselves in a position where they are always giving gifts to others, while simultaneously and consistently refusing to accept gifts from others,

---

3. See Litz et al., "Moral Injury and Moral Repair in War Veterans."

III. MUTUAL CARING

suggests that their giving might be more related to enforcing the kind of power dynamics they prefer to inhabit than it has to do with love). Accepting a gift is, in fact, an expression of vulnerability, and one that has the potential to counter the power dynamics that are operative in so-called caring professions. Consequently, we need to learn to be as thoughtful, empathetic, creative, and sensitive when receiving gifts as we are when giving gifts.

Because of this, how we go about receiving gifts can look very different with different people. For example, I once knew a fellow who would sometimes come to see me when he needed a bit of money—sometimes for medication, sometimes so he could get out of town for a while when things were getting hot. We had built up a relationship of mutual trust, and I could usually help him out. I understood that it was hard to find social services that had funding designated for such things.[4] This continued sporadically over some time and then, just before Christmas one year, I came into work and discovered a card had been slipped under the door of my workspace. In it was a letter from this man, wherein he expressed his gratitude for my friendship and wished me and my children well. Also included in the card were two Percocets (i.e., a medication that is a mixture of oxycodone and acetaminophen). Knowing what this fellow has done in order to hustle in whatever ways he needed to hustle to get this medication, and knowing how sick he can be without it, I believe that this is one of the most generous gifts I have been given. Consequently, although technically I was required to report this to my supervisor, hand in the percs so that they could be returned to a pharmacy, and then lecture this fellow about boundaries and what is and is not appropriate in a social service environment, I knew that this response would be deeply dehumanizing, would belittle his sacrifice, would demonstrate my refusal to respect him as a fellow human being, and would show that I cared more about following the rules of the system that oppressed, dispossessed, colonized, and abandoned him and his people,

---

4. No social services are receiving funding to help people purchase medication that doctors have denied them and it's hard enough to get people out of town when they fit the victim narratives encouraged by social services—it's impossible to get people out of town, at least via the official avenues, when people not only do not fit but actually challenge or contradict that narrative. Imagine, for example, a social service providing funding so that a person who has warrants out for his arrest due to not showing up at court in relation to petty property crimes and possession-with-intent charges—stealing from Wal-Mart, having a gram of crystal meth in their possession and so on—who wants to leave the province and first spend some time caring for his sick mother before he comes back and turns himself in to do his time. No social service would fund this and, in fact, a good many of them would secretly call the police to report the fellow and then they would try and keep him there until the police arrived to arrest him.

than I cared about him. So I did nothing of the sort. The next time I saw him, I thanked him.

However, there have been other situations when I chose to refuse gifts but, even while doing so, I have sought out ways to affirm the dignity, humanity, and generosity of those offering the gifts. I have mostly done this in situations where relationships of mutual trust, respect, and admiration had not yet been established, and in situations where gifts seemed to be a component of the kind of credit-and-debt cycle that I wished to avoid. Thus, for example, when I have provided assistance to some of the more well-connected members of alternative economies and alternative courts of justice (like gangs that are not as well-funded or as well-protected as the police), these members frequently offered to do me favors or give me some kind of gift in return for the service I provided. Mostly, people make this offer because they are kind and because they also are not accustomed to relationships or economies where people receive things free of charge (gangsters are like bankers—they are accustomed to there always being strings attached, and they have also learned that a lot more is said in the small print than one is wont to notice in the large print). Sometimes, they wish to do something for me because they feel that they may now be indebted to me (especially if I provide a service outside of what is usually offered by other social services), and they demonstrated their strength of character by showing that they always pay their debts promptly and in full. While this is admirable, this situation is potentially dangerous—if I accept this economy of debt and repayment, and if I accept a favor or gift in return, this favor or gift may exceed the gift I originally gave. As a result, I would then be in debt to the giver of that gift and what I may subsequently be asked to do to pay that debt, or what may happen if I refuse to pay that debt, may well be more than I can handle. Therefore, I seek to avoid this kind of economy altogether. In such situations, I find it useful to emphasize that, as a person who is paid to be present in the space, I already receive compensation for the work that I do and, as a result, nobody is indebted to me. I am simply doing the job that I am paid to do. However, I go on to say, if people wish to insist on expressing their thanks in some other way, I would be happy to have them shake my hand and say thanks. In fact, I would be honored if they would do this. Time after time, I have seen the effectiveness of this approach. People are able to break out of a credit-and-debt-based way of being in relationship with others. People, especially but not exclusively old-timers or those who remember old school codes of honor, remember that shaking a person's hand can mean a lot more than just a formal nicety. It can also be a way of showing respect, of affirming a person's dignity, of recognizing the shared and equal humanity of all involved, and of honoring a person's

III. MUTUAL CARING

word. Because, for many on the street, their word is their most prized (and sometimes only meaningful) possession. To shake a person's hand when they thank you is to say that you take them at their word and honor their word. For many, especially men who have been criminalized and cast aside by others, this is no small thing. It demonstrates that I view them as honorable men. Consequently, what at first has the potential to further belittle and dishonor a person—i.e., the refusal of a gift that they offer to give—can be transformed into something that accomplishes all that we hope to accomplish and communicate about mutuality and care when we give gifts to each other.

C. Affirming

Honoring people also means going beyond the rhetoric of "acceptance" that is celebrated and held up like a badge of virtue within liberal discourse and social services. Of course, acceptance itself is not a bad thing—and, in fact, it can be a profoundly life-saving thing when experienced in certain ways by people who know what it feels like, day after day, to not be accepted. However, acceptance often operates in a watered-down and passive sense in the so-called caring professions (and, in fact, passivity is connected to the etymology of the word, which has connotations of "receiving without effort" and simply taking or agreeing to what is offered). It is a sad commentary on our society that even this watered-down and passive acceptance is experienced as potentially life-saving. Because, frequently, what does such acceptance mean? It means that those doing the accepting refuse to actively participate in the abuse of those whom others reject. Often, however, there is still a component of judgment involved in this acceptance. For example, in programs that are invested in making people stop taking medications because they operate from an addictions-based paradigm and are fighting a war on drugs (which, in actual fact, is a war on people—mostly adults—who engage in personal self-care and healthcare in ways that the State says are disallowed), people frequently receive the message that "we accept you *even though you are not clean*." Or, to pick another example, conservative Christians who work with Queer youth often hold an unexpressed belief that Queerness is somehow wrong (if not a deliberately sinful act then, at least, a sign of the "fallenness of creation" and a "symptom of the universality of sin") but they recognize that they (the Christian youth workers) are not without sin themselves and, as a result, will not "throw stones." In these, and other similar instances, acceptance is something done *despite* who the person being accepted is. It is a condescending act of noblesse oblige. It then signals the superiority of the one doing the accepting and establishes the indebtedness of the one being accepted.

C. AFFIRMING

However, those who understand more about the depths of acceptance understand that it cannot remain passive and it cannot be something we do despite who we truly (secretly or not-so-secretly) believe others are. It must move beyond the level of simply refusing to actively, aggressively, and deliberately abuse others. Here, we shift from focusing on accepting others as they are to *affirming* others as they are. Affirming is much more active than accepting and, unlike acceptance, which indicates receptivity to whatever is being offered, affirming contains the idea of making firm, of strengthening, of steadying, and of holding in a supportive way. As such, affirming is a way of *confirming*—in the same way that one would make a solemn declaration before a court—that those with whom we interact are honorable (i.e., worthy of being honored), *just as they are*. Thus, to reframe the examples provided above, when engaging with people whose way of taking their medications has been criminalized, I do not say, "I accept you despite the fact that you are not clean." Instead, I say that, "you don't need to get clean because *you were never dirty to begin with*" (a statement I once saw in sidewalk art and one that has some traction within groups of people fighting to end prohibition). Similarly, over against the Christian youth worker who accepts Queer youth despite the fact that their Queerness is taken as a marker of sin's influence on the world, truly affirming those youth, in all their Queerness means recognizing Queerness is something that, in and of itself, is wonderful and worth celebrating (and, to be fair, some Christian youth workers do this and celebrate Queerness as one part of the wonderful creativity of the Creator and what it means to be made in the image of the Creator). Thus, affirmations both acknowledge and strengthen. When a person is consistently told they are dirty, they are undeserving, or that they deserve to be abandoned or harmed, they often come to believe these things. Affirmation strengthens their ability to fight against these lies.

In this way, affirmation has the potential to take us beyond the "strengths-based" language that is now so common in social services—but only because the way in which that language is deployed inclines towards a form of pragmatism or utilitarianism that does not quite get to the core of what we want to express when we affirm others (and what we want to experience when we are affirmed by others). Again, as with acceptance, there is nothing inherently wrong with a "strengths-based approach." Furthermore, thoughtful practitioners of this approach are able to use it in ways that are very deeply affirming of who people are. Problems only arise when strengths-based approaches are narrowly focused (as they all-too-often are) upon the kinds of strengths that people might possess that would permit them to adequately perform the roles assigned to them by neoliberal distributions of power, property, and labor. Because, ultimately, affirmation is about affirming *the core of who people experience themselves as being* (regardless of whether or not such a core exists as a "real thing"—and regardless of how that "thing" is constituted—most everyone experiences themselves as being the kind of being that is or has such a core). Over the years, I have found there are three especially meaningful ways in which affirmation can be communicated. These are: affirming a person's specialness (belovedness), affirming a person's worthiness, and affirming a person's inter- and intra-connectedness. I will now explore each in more detail.

i. Specialness (Belovedness)

One of the outcomes of childhood abuse is the belief, held by abused children, that they deserve to be abused, that they are to blame for the abuse, and that if there is anyone who is broken, faulty, dirty, compromised, or worthless, it is them and not the adults who abuse them. This is so for at least two reasons. First, and most importantly, young children are so full of love and good intentions that they cannot fathom the idea that adults would hurt them if they did not have something deeply wrong with them (the children), and they continue to be so full of love and good intentions that, no matter what evidence accumulates to the contrary, they will default to believing horrible things about themselves so that they can continue to valorize and exonerate their abusers. To me, this is one of the most heart-breaking things about childhood abuse—the ability of children to love unconditionally, over and over again, no matter what, and the ways in which abusive adults exploit this, causing what is frequently irreparable harm to those who only deserved to be loved unconditionally in return. Secondly, of course, is the massive power differential that exists between adults and children. This not only makes the abuse possible but gives adults hegemonic control over the narrative that is created about the abuse, about the relationship between the abuser and the abused, and about the moral character of the people involved. This is a narrative that outsiders then find most compelling or plausible (like the Christian pastors who said I was the one who needed to apologize to my father after he made me homeless, rather than saying my father should be the one to apologize to me). But, and this is the especially insidious element, it is also a narrative that the children being abused find most plausible. In this way, they internalize the discourse of their abusers. It's a devastating combination: children love—easily, quickly, repeatedly, unconditionally—and abusive adults take advantage of that to both abuse children and make the children they abuse love them. Heather O'Neill summarizes this well in *Lullabies for Little Criminals*: "No matter how scuzzy or crazy [sic] their parents are, kids still try to make them feel good about themselves." And again: "She was one of the worst breed of parents going, the ones who are really mean but then don't even give you the satisfaction of being able to hate them. They just break your heart. They were able to do whatever they pleased and then still have you love them."[1] Ain't that the truth?

Having grown up in an abusive home, I am intimately familiar with these dynamics. Long before my father kicked me out and abandoned me to whatever I might encounter on the street, I had internalized the belief that this was the kind of treatment that I deserved. Consequently, when I was deprived of house and home, I did not question it or fight against it. I was guilty. I was shameful. I was inadequate. I deserved to be punished, to be rejected, to be left for dead. The world would be a better, purer, holier, safer, healthier place without me. I was so convinced of this that, after my father left me for dead, I began to self-harm or look for fellows who might be inclined to punch me out late at night, because I felt that was what I deserved. My feelings of guilt were so overwhelming and so entrenched in my form of embodiment, that I needed some way to feel as though I was bodily paying for my sins.

I think many others who are abused when they are children develop similar patterns. It's not so much that we become self-destructive as that we are accustomed to being destroyed, and that we believe that we deserve to be destroyed and that something is wrong with the world if we are not being destroyed. Self-harming, or finding others who will harm us, actually becomes a form of self-*soothing* because it provides expiation for the guilt we have been taught to internalize since the day we were born or, as my mother later told me, since my first "spanking." Extensive studies demonstrate that children experience spanking in *exactly* the same way as other forms of physical abuse and that spanking produces *exactly* the same outcomes as other forms of physical abuse, meaning that my first spanking was really my first *beating*. I received this beating when my father was changing my diaper before I was old enough to walk or crawl. My mother recalls that I had become "fussy"—and so my father "spanked" me, and after that I never fussed when getting my diaper changed. Already, as an infant, I was taught that it is safer to freeze in terror than resist when people do things to your body that you do not like—a response it would take me most of my life to learn to overcome, and one I still have to consciously fight against today.

My feelings of guilt, shame, worthlessness, and disgust about myself were especially strong after my father made me homeless because I blamed

---

1. O'Neill, *Lullabies for Little Criminals*, 12.

1. SPECIALNESS (BELOVEDNESS)

myself for becoming homeless.[2] I blamed myself for the tears my mother shed when I was leaving. In fact, this was one of the most painful ways in which I internalized the discourse of my abuser: when the abuse I experienced also hurt others, I blamed myself for the hurt that they experienced. Thus, I believed that I had ruined my family and that, forever after, things could not be the same. They would always be stained, always be broken, always be compromised. As a result, I believed that I was worse than worthless—I was a fucking piece of shit. It wasn't that I had no value, I actually had a negative value. My presence wasn't negligible. By being present in the world, I actually made things worse. I hurt those who loved me, I betrayed those who trusted me, and I let down those who counted on me or expected anything good from me.

I believe I would still be living in very different circumstances (if I was living at all), if I had continued to believe all of those things about myself. I know many people who have spent their lives forcibly deprived of housing, and who have persistently soothed and harmed themselves with various substances, practices, or ways of being in relationships with others, because beliefs like these ones were carved into their bodies (they've shown me their scars) and their identities (they've shown me their hearts), when they were very young and they never escaped from them. I see myself in many of these people and many of them see themselves in me.

However, I was fortunate. Not too long after being deprived of housing, I had a very unusual experience that completely transformed the ways in which I perceived and related to myself. I have gone back and forth with how much I share about this experience with others over the years but, as I was recently reminded while reading Helen Knott's memoir, *In My Own Moccasins*, unusual experiences that end up being transformative are actually not nearly as rare as those who drift through life from dominant, secure, and comfortable positions tend to assert.[3] Many people I know, people not inclined to believing anything out of the ordinary, people who value "reason," "objectivity," "critical thinking," and so on, have had their lives transformed by unusual, seemingly inexplicable, experiences and encounters. These can

---

2. Context: my father kicked me out because he discovered that, even though I continued to get high grades, I was skipping classes and had forged both his and my mother's signatures on many notes. Later, he told me that he was convinced that I would start writing cheques in his name and so that was why he decided I had to be abandoned and left for dead; I am unsure as to how to evaluate the possible truth-value of that post-dated explanation but I do know that my relationship with him was such that I was certain that he was going to kick me out that afternoon when I got home. I told my friends it was going to happen although, given how little trouble I caused anyone, they found it hard to believe me.

3. See Knott, *In My Own Moccasins*.

occur through dreams, through experiences had while engaging with different plant-based medicines, through random encounters with mysterious strangers who know things that seem impossible for strangers to know and who only appear once and then never again, through books falling open to just the right passage at just the right time, through guns misfiring, through what they take to be some kind of visitation from a dead relative or friend or spiritual being, through what they experience as miraculous answers to prayer or signs from the god to whom they pray, and so on. I am not invested in any particular kind of interpretation of such experiences (i.e., I have little interest in evaluating their so-called "truth-value," or trying to see how these claims fit into some kind of meta-narrative or metaphysics that I use to evaluate every system of meaning). It is hard to *make sense* of such experiences. In fact, if one is limited by the lenses provided by the epistemology that dominates our status quo, I don't think one can make much sense of them. They are fundamentally nonsensical. However, and this is the critical point, it is also equally hard to deny that they occur and that, whatever they might be, *people experience them as profoundly transformative* (but, of course, we should never forget that this is true of so many other things that we take for granted; existence, life, consciousness, love, desire, mattering—we also lack clear, sensible explanations for these things). Sometimes I wonder: if we weren't made to feel ashamed for having and valuing nonsensical experiences, just how many people would share stories like these? I suspect we might be surprised by the answer to that question.

As for me, this is what occurred. Some months after I had been made homeless by my dad—months spent couch-surfing, walking empty streets at night, being booted from one coffee shop to the next every time I fell asleep, trying to sleep on or under the shelter provided by the playground equipment at a park—a friend's parents offered to pay for myself and their son (my friend) to attend an event hosted by a charismatic religious group in Toronto (this was in 1998, and the event was part of what had become known in some circles as "the Toronto Blessing"—an occurrence much debated by theologians, sociologists, and religion scholars since it occurred). I had no experience of such charismatic religious settings but chose to attend the event. I found the environment to be both unsettling and exciting. I was not sure what to think of it or what to expect from it. What did I know? I knew that my life was unbearable. I knew that I needed help. I believed that help was out there . . . somewhere. So, I tried to be open-minded in the midst of an environment that was very unusual to me.

And it was there, on the floor of a former convention center converted into a church—little more than carpet placed on top of concrete and rows and rows of stackable chairs—that I had my inexplicable, nonsensical

I. SPECIALNESS (BELOVEDNESS)

experience. It is hard to describe. A pastor had reached out to pray for me (specifically mentioning something about knowing the love of God as a father who tenderly cares for his children—a patriarchal image of the divine that I have since rejected but one that connected with me very much at that time of life) and, unbeknownst to me, I fell in a swoon or a trance of some kind. Essentially, I felt as though I was met by a love so large, so all-encompassing, so tangible, and so strong that it forever after changed the way in which I understood myself. Sometimes, I describe this experience by saying that it felt as though a blanket of love descended upon me, wrapped itself around me, and transported me to a reality more real than what I had experienced up until that point. In that reality (and thus also in all realities), I realized that I was *beloved*. Furthermore, this belovedness was not a status that was granted to me based upon the ones who loved me. It was not conditional. It was not the kind of thing that could be given and then taken away. Rather, it was intrinsic to who I am. To be, I realized, is to be loved. And we are beloved because, who we are, all of us, in the core of our being, is *lovely*. This is what I experienced on the floor of an old convention center where I lay, unconscious or in an altered state of consciousness, for about an hour before opening my eyes and asking, "What am I doing on the floor?"

A nonsensical experience, indeed! But it is equally difficult to describe how transformative this experience was for me. To go from being absolutely convinced of one's own status as garbage, as a pollutant, as a fuck-up, a failure, and a cause of harm, to being absolutely convinced of one's own status as beloved, as lovely, as, in fact, a gift to the world, is the kind of thing you can only really understand if you have experienced it yourself.

This is part of the reason why I believe the language of trauma is applicable to love. What makes trauma traumatic is that it fundamentally alters your conception of the world and the core beliefs you hold about yourself, others, what is right and wrong, what is possible, what is safe, and what is not. Judith Hermann's formative work on trauma is instructive in this regard. She defines trauma in this way:

> trauma is an affiliation of the powerless. At the moment of trauma, the victim is rendered helpless by overwhelming force ... Traumatic events overwhelm the ordinary systems of care that give people a sense of control, connection, and meaning ... Traumatic events are extraordinary, not because they occur rarely, but rather because they overwhelm the ordinary human adaptations to life.[4]

---

4. Hermann, *Trauma and Recovery*, 33.

Trauma, then, is not a synonym for "something that must be super, really, very extremely painful or bad." Rather, trauma refers to the ways in which our experiences can or cannot be integrated into the systems of meaning in which we participate, the sense of identity and belonging that we develop over time, and the general expectations we have of the world. In other words, what makes trauma so traumatic is not so much the ways in which it changes us, as the ways in which it changes *everything else* and *our relationship with everything else*. Thus, while we are accustomed to focusing on trauma as a strictly negative thing (for violence, abuse, sudden losses, and the ongoing experience of pain, suffering, and isolation can radically change us and our understanding of the world around us in these ways), I believe that encountering a love so overwhelming that it transforms the system of meaning in which we live, that it alters the ways in which we feel connected to others, and that it shifts the ways in which I adapt to the world around me, is also a form of trauma. A good trauma! The kind of trauma that, as I have seen time after time, actually holds the potential to be more powerful than *all* other forms of trauma.

When I learned this about myself, I also realized that this is true of everyone else—my status as beloved is not unique to me, it is at the core of all of us.[5] And those who have been oppressed and abandoned by others, those who have been made to feel like they are human waste, are those who are most in need of coming to know and understand this. Consequently, it is this sense of one's intrinsic belovedness that I have sought to share with others over the twenty-seven years that have passed since I first came to know myself in this way. Recognizing, welcoming, acknowledging, affirming, honoring, and celebrating the belovedness of those whom we encounter in our efforts to be good company to and with others is, in my opinion, the truly transformative core of our work. Over the years, I have learned that, with enough time, connections, smarts, and effort, I can help anyone gain some kind of financial stability, some kind of housing, and some kind of security in terms of basic needs, but unless we help people to understand, perceive, and *relate to themselves* in new ways, then frequently we are not getting at the core of what makes people's sufferings unbearable. Almost inevitably then, no matter what circumstantial changes have taken place, people return to other things, patterns, relationships, and comfort zones, that both soothe and affirm the destructive narratives they have been taught to believe about themselves. Helping people to come to know themselves

---

5. This is something Henri Nouwen also tries to communicate in his book, *Life of the Beloved*.

I. SPECIALNESS (BELOVEDNESS)

as beloved is often the difference between assisting with bare survival and contributing to our collective participation within the abundance of life.

While the language of belovedness resonates with me personally, I think another way of speaking about this is to refer to a person's intrinsic *specialness*. Adults, particularly cis-men in our culture, frequently take a belittling and condescending attitude towards the language of specialness. I suspect that this is the case because when they were children their desire to have their own specialness acknowledged went unmet. As bell hooks and Jennifer Siebel Newsom so convincingly demonstrate, the production of men in our culture is premised upon *the devastation of boys*.[6] Men who mock specialness were taught that specialness was a thing that had to be earned, that it was reserved for an exceptional few and that, short of living up to those standards, you deserved to be neglected, ignored, forgotten, or shit upon. And, having subsequently been shit upon, they go on to shit upon others ("hurt people hurt people" as trauma-informed social workers repeatedly remind us).

I believe that there is a very deep woundedness here, an intergenerational transmission of a brutal form of trauma, that cannot be healed outside of the recognition that specialness is, in fact, one of the few non-negotiable, sine qua non elements of existence. There is nothing wrong with longing to be special. What is wrong—what is heart-breakingly wrong—is dismissively sneering at children who receive awards for specialness just because, when we were children and we longed to be acknowledged in that way, we were mocked, laughed at, told to "toughen up," told to "be a man," told to "stop being a little bitch," or a "mama's boy," and trampled into the dirt (even now, at forty, I can still remember the look of total *disgust* that broke out on my father's face when he saw me being a boy who cried—do you know what it does to a child who longs to be loved by their parent when that child is treated as an object of abject disgust?). And it is just as wrong to also refuse to acknowledge the special hopes, dreams, and hurts of our children. Few things cause such long-lasting harm as this replacement of acknowledging, treasuring, and caring for the specialness inherent in others with the treatment of others as objects of disgust (which, precisely because they are objects of disgust can then be abused and discarded without further thought or consideration).

Being treated as something disgusting—as something offensive, repugnant, and loathsome—is a familiar experience to those who are oppressed, abandoned, and left for dead in our society. It is something they experience every day. This, then, is what we are up against when we try to honor people

---

6. See hooks, *Will to Change*; Newsom, *Mask You Live In*.

and seek out ways to communicate to them that they are special and that they are beloved, exactly as they are right now, exactly as they have always been, and exactly as they will be. Ensuring that we are doing this well is not one of the things tracked by social and other services. In fact, many services reinforce the punitive, performance-oriented understanding of how much value people have and whether or not they deserve to be treated well or poorly. "If you bring a needle into this shelter, you *deserve* to be deprived of the only bed available for you to sleep in." "If you have a beer, you *deserve* to be kicked out of this program." "If you do what we tell you to do, if you go where we tell you to go, if you stop doing the things we don't want you to do, if you stop being friends with your friends, if you express gratitude for what we do, if you apologize to us for everything you have done and been up until now, and if you never ask for more than the smallest amount that you might need in order to not starve or freeze to death, *then* you deserve to receive help." And so on. We must fight against this structural (but still deeply personal) form of oppression by the ways in which we go about being in relationships with others, the actions that we take, the priorities we make, and the ways in which we go about structuring our collective life together. To help myself in this process, I frequently ask myself questions like these: "Does the way I treat people communicate to them that I view them as possessing an intrinsic specialness and belovedness or does it affirm other more harmful beliefs they have inherited about themselves?" and "Given what people have been taught to believe about themselves, what can I do to not only present them with a different message but also present that message in a way that they find plausible or even compelling?" It is questions like these that have led me to many of the conclusions that I am sharing in this book. Furthermore, constantly asking myself these questions have also led me to affirm the *worthiness* of others—something that operates in a different register than the language of specialness or belovedness.

ii. Worthiness

When I say that belovedness and worthiness operate on different registers what I mean is this: belovedness is something that is operative prior to and outside of the formation of any kind of *judgment*—it speaks to "the bones of existence," the way things are—whereas worthiness is premised upon making a (positive or negative) judgment about someone. The relationship, here, is something like that which exists between love and justice, or justice and the law. These are different enframings, which, despite our best efforts to coordinate them, never actually line-up completely with each other even if one is consistently presented as the foundation or justification for the other. Hence, love undergirds justice and justice undergirds the law even though, as we frequently discover in practice, love also sometimes exceeds, overrules, or operates outside of the domain of justice, and justice sometimes exceeds, overrules, or operates outside of the rule of law. Thus, belovedness is not a thing that exists on a sliding scale where a person is deemed to be more or less beloved based on whatever circumstances or attributes are deemed relevant. Belovedness is what it is because we are what we are—as I stated above, to "be" is to "be loved," to be lovely, to be beloved, to be special. Belovedness, then, is rooted more in metaphysics than ethics (even though it is somewhat silly to try and suggest that metaphysics and ethics can exist independently of each other). Worthiness is something different. It is related to judging, to evaluating, to the weighing of evidence, and to coming to conclusions based upon those things.

Now, of course, the affirmation of belovedness is something that should tip the scales when these kinds of evaluations are made. Hence, belovedness relates to worthiness, even if it operates in a different register. The problem is that, in general, our culture brackets out the question of belovedness when making its evaluations about worth (it pretends we can make an evaluation in relation to one of those things in a way that neither affects nor is affected by how we feel about the other thing). Here, again, the relationship between justice and the law provides a parallel example. Justice *should* tip the scales when the law makes its evaluations but, in actual fact, it is all too often money that does this. Thus, when it comes to the rule of law, you usually get as much justice as you pay for. When this occurs and becomes the norm (as it has in our context) a fundamental perversion of justice has taken place. Injustice is portrayed as justice. The increasing militarization of the police, the ways in which municipalities are continually expanding their budgets for policing while simultaneously cutting almost every other area of funding (except for corporate kick-backs and tax breaks), and the ways in which those of us who are too impoverished and dispossessed to be able to afford even the semblance of justice are increasingly targeted by the police, helps to show that those who benefit from this perversion of justice realize that the rest of us are not so easily fooled. Ultimately, the enforcement and implementation of injustice as justice relies upon brute force.

However, a similar perversion occurs when neoliberal standards of worth are used to determine the extent to which a person is considered beloved. If you are rich, if you make playthings for other people who are rich, and if you help the rich get richer, you will be treated as beloved while you are alive and universally mourned and eulogized when you die, even if you never did a single thing worth mentioning for those who are not rich (the saintly memorialization of Steve Jobs, a selfish prick if ever there was one, is a prime example of this). But if you do not do this, if, in fact, you do not or cannot even play the role assigned to you no matter how lowly and live as a "contributing member of society" (i.e., someone who works for wages, who pays taxes, who pays rent, and who accumulates credit-debt) then you are worthless or worse than worthless—you are taken to be "a drain on society" who exploits the kindness of those who claim to be both morally and financially superior. In this way, corrupt notions of worth are used to annihilate belovedness as a categorical imperative and, instead, make it conditional upon the anthropologies, ethics, and enframings favoured by neoliberal dispossessors.

When we refuse this reversal and interpret worth via belovedness, we come to very different conclusions. In fact, we judge the situation in which we find ourselves, and we determine that those who come to us seeking good company, *deserve* the very best treatment and the very best care. Those who are oppressed, those who are colonized, those who are criminalized, those who are dispossessed and impoverished, those who are abandoned and left for dead, are always "more sinned against than sinning," and this is just as true in social services and healthcare institutions as it is in any other environment. Therefore, it is of the utmost importance that we remember

II. WORTHINESS

that when such people come to us seeking help, we are not condescending to serve them. We do not serve them because, in our great nobility, we go out of our way to show them grace. Quite the opposite, in fact. We must ensure that we do our *very best* work so that we treat those who come to us seeking help how they *deserve* to be treated.[1] Therefore, when people come to me to express their gratitude, I try to communicate to them something like the following:

> While I sincerely appreciate and accept your thanks, you need to know that I am doing nothing more and nothing less than my utmost to honor and respect you *by treating you the way in which you deserve to be treated*. I don't deserve any special praise for this but, rather, want you to know how grateful I am that you chose to be vulnerable with me, share your life with me, and gift our community with your presence. I know many people, including many other people who claim they are here to help, have betrayed your trust, have hurt you, and have not treated you the way in which you deserve to be treated. So, really, I am just trying to show that I am worthy of the trust you have placed in me. Thank you for that.

This kind of communication needs to occur in both word and deed (it needs to be an *embodied and active* proclamation). And, in fact, doing our very best work with and for those who come seeking assistance from us is one of the most powerful ways to communicate to them how we assess their worth. For all kinds of reasons, those who are oppressed, colonized, dispossessed, and abandoned are forced to accustom themselves to people doing subpar work on their behalf. Whether this is because social workers are overwhelmed by increasingly large case loads, or shelters have a reduced capacity to take people in, or the social assistance worker feels that their clients haven't produced adequate proof to demonstrate that they aren't just scamming the system, or because moralizing do-gooders find that the objects of their charity speak in a way that feels too abrasive, the left-for-dead are accustomed to having their needs neglected, ignored, forgotten, put off, or only poorly met. Consequently, if we are to be good company to and with those who are treated in this way, it is essential that we do our very best work, that we respond promptly, efficiently, and effectively to requests for help (and, if we are unable to do this, and are unable to learn how to do this, that we quickly and effectively connect people to those who can help in this

---

1. Although, beware! Those who are unaccustomed to being treated in this way may wish to then praise us for acting in this way and see us as especially noble patrons. This can lead to inflated egos and make us drift towards the kind of patronage favoured by oppressive systems.

way). As I tell the workers that I train, if we do this—simply follow through on what we say we will do and follow through quickly and well—we will be offering better care to people than what they receive almost everywhere else from almost everyone else.

In order to help myself determine whether or not I am meeting this standard, I spent many years asking myself, "would I be doing anything different right now if this person was one of my siblings?" Often, I found the answer to that question was "yes" and I have found that answering "yes" has led me to change my course of action (I say "often" but not "always" because there are still real differences of trust, intimacy, and risk that are present between those whom one has known all of one's life and those whom one is just getting to know). Thus, for example, I remember one slushy night in Vancouver when the temperature had dropped below freezing and the wind was blowing hard and I was riding the bus home from a late shift when I saw a young woman who was riding the bus with no shoes or socks on. I was tired and didn't feel like walking barefoot for the two blocks to my apartment, plus; even though I had other shoes at home, I really liked the boots I was wearing. However, knowing that I would not hesitate to give my boots to one of my siblings if they had need of them, and knowing that I had no good reason not to treat this young woman like my sibling, I gave her my boots and socks, and got home just fine. And I share this story, not to say, "look at how noble or good or generous I am!" but to suggest that, doing such things is, in fact, treating others *as they deserve to be treated*. Treating this person in this way does not make me a saint, it just means that I'm trying to not be a total fucking asshole, even if our society makes it so easy for us to be total fucking assholes that we frequently don't even notice or, worse yet, feel virtuous, when we are acting that way.

It is here, within the acknowledgment of worthiness, that we also give meaning to the ways in which we talk about treating others with "dignity" and "respect." Dignity, by definition, refers to a person's "state of being worthy." We demonstrate our true beliefs about a person's state of worthiness not by endlessly issuing statements that we "affirm their dignity" but by how we treat them, by the circumstances and environments in which we place them, by how we help or do not help them, and by how much time we spend with them. So, for example, if you want to know what a homeless shelter really thinks of the dignity of those whom they claim to serve, don't look at the statements they post online—look at the state of their washrooms, mattresses, and lockers. If you want to know what a social assistance or disability support worker really thinks of the dignity of a "client assigned to their caseload," watch how they treat a client when that client is upset or frustrated. If you want to know what a child protection worker really

II. WORTHINESS

thinks of the dignity of the parents they are required to support, observe how quickly they do or do not call the police for support when they (the workers) do not get their way. If you want to know what a nurse or a doctor really thinks about the dignity of their patient, listen to the way they talk to a person who has a spinal infection and who suffers from chronic pain, but who is flagged as a "substance abuser," when that person asks for something to help them endure their pain. What quickly becomes apparent, if you do, is that much of the talk about dignity that is put forward by poverty pimps and managers within "caring professions" is a hustle used to draw in funding dollars (and to help people who harm others feel like they are helping others), and not actually a meaningful practice that relates to how they treat people. Thus, dignity, like love, is something that only gains meaning in our actions, in how we actually treat others, and in how they experience our treatment of them.

Respect, too, is something we must negotiate with care. While dignity features prominently in the language games played by service providers, respect is a central motif internal to many of the cultures that form on the fringes of society. Having been dispossessed, incarcerated, deprived of housing, criminalized, colonized, and left for dead, people frequently feel that all they have left is their respect—both their self-respect and ensuring that others are respecting them in the ways in which they feel they deserve to be respected. However, because notions of respect that are operative on the streets are so infected by the kinds of respect imposed by abusers—from the police, to prison guards, to staff members at other disciplinary institutions—respect tends to be treated as a limited good within an economics of austerity. There is not enough to go around. As a result, respect is won or lost agonistically. You gain respect by demonstrating you deserve to be respected more than someone else—you lose respect by showing that you can be respected less than someone else. Furthermore, because one can often not do much about the ways in which one is brutally disrespected, abused and harmed, by abusers like cops, prison guards, security guards, doctors, social workers, and so on, the search for respect frequently produces lateral violence wherein people assert themselves, refuse to put up with any more insults or harm, and treat others the ways in which they have been treated.[2] This is why disrespect is regularly met with violence that appears disproportionate to those who do not understand or have to live and survive within these cultural dynamics.

---

2. For more on "respect" and the role it plays in the culture of young crack dealers in New York City (an example that can be expanded to other cultures), see Bourgois, *In Search of Respect*.

Affirming worthiness via belovedness is one way to circumnavigate these dynamics and move respect from an economics of austerity to an economics of abundance. When we care for one another, when we share with one another (when each gives according to their ability and receives according to their need), there is, in fact, enough for everyone. Here, two things must be avoided: we must ensure that we do not disrespect people, while also ensuring that we do not replicate abusive hierarchies of respect that are often operative in liminal groups that have been targeted and infected by some of the worst elements of mainstream society. Thus, for example, when a large ex-lifer covered in gang tattoos and sporting through-and-through bullet scars from a shoot-out with a tactical police unit comes to me for assistance, I make sure to treat this man with the utmost respect (doing all of the things I have described above). And when a small man who hasn't showered in days, who is psychotic and smells like shit and rotting flesh, who is regularly driven from shelters because of his personal hygiene (even though poor personal hygiene can be a defense mechanism frequently practiced by survivors of sexual abuse), I also make sure that I treat this man with the utmost respect and unconditional positive regard.

Here, those who are paid to be present in community spaces must avoid two temptations. First, they must refuse to engage in the abuses of power that are taken for granted and treated as norms within other social services and institutions. Second, they must also avoid becoming personally invested in street notions of respect. I have seen those who are paid to be present in community spaces fall for both of these temptations. Even those who do not get off on being in a position where they wield power over others can slowly drift towards adopting harmful elements of street culture (which, it should be noted, also has many good elements and so, for those who recognize this, the temptation is to uncritically accept *all* elements). However, one of the strengths of those who are paid to be present in a space is that they do not have to live within this code of respect. Thus, for example, I can continue to caringly engage with an upset person who calls me a goof (local prison slang for a pedophile—a term that is traditionally only employed if a person wants to transition from throwing words to throwing hands), without then feeling as if I must resort to violence to maintain my honor. Not being bound by this code allows me much more freedom to resolve conflicts and pursue outcomes that are at least satisfactory if not beneficial to all parties involved. I don't have to be sidetracked or subverted by a focus on maintaining my status within a hierarchy where everyone is punching down. Another example of how operating outside of this code can be beneficial to the community is the way in which paid staff members, while assiduously working to avoid ever placing calls to the cops, can still talk to the cops if the cops come creeping around a community—others in the community may operate by a strict code of refusing to ever talk to cops (or, at least, ever being seen by others when talking to cops) but those who are paid to be present can talk to cops in order to try and keep the community safe from cops. This is an activity that is both encouraged and appreciated by those who would never talk to the cops.

In fact, refusing to operate by this street code of respect—even though you might be in a position of power or authority that provides you with the opportunity to exploit it—is one of the most significant ways to communicate that you are serious about your commitment to acknowledging the worthiness of everyone who is involved in the community. Few things are so convincing to others about your commitment in this regard as refusing to respond to abuse with more abuse. This does not mean that people are not held accountable for abusive actions (more on that in the sections below regarding "Destructive Companions"), but it does mean that even when people are abusive, we respond with a desire to care for, and well-treat, everyone including people who are angry, upset, scared, violent, or abusive. In fact, this is especially important for our efforts to communicate to people our sense of their worthiness because, frequently, people are never more convinced of their own worthlessness, than when they act in these ways. After a violent outburst, people frequently feel shame, remorse, and self-loathing and, in fact, will then feel like their actions demonstrate that they deserve to be treated and harmed in all the shitty ways in which they have been treated and harmed. Therefore, responding with compassion and consideration to people when they are at (what they perceive to be) their worst, becomes one of the most powerful ways of communicating to people that who they are, in all that they are, is someone worthy and deserving of care. This does not mean that people are not held accountable for harmful actions, and it also does not mean that people are not sometimes asked to leave the community (as we will see in the section below about "Exiling"), it just means that our first response to potentially harmful situations or individuals is to avoid contributing to further harming anyone.

iii. Inter- and Intra-Connectedness

"Existence," quantum physicist and feminist social theorist Karen Barad reminds us, "is not an individual affair."[1] We are, all of us, *entangled* and, as such, are not simply intertwined with one another "as in the joining of separate entities," but, in fact, "lack an independent, self-contained existence."[2] Barad then uses the term "intra-action" to express what she means by this:

> The neologism "intra-action" *signifies the mutual constitution of entangled agencies.* That is, in contrast to the usual "interaction," which assumes that there are separate individual agencies that precede their interaction, the notion of intra-action recognizes that distinct agencies do not precede, but rather emerge through, their intra-action. It is important to note that the "distinct" agencies are only distinct in a relational, not an absolute sense, that is, *agencies are only distinct in relation to their mutual entanglement; they don't exist as individual elements.*[3]

For Barad, following in the steps of Niels Bohr, it is the "Observer Effect" that makes this especially apparent. Recognizing, for example, that light can be observed as both a particle and as a wave (depending on the apparatuses used to study light), or that the more precisely we can measure something's velocity the less precise we can be about its location or, conversely, the more precisely we can locate something, the less we are able to determine its velocity, helps to demonstrate how individual entities only emerge in and through the ways in which they are entangled. Hence, Barad goes on to argue that this "entails a rejection of the classical metaphysical assumption that there are determinate objects with determinate properties and corresponding determinate concepts with determinate

1. Barad, *Meeting the Universe Halfway*, ix.
2. Barad, *Meeting the Universe Halfway*, ix.
3. Barad, *Meeting the Universe Halfway*, 33.

III. INTER- AND INTRA-CONNECTEDNESS

meanings independent of the necessary conditions needed to resolve the inherent indeterminacies."[4] Consequently, "[a] *phenomenon is a specific intra-action of an "object" and the "measuring agencies"*; the object and the measuring agencies emerge from, rather than precede, the intra-action that produces them."[5] As such, Barad encourages us to rethink existence as something that occurs within "*a relationality between specific material (re)configurings of the world through which boundaries, properties, and meanings are differentially enacted.*"[6] Furthermore, this leads Barad to the following conclusion about reality itself: "Reality is . . . not a fixed essence. Reality is an ongoing dynamic of intra-activity . . . humans (like other parts of nature) are *of* the world, not *in* the world, and surely not outside of it looking in. Humans are intra-actively (re)constituted as part of the world's becoming."[7] Living in an ethically responsible manner, then, "entails an ongoing responsiveness to the entanglement of self and other, here and there, now and then."[8]

I am drawn to this understanding of reality, in part, because it fits so well with the Indigenous conceptions of the land, and what it means to be *of* the land, that I described above (in the "Acknowledging" chapter). It is fascinating to me that the most cutting-edge, up-to-date areas of science—especially as they pertain to matter, meaning, relationality, and life—are actually aligning with what Indigenous people have believed for millennia (and, I think, what European people also believed thousands of years ago, before they were colonized and went on to colonize others). The inter- and intra-connectedness that is constitutive of the kinds of political structures that are Indigenous to Turtle Island, which we also saw as constitutive of who we are as organisms, i.e., as ecosystems with consciousness (as per the "Honoring" chapter), this same inter- and intra-connectedness also appears to be constitutive of *reality* itself.

All of this flagrantly contradicts the glorification of the individual—a narrative that has been instrumental to and within the rise of modernity and the various permutations of oppression that have accompanied it. First with nation-states, then with colonial empires, and then with the globalization of racial capitalism under the rule of transnational corporations, modern imperialism has increasingly devastated previously existing communal bonds and ways of structuring life together, in order to produce individual

---

4. Barad, *Meeting the Universe Halfway*, 127; emphasis removed.
5. Barad, *Meeting the Universe Halfway*, 128.
6. Barad, *Meeting the Universe Halfway*, 139.
7. Barad, *Meeting the Universe Halfway*, 206.
8. Barad, *Meeting the Universe Halfway*, 394.

workers and consumers who can facilitate the maximization of profits for corporate shareholders. From the rugged individual who pulls themselves up by their proverbial bootstraps, to the entrepreneurial individual who maximizes their own commodification by successfully transforming themselves into a brand, we are consistently presented with narratives and images that encourage us to view, understand, and identify ourselves in isolation from others, in distinction from others, and over and against others. In this context, it becomes natural to first and foremost view ourselves as individuals and then, only secondarily, view ourselves as a member of this or that family, community, group, population, market, or history. However, as we have now seen, this is incongruent with quantum physics, with anthropology, with biology, and, despite those who are born rich who gloat about "the survival of the fittest" (by which they mean "the most ruthless" and not "those who find the best fit within their current, dynamic ecosystem), it is even incongruent with evolutionary science. It is, however, very congruent with regimes based upon capital accumulation that require the vast majority of life and living beings to be treated as disposable, as objects to be consumed, as sources for profit-extraction, and, once this has been done to the fullest extent possible, as trash. Hence, we along with the rest of the world, are, quite literally, *wasted*—as isolated individuals, we are emptied out, made desolate, and transformed into refuse.

One of the most prevalent and painful immediate consequences of this is that loneliness and feelings of lostness become ubiquitous among those who inhabit this narrative. It is a banal but no less tragic observation that, in our context, we live in close proximity to higher numbers of people than ever before but also experience higher levels of loneliness than at any other time in our history.[9] In reflecting on these things, I often find myself thinking about the suicide note Amanda Todd posted online shortly before she died (due to the vicious and absolutely unrelenting bullying she experienced both on- and off-line). In this note, which has now been viewed more than thirty-five million times, she writes: "I have nobody. I need someone."[10] *Millions* of us watched this and thought, "yes, I too, know how it feels to feel that way."

We feel lonely and we feel lost, and we always will feel this way to a greater or lesser degree when individuality becomes a goal, marketing strategy, or mandate, because *belonging is something we only experience in relationship with others*. Belonging is a product of inter- and intra-connections

9. In observing this interweaving of the banal and the tragic, it is also worth noting that the banalization of tragedy is another fundamental component of the fracturing of our collective life together and the reduction of people to human waste.

10. See TheSomebodytoknow, "My Story" (major content warning).

III. INTER- AND INTRA-CONNECTEDNESS

and, if those connections are destroyed or denied, then we become disoriented and cannot discern if or where or how or to what extent we belong. We become unsettled, anxious, uncertain, and sad but often, given how crowded our lives are, without being able to name the cause of our sadness, anxiety, and unsettledness. We are taught that our distress is, perhaps, related to existential angst, or melancholia, or some kind of neurochemical imbalance, rather than being related to the life-destroying and life-denying ways in which we are (literally and metaphorically) broken apart and isolated from one another, so that a very few people can get very rich.

Learning to rediscover the inextricable ways in which we exist in relationships of inter- and intra-connection provides considerable and perhaps unexpected relief from these things. The discovery that we are so intimately connected with others that, in fact, the boundaries between ourselves and others become porous and blurred, that we, in fact, *co-constitute one another*, shows us that there is a place where we fit and where *we belong*. As we learn to recognize, acknowledge, and deepen the relationships that constitute us, we discover ourselves to be more and more *at home*.

Having been personally deprived of housing and family, I deeply resonate with the longing to be-at-home but I also believe that my personal experiences in this regard have given me (and others who share this experience) some insight into some of the more general dynamics of the culture that arose from the nexus of patriarchy, imperialism, settler colonialism, and racial capitalism. By transforming place into property, ecosystems into standing reserves of natural resources, bodies into labor power, and mutual aid into personal advancement, our sense of being at home in the world and with one another is assaulted, eroded, and degraded. The globalization of neoliberalism and the digital transformation of the economy has only further uprooted profit-making, investments, and asset acquisition, which has also created an uprooted global labor market and human migrations on a scale that is hard to imagine (leading to the increasing militarization of borders, from Trump's wall, to the fortification of Europe, to the establishment of what are essentially for-profit penal colonies on islands off the coast of Australian-occupied territories). Thus, capitalists, like imperialists and colonizers, travel the world, deny the rights of others to their own homelands, mock notions of being-at-home as infantile mystifications retrojected onto some kind of imagined past, and do all they can to destroy any kind of rootedness.[11]

---

11. This, despite the ways in which it has been co-opted and branded, is why the language of radicality still makes sense in relation to resistance given that the word "radical" refers to *going to the roots*.

However, recognizing these things means that we also must avoid the violence and hubris of those like imperialists or colonizers or capitalists who feel they can go anywhere and claim that place as their home or, more properly, claim that that place belongs to them. For, as I have argued elsewhere, one of the transformations colonizers bring with them is the transformation of *personal belonging* into *personal belongings*, so that "home" transitions from being a local network of connections in which I belong to being a place that *belongs to me*.[12] Inter- and intra-connectedness counter this possessive narrative and are shown to be rooted not only in space and place but also in time and history.

Along with establishing a sense of belonging or at-homeness, inter- and intra-connectedness establish relationships that involve both *responsibility* and *accountability*. To be responsible for someone or something is to have an obligation that must be fulfilled to that person or thing. To be accountable to others means, quite literally, "to be liable to be called to account." It means recognizing that there are those who have the authority to ask you to make a statement explaining your conduct in the context of a reckoning (and, it should be noted, the people with the authority to do this are those whom we serve, not those who write our paychecks). Hence, belonging is both a liberating thing—one that frees us from uprootedness, loneliness, and dread—but also an obligatory thing. It gives us roots, which fasten and bind us to certain places, certain neighbors, certain relationships. Or, more accurately, it reveals the network of relationships in which we are always already and inextricably bound. Thus, for example, adults are responsible for children and should also be accountable to them; humans are responsible for and accountable to the land and the other beings who are of the land; the living are accountable for what they do as the present participants in the dynamics created by their ancestors, and are also responsible for what kind of dynamics they leave for their descendants; and so on. It is especially important for members of dominant and oppressive groups to realize this. To be identified as White, or as a cis-male, or as a colonizer, or as a member of the upper class means that one cannot escape from the dynamics established by White supremacy, heteropatriarchy, colonialism, or theft simply by saying, "but I'm not racist!" or "#NotAllMen" or whatever else. To be White and cis-male is to inherit the blood-soaked privilege of Whiteness and cis-maleness, and the same goes for people born into other dominant and oppressive groups regardless of how well-intentioned, woke,

---

12. See Oudshoorn, *Magnificent Work*, especially Part IV. See also Nichols, *Theft Is Property!*

or kind-hearted they might feel themselves to be. The object, then, is not to become reconciled to these dynamics but to *engage in a reckoning that changes them.*

Learning to be responsible for oneself, opening oneself to being held accountable by others, and encouraging others to do the same is very difficult work—in fact, in my opinion, it is some of *the most difficult work.* Frequently, those who wield power over others feel they have no good reason to do this work (they can always just go and find another victim) and those who are accustomed to others abusing them by wielding power over them often feel that they are more wronged than wrong (which is generally true) and so it is unfair and a misplaced and potentially oppressive priority to turn attention to ways in which they need to take responsibility or be held accountable (which is not necessarily true in this or that specific relationship or situation). Furthermore, this kind of work is especially difficult in communities of people who are oppressed both because of the ways in which lateral violence and intersectional complexities problematize any simplistic dualism between "oppressed" and "oppressor," "abuser" and "victim" (many people are both in different ways at different times or even simultaneously) and because the traditional ways of holding people responsible or accountable are, themselves, part of the system of oppression (police, prisons, and all of what Foucauldians refer to as the juridico-political system and the carceral state). This is very messy, very challenging, very sensitive, and very important work. Thankfully, it is something that communities of oppressed people have been exploring very thoughtfully and practically for many years. From colonized Indigenous nations practicing restorative justice within emancipatory spaces liberated by militant land defenders, to impoverished Black communities developing transformative justice and their own neighborhood support groups, to Queer anarcho-feminists who have developed caring but firm communal structures to makes spaces safer, there are rich histories we can (and should) learn from. I will not try to summarize all that we can learn from these (continually developing) traditions here but there are three points I wish to emphasize (and will return to these themes in more detail in the sections below, entitled "Alternate Courts of Justice" and "Restoring Ecosystem Thriving").

First, acknowledging how histories and experiences of oppression are significant factors in producing people who abuse, and desiring to prevent people who abuse from being further abused in racist and colonial justice systems, should never prevent us from centering the voices and needs of those whom they have abused. While this makes immediate sense on paper, it is often a difficult thing to implement well in practice. This is so for at least two very different reasons. On the one hand, there is the fact that patriarchal rape culture inclines towards empathizing with, believing, and exonerating violent men. On the other hand, there is the fact that victims and survivors, themselves, are often colonized by violent (punitive and retributive) understandings of what justice looks like. So, while we may all nod our heads and say, "yes, of course," when we are called to center the voices and needs of victims and survivors, in actual practice we all too often prioritize abusers' voices and needs or we all too often think we know better than what victims and survivors say they need because what they ask for conflicts with our own moral codes.

This leads to the second point I want to emphasize: that communities, themselves, need to understand how they, as a collective, share in the responsibility for what occurs in the lives of their members and how communities, understood as a whole, must be held accountable for the ways in which they contribute to harms that occur. In this regard, I was especially struck by the work of Cyrée Jarelle Johnson in her contribution to *Love WITH Accountability: Digging Up the Roots of Sexual Abuse* (edited by Aishah Shahidah Simmons). Having observed some of the ways in which transformative justice practitioners have failed to properly care for victims of sexual violence and, in fact, have actually helped to protect men who sexually abuse children, Johnson writes the following:

> Personally, I believe that the accountability model is a conservative and confessional one. It stops at the level of admitting to the violence—an important step but only the first one ... I don't need anyone to confess their guilt publicly—I already know who harmed me, and in many cases, *so does everyone else*. I need a community where everyone recognizes the role they played in that violation.[13]

What Johnson forces us to confront is the recognition that, almost always, when abuse occurs, there is someone else, or several other people within the community, who are aware of the abuse or who suspect that abuse is taking place, but who do not respond adequately to that knowledge and, as a result, who either actively or passively facilitate the abuse and the broader

---

13. Johnson, "Social Silence and Sexual Violence" in Simmons, *Love WITH Accountability*, 58; emphasis added. This is an important criticism, especially in Canadian-occupied territories where the performance of a confession or an apology is often substituted for meaningful acts of restitution or for structural changes that would uproot oppression (thus, for example, the Royal Canadian Mounted Police [RCMP] apologized for the ways in which it contributed to Canada's Indian Residential School system, but it did this while its membership continued to murder Indigenous men, rape, murder, and disappear Indigenous women and girls, and criminalize Indigenous peoples at massively disproportionate rates).

III. INTER- AND INTRA-CONNECTEDNESS

cultural dynamics that make abuse so ubiquitous. Thus, a commitment to the pursuit of accountability does not only seek to hold specific individuals accountable. It recognizes, as I have argued here, that individuals are not beings that exist in isolation from others but are beings *co-constituted with and among others* and, as a result, accountability is something that must be examined in relation to other parties in that network and in relation to the network as a whole. This forces us to ask hard questions about ourselves and, again, open ourselves up to the voices and needs of those who have been harmed.

Third, this means that we need to very deliberately structure our community spaces so that *mutual* accountability becomes possible. This is especially the case in communities where some people are paid to be present while others are not. Those being paid to be present must be as open and as easily held accountable by the community as any other members. This means reorienting how power is distributed in community spaces and developing ways to disrupt the correlations we make between payment and power. This means challenging expectations *on all sides*. For, just as much as some paid workers want to feel a disproportionate sense of power, there are also other community members who come to such spaces for support who want paid, authoritarian workers to act like cops and punish those who make them feel uncomfortable. As I said, this shit is complicated, and each local community, with its own unique dynamics, specific experiences, histories, strengths, and challenges must find its way to work through them. There is no "one size fits all" answer to these matters and there is every likelihood that we are going to make a lot of mistakes (especially early on) as we try and move further in this direction and liberate ourselves from other more oppressive ways of structuring our lives together. This should not cause us to lose heart. We *can* go good places together and it is precisely the recognition that we are *together* and desire to go in this direction *together* that will get us there.

D. Celebrating

We honor others by trusting them, by working together with them, and by affirming them, but we also honor them by celebrating them and by celebrating with them. The company we offer is fundamentally incomplete if we are missing this element. Originally, "to celebrate" referred to the idea of commemorating, honoring, or singing the praises of someone or something with demonstrations of joy.[14] By definition, celebrating was something that was done publicly, collectively, and joyfully but, also, with a sense of solemnity that was frequently ritualized and incorporated into the ways in which communities marked time. Thus, for example, within Christendom, the Roman Catholic Mass was described in Latin as something that is "celebrated" (celebratus) from the mid-fifteenth century onwards.

These, then, are things we must learn to practice and incorporate into our manner of being together with others. It is not enough to simply try to assist others or to treat others professionally and politely (wherein, as already noted, professionalism and good manners are usually performed via a passive refusal to engage in subjective violence directed at others even if one is still implicated in structural, objective violence). We must also celebrate others. We must greet them joyfully. We must do this publicly—those who are around us should know the joy we feel when greeting our loved ones and they should also know that they will be greeted joyfully by us when they come to see us. However, this joy is not trite or flippant. It is not forced or artificial. It is a serious thing. It is serious because the joy arises from our awareness of the specialness, belovedness, worthiness, and inter- and intra-connectedness of those who come to be with us. It is a *privilege* for us to be here, now, with this person, and we honor others by celebrating the fact that *they have honored us with their company*. So of course we celebrate

---

14. Or, depending on the context in which the celebration takes places, sorrow and regret—something I will explore in more detail in the chapter called "Commemorating."

D. CELEBRATING

this, and we do this exuberantly, profusely, publicly (like a parent applauding their child at the school talent show, like a child rushing to their parent when their parent returns from a trip, like old friends being reunited after the war—how could we not celebrate this exuberantly?) but, given what all is connected to this, we also do this seriously. After all, if we do not take it seriously, and if we do not celebrate others, then we are sending them a message that may very well harm their sense of themselves as special, beloved, worthy, and connected. In the three sections that follow, I will talk about how we celebrate others through marveling, thanking, and grieving.

Before getting to those themes, however, it is necessary to yet again go back to basics that have been forgotten, neglected, or deliberately ignored by so many institutional service providers who support and contribute to broader death-dealing structures within our society. One precursor to the ability to celebrate other people well is the recognition that *other people matter*. Celebrating people means affirming that they, in their specificity, matter—and that they, in their specificity, matter a great deal. Here, I am not proposing some kind of affirmation of the bleached-out and (as we will see) abusive statement that "All Lives Matter." Rather, recognizing the very real dynamics of oppression, dispossession, abuse, racism, colonization, and abandonment that are definitive of our time—a time when some lives are treated as disposable or worse, while other lives are treated as sacrosanct and inviolable—means that we affirm statements like the following: BLACK LIVES MATTER. To proclaim that "Black Lives Matter" is not a comment on any other race or whether they matter or not. It is simply to draw our attention to the fact that Black lives have systematically, time after time after time, been treated as disposable, as refuse, as criminal, or as "vulnerable to dying in unexpected ways." Thus, there is a need to draw attention to the fact that Black lives do, in fact, matter. And they matter a great deal. To respond to this by saying, "well, wait a minute, *all* lives matter," is akin to suggesting that the fire department should stop at every house in a city rather than going to the house that has been set on fire by a group of arsonists. "Yes, okay, we know your house is important, but there's one house in particular that some people are trying to burn down and that's the house we need to pay attention to at the moment." To try and draw attention elsewhere is, in fact, to help ensure that the burning house continues to burn until nothing is left. If the fire department stops at every house, then the burning house will be ashes by the time they arrive—which, it should be noted, is well-known by a good many people saying "All Houses Matter." And, of course, this is how the statement "All Lives Matter" functions. It tries to draw us back to supporting the status quo where Black people are routinely oppressed, targeted, abused, and left for dead, simply because they are Black.

The violence here is monumental. One gets a sense for it by attending to the dying words of those murdered by police officers. The dying words of Elijah McClain, a Black, twenty-three-year-old massage therapist in Aurora Colorado, were captured on the body cameras of the three White police officers, Nathan Woodyard, Jason Rosenblatt, and Randy Roedema, shortly before they turned off or discarded those cameras. This is what Elijah said:

> I can't breathe. I have my ID right here. My name is Elijah McClain. That's my house. I was just going home. I'm an introvert. I'm just different. That's all. I'm so sorry. I have no gun. I don't do that stuff. I don't do any fighting. Why are you attacking me? I don't even kill flies! I don't eat meat! But I don't judge people, I don't judge people who do eat meat. Forgive me. All I was trying to do was become better. I will do it. I will do anything. You all are phenomenal. You are beautiful. And I love you. Try to forgive me. I am a mood Gemini. I'm sorry. I'm so sorry. Ow, that really hurt. You all are very strong. Team work makes the dream work . . . (crying) . . . oh I'm sorry. I wasn't trying to do that. I just can't breathe correct (proceeds to vomit from the pressure on his chest and neck).[15]

Nate, Jay, and Randy claim that their body cameras were knocked off in the "struggle" (which was really a beat-down, a murder) but this claim is contradicted by evidence captured on camera (by a cop who arrives later) which shows this late-arrival being directed to point his camera away from the sight of Elijah vomiting while one of the original trio applies a chokehold. Paramedics assisted Nate, Jay and Randy in this murder. As Elijah struggled to breathe with three large men "restraining" him (i.e., suffocating him), the (unnamed) medics injected Elijah with 500 milligrams of Ketamine—an animal tranquilizer known for putting people into terrifying "K-holes"—which stopped him from struggling and, shortly afterwards, with the assistance of the police, stopped him from breathing and then, with further assistance from the police, stopped his heart from beating. Elijah was kept on life support but pronounced dead at the hospital a few days later (while his body was still covered with bruises and abrasions, including hemorrhaging that occurred on his neck due to the cop-applied chokehold). That was what happened to Elijah McClain, a young man who spent his lunch breaks playing his violin for cats and dogs at the local animal shelter because he believed it helped to ease their distress—but who was murdered because

---

15. This went viral on social media and has been subsequently verified as an accurate transcript by various fact-checking sites.

D. CELEBRATING

he was Black, had anemia and social anxiety, was cold, liked music, danced awkwardly, and went to the store to buy his brother an iced tea.

Elijah was murdered about a year before the murder of George Floyd. Held up at gunpoint, beaten in a police vehicle, and then forced to the ground, where a White police officer, Derek Chauvin, spent eight minutes and forty-six seconds kneeling on his neck (with the support of three other cops—Thomas Lane, J. Alexander Kueng, and Tou Thao), George Floyd, a forty-six-year-old Black man who had moved to Houston in order to improve his relationships with his daughters, a man who was known for standing up for others and loving "people that were thrown away," said the following before he died:

> it's my face man
> I didn't do nothing serious man
> please
> please
> please I can't breathe
> please man
> please somebody
> please man
> I can't breathe
> I can't breathe
> Please
> (Inaudible)
> man can't breathe, my face
> just get up
> I can't breathe
> please (inaudible)
> I can't breathe shit
> I will
> I can't move
> mama
> mama
> I can't
> my knee
> my nuts
> I'm through
> I'm through
> I'm claustrophobic
> my stomach hurt
> my neck hurts
> everything hurts
> some water or something

> please
> please
> I can't breathe officer
> don't kill me
> they gon' kill me man
> come on man
> I cannot breathe
> I cannot breathe
> they gon' kill me
> they gon' kill me
> I can't breathe
> I can't breathe
> please sir
> please
> please
> please I can't breathe[16]

And then George Floyd—known as Floyd to his friends—closed his eyes, stopped talking, and died. Aided and abetted by Tom, Alex, and Tou, Derek murdered Floyd. And everyone saw it happen, and nobody with the power to address it did anything about it, not until cities were literally burning for weeks, and, even then, it remains to be seen if the response that has now been made will bring any kind of "justice" to bear on what happened.

Eric Garner and Freddie Gray also said "I can't breathe" before being murdered by Daniel Pantaleo with the support of Kizzy Adonis of the NYPD, and by Brian Rice, Alicia White, William Porter, Garrett Miller, Edward Nero, and Caesar Goodson of the Baltimore PD. Meanwhile, the last known words of Amadou Diallo—Amadou, who was shot forty-one times without any warning by four plainclothes NYPD Officers, Edward McMellon, Sean Carroll, Kenneth Boss and Richard Murphy, because he was reaching for his ID to give to them—his last known words were: "Mom, I'm going to college."

According to Timothy Loehmann, the White police officer who murdered twelve-year-old Tamir Rice because Tamir was a Black boy playing in a Cleveland park, Tamir didn't have any last words. "He just moaned." What Tim did not mention is that Tamir lay on the ground moaning for a full four minutes before receiving any kind of medical attention (during that time, a large, cis-male cop pushed Tamir's fourteen-year-old sister onto her back, lunged on top of her with his full weight, and then locked her in a squad car—and the medical attention Tamir received, when he did receive it, was not from one of the cops involved). Tamir died in the hospital the next day.

---

16. This, too, went viral on social media and has been verified as authentic.

D. CELEBRATING

This is the reality of what we are up against when we try to tell people—*You matter. You Matter.* This is why it is so essential that we celebrate those who have been and are oppressed and who come to us seeking good company. It's not enough to be "polite" or "professional." We must *celebrate* people—especially those who have consistently received very powerful messages from the world around them that they *do not matter at all.* That, in fact, they matter so little that they can be a small child playing with a toy and be killed and the killer can get away with it, that they can be shot eight times in their sleep (Breonna Taylor was murdered in this way by Jonathan Mattingly, Brett Hankinson, and Myles Cosgrove of the Louisville Metro PD), that they can be shot dead through their bedroom window while playing video games with their nephew (as occurred when Aaron Dean from the Fort Worth PD murdered Atatiana Jefferson), that they can be home alone in their own apartment minding their own business (Amber Guyger from the Dallas PD murdered Jean Botham when she walked into his apartment claiming that she thought it was her own apartment and claiming, also, that she feared for her life); that they can be a man celebrating his wedding ("I love you, too" were the dying words of Sean Bell, 23, who was murdered on the day of his wedding by NYPD officers who fired fifty bullets at him—Paul Headley fired once; Michael Carey fired three times. Marc Cooper shot four times; Officer Gescard Isnora fired eleven times; and Michael Oliver emptied two full magazines, firing thirty-one times, pausing to reload at least once), and, really, they can be shot and murdered for any or no reason at all and the murderers will walk away without facing any consequences. When this is the case, we must go above and beyond to show people that they matter, to affirm their mattering, and to celebrate them.

In this regard, we absolutely must go beyond the general statement-making that social services like to make in order to wave their own flags, signal their own virtue, and retroactively exonerate themselves when a large amount of public attention and pressure is brought to bear on a certain issue. For example, in Canadian-occupied territories, as public funds were diverted from social services into police budgets in order to facilitate the militarization of the defense of private property required by austerity budgets, and as police departments simultaneously rebranded themselves as "services" rather than "forces" (further wedding the medical model of care to the carceral model of the State), police officers have been increasingly deployed in "wellness checks" for people "acting strangely" or experiencing some kind of "mental health crisis." One of the results of this is that cops frequently manhandle, assault, shoot, and kill those whom they have been called to support (often leaving mothers, siblings, friends, and lovers to deal with the fall-out of having called 911 for help only to end up seeing their loved ones abused and murdered right in front of them). This has been ongoing for quite some time, but the recent uprising against the racist and lethal use of violence by cops against Black folx has brought a renewed level of public scrutiny. Thus, in the province where I reside, it has become known that, in less than two months, police officers have murdered at least four people from racialized groups when they (the cops) were called to do "wellness checks" on these people. Those murdered were: D'Andre Campbell, 26, who had called the police himself to ask for help and who died from two gunshots to the chest, fired by an unnamed Brampton Police Officer, in the presence of two of his sisters and his younger brother; Caleb Njoko, 27, who somehow managed to "fall" out of his mother's apartment on the fifteenth-floor after unnamed officers from the London Police forced their way in and confronted him about his wellness (Caleb was still recovering from being assaulted be police in a previous interaction); Regis Korchinski-Paquet, 29, who was thrown from her twenty-fourth floor balcony by unnamed officers from the Toronto Police; and Ejaz Choudry, a 62-year-old father of four, who was shot and killed by unnamed Peel Police officers who had refused to permit Ejaz's family members to try and assist him in receiving help during a wellness check (additionally, as I was in the midst of writing this chapter I was notified of two further beat-downs—one where Lacy Browning, an RCMP officer in Kelowna dragged a young woman, a nursing student named Mona Wang, in cuffs and on her face, across the floor before standing on her head as a part of a wellness check; and one where Shanna Blanchard, a personal trainer in Nanaimo, was knocked unconscious, had both her eyes blackened, her nose broken, and two teeth knocked out, by two unnamed RCMP officers doing a wellness check).

In response to these "wellness check" murders and assaults, the largest community mental health organization in Ontario—the Canadian Mental Health Association, an organization that has a long history of working collaboratively with the police—released the following statement from their CEO:

> It's sad, heartbreaking and incredibly upsetting that once again an individual experiencing distress has died after a police response to a mental health crisis call. It's frustrating to reiterate our recommendations to the media, the public and government about what changes are required to support those who need help at the most critical point in their lives.
>
> Since April, four racialized Ontarians—D'Andre Campbell, Caleb Njoko, Regis Korchinski-Paquet and now Ejaz Choudry, a 62-year old husband and father of four—have lost their lives in a way that's becoming alarmingly common. The family of each

D. CELEBRATING

one of these individuals, and in the case of Mr. Campbell himself, had reached out for help only to end up dead after a police interaction.

It's easy to point fingers and lay blame with police, but these tragic events are a painful reminder of how our health, justice and social systems are failing those living with mental health or addictions conditions.

Having 911 as the de facto crisis line is problematic to begin with, but it's the reality. This is why we've long held the view that all communities in Ontario should have the resources to put enough mobile crisis response teams on the road 24 hours a day, seven days a week, as a first response model. These teams typically include a mental health professional, such as nurse or social worker, who rides alongside a specially-trained police officer.

...

Our experience, and our partnerships with police services across Ontario, has shown us that police also want additional MCRTs on the road, as well as increased training for all frontline officers to help them support people in distress.

...

There are shining examples that exist, such as in London, Ontario, where our branch of the Canadian Mental Health Association has a standalone 24-hour crisis center where individuals can walk in and receive crisis services and where police and paramedics can take people in distress. There, staff can help de-escalate and prepare a care plan, connecting a person to mental health resources. Between March and May, there were 644 visits to this crisis center, including 120 times when police or paramedics delivered someone experiencing a crisis.

But examples like this in London are few and far between. The resources just aren't available. Even if these programs do exist, the public largely isn't aware of them.

That's because the mental health and addictions system has been chronically underfunded compared to the physical health system, and as such it is difficult to navigate for the average person. If you break your arm, you go to the hospital. Our goal is to help inform the public that community-based agencies are here to help when they're struggling with their mental health.

...

Our goal should be to support people at all points on their journey of recovery from mental health and addictions issues so that they can lead meaningful and productive lives and avoid crisis situations.

Otherwise, we will find ourselves here again, faced with more tragedies and filled with more anger and frustration.[17]

To the general public, this statement may seem thoughtful, sensitive, and well-stated. But, under closer scrutiny, serious problems appear. Note, immediately, how this statement twists and turns and strains to use *any word but murder*. Thus, it states that "an individual experiencing distress *has died* after a police response" (emphasis added) and goes on to name others who "*end up dead* after a police interaction" (emphasis added). We see similarly tortured rhetorical tactics deployed in an earlier statement this organization made in relation to the Black Lives Matter uprising where, for all of its self-proclaimed affirmation of anti-racism, and all of its self-righteous assertions about having always been an anti-racist organization, in a more than four hundred word statement, the organization never actually says, "Black Lives Matter."[18]

Fundamental to both statements is the assertion and defense of the organization itself and the declaration that they (CMHA-Ontario) have always been on the right side of this issue and, in fact, that these tragic events would not be happening if the government had listened to them (hence, for example, the *very first paragraph* of the statement quoted above makes this clear when it declares that it is "frustrating to reiterate our recommendations to the media, the public and government about what changes are required to support those who need help at the most critical point in their lives"). This is both a defensive maneuver—one intended to prevent, a priori, any critical kind of attention being applied to this organization (given that social services who collaborate heavily with police and the goals of policing have been facing more public scrutiny)—and an offensive (in both senses of that term) statement intended to boost the brand equity of the organization and, rather than contribute to supporting the goals of those organizing with Black Lives Matter, co-opt that agenda and redirect funds to the coffers of the organization. Thus, in a statement that is remarkable for its naïveté of how deeply offensive it is in the context of police officers murdering Black, Indigenous, and other People of Color/members of racialized groups, the organization goes on to suggest that what, in fact, is needed is *heightened collaboration* with the police and *further funding for police budgets* in order

17. See Canadian Mental Health Association, "CMHA Ontario Responds."
18. Canadian Mental Health Association, "We Need to Do More and We Need to Do Better." The absence of the statement that "Black Lives Matter" is especially striking given that this statement also asserts, without any sense of irony, that: "We stand with those who continue to speak out and will use our platform to amplify their voices." It is odd, almost to the point of appearing duplicitous, to make this claim without also affirming the central declaration of those whose voices they claim to amplify.

D. CELEBRATING 131

to assist with this. This tactic of police reform and education has, time after time, been conclusively demonstrated to produce no meaningful change.[19]

The statement from CMHA-Ontario moves rapidly from virtue signaling (expressing outrage and mourning about the fact that people seem to keep oh-so-mysteriously and inconveniently dying when the police engage in wellness checks), to praising their own collaboration with the police and calling for further funds to improve that collaboration (for, as the CEO asserts in one of the most tone deaf and offensive parts of the statement: "It's easy to point fingers and lay blame with police, but these tragic events are a painful reminder of how our health, justice and social systems are failing those living with mental health or addictions conditions"). In other words, holding killer cops responsible for killing people isn't the answer—giving more money to this organization, and the "shining example" they provide of bootlicking, is said to be the answer! In a context where others are calling for disarming, defunding, abolishing, or straight up fucking the police because of the anti-Black (and other) violence that is deeply and inextricably engrained in the culture of policing, this organization boldly continues to support the police and the system as it is, while simultaneously posturing as though they are supporting those who are murdered by the police and as though they are the solution to the broken system (that, in fact, they are trying to maintain).

Another conclusion that is difficult to escape, once one has spent some time examining these things, is that liberal tolerance, if it means anything at all, is simply the remarkable ability of liberals to tolerate a violent system so long as it leaves them alone and so long as it permits them to feel like they are not personally involved in violence but are, in fact, good people. Thankfully, however, there are those with a better understanding of what it means to grieve, rage, work, and fight alongside of those who are oppressed. Take, for example, the following statement made by SafeSpace London, a collective of current and former sex workers who run a community space to support sex workers:

> Black Lives Matter.
>
> Police in Canadian-occupied territories are, and always have been, one of the key institutions responsible for building and maintaining a national culture that is thoroughly racist. The

---

19. For one poignant example of how police forces resist changing based on things like sensitivity training or further education, see Doe, *Story of Jane Doe*. More systematically, see Vitale, *End of Policing*. For histories of policing that helps to explain this factor see Williams, *Our Enemies in Blue* and Maynard, *Policing Black Lives*.

police are a brute force, not a "service," and they are deployed to maintain structural racism, uphold White supremacy, and legitimize settler colonialism. This has resulted in decades of police violence directed at Black people—violence that White people and those who find ways to get rich within racist societies, have long ignored or denied.

We acknowledge that nobody—not one single person—who is not a Black person (a Black person regularly and routinely at risk of being raped, murdered, robbed or beaten by the police), has any authority to tell Black people how they may or may not protest or resist the lethal force deployed against them. We support the Black Lives Matter uprising, no matter what means are used in the pursuit of justice, restitution, and equitably sharing the abundance of life that should be available to all people but which, in fact, is regularly hoarded by a very few, mostly White, people (who the police then serve and protect—and who allow the police to do whatever they like to Black people so long as the police continue to serve and protect their interests).

We deny the legal authority the police claim to have to kill us or force us to do what they want, and we deny the moral authority the Canadian state claims in order to enforce White supremacy and normalize structural racism.

We call-out local non-profit and charity organizations who benefit materially or otherwise by maintaining "collaborative relationships" with police rather than disrupting the status quo. We see you.

This has gone on for far too long. Disarm and defund the police. Free Black prisoners. Pay restitution to Black communities that police have assaulted on behalf of wealthy, White interests. We support those who call for these things, regardless of their tactics.

Black Lives Matter.

See you in the streets.[20]

Comparing the statement from CMHA-Ontario with the statement from SafeSpace London is instructive. It demonstrates why people involved in struggles at the grassroots level, and why people who experience oppression, have increasingly created a distinction between "accomplices" and "allies." From this perspective, "allies" are those who will tell anyone and

---

20. Posted online on the SafeSpace London Facebook page on June 5, 2020. Full disclosure: as a member of the SafeSpace Board of Directors, I helped draft this statement.

D. CELEBRATING

everyone that they are on the side of those who experience oppression, but who actually do little to challenge themselves, to check their privilege, to risk anything, or to make a meaningful difference. "Accomplices," on the other hand, are those who are willing to put themselves in harm's way, who are willing to suffer as a result of their solidarity, and who will put themselves on the line, in acts of lived solidarity with those whom they support.[21] It is important to recognize this here because celebrating people does not just mean cheering them on from a safe distance—*truly celebrating people means getting in the thick of things with them*, running down alleyways together, de-arresting one another, and laughing at the cops together afterwards. Celebrating people means celebrating *with* people—celebrating the things that matter *to them*, their victories, their achievements, who they've become after all they've been through. It means celebrating when someone finds a street-level pharmacist who they can trust to provide them with a safe supply of their medication. It means celebrating when someone else finds a birthday present for their kid at the street market outside of the local shelter. It means celebrating when someone gets an extra-large tip from a john. Checking privilege means checking your values and asking yourself—do I value this person as much as I say that I do, or do I, in fact, value some other things more dearly and, as a result, refuse to celebrate them and the things they celebrate?

For example, when LA exploded after the video of the Rodney King beating surfaced in 1994, and an unknown Black man declared, "Burn motherfucker, burn!" can I respond to that declaration with a resounding, "Fuck, yeah!"? Or, in 2020, can I celebrate when I see the Third Precinct police station in Minneapolis burn to the ground? Can I commemorate this event, honor those who participated in it, sing their praises with public demonstrations of joy—or am I just contributing to policing them as I try to insert myself into events in which I have not participated in order to feel good about myself or boost my own brand status? What you choose to celebrate or not celebrate, what you celebrate publicly and what you celebrate privately, and who you choose to celebrate and celebrate with, reveals a great deal about your allegiances. And here's the thing: we are all well past the point of being fooled by those who say one thing in private but never show up in public. And we all now know that those who claim to be neutral in the context of oppression are ever and always on the side of the oppressor. Either you're with us or you're against us, and if you find yourself paralyzed and panicky when confronted by the reality of having to pick a side, then, at the very least, *get the fuck out of the way*.

---

21. For more on this, see Milstein, *Taking Sides*.

i. Marveling

In France, in slightly more formal settings, if you wish to say that you are delighted to meet someone, you might use the word "enchanté." This would translate into English as "delighted" (with the "to meet you" part being implied) but, more literally and archaically (in both English and French), the word communicates the idea of being *enchanted* by someone. To enchant someone expresses the idea of delighting, "affecting with great pleasure," charming, or fascinating them with your company and, more literally, refers to act of casting a spell ("practicing sorcery or witchcraft") on someone—bewitching them in a way that is alluring. Here, the roots of the word also carry musical connotations (with "chant" from "en-chant" being entomologically rooted in the notion of "singing"). Much of this still carries forward in the ways in which we speak about songs or musicians as charming, as alluring, as magical, and so on. Very literally, traced back to the Latin ("in" + "cantare") to enchant someone means to *in-sing* them. It is to draw them into the song that you are; it is to open them up to the song that you sing, or, perhaps, to discover that you are both singing the same song (or, at least, discover that your songs are in harmony). Hence, more colloquially today, we speak of "vibing" with someone or "being on the same wavelength." Thus, over a long period of time, the language used to communicate this concept changes but the core motif—enchantment, in-singing—remains remarkably the same.

It is useful to remember this as many people are now exploring what it might mean to "re-enchant" the world. Or, more properly, more people are recognizing that industrial (and post-industrial), capitalist, imperialist, and colonial efforts to dis-enchant the world have failed to create life with meaning and have done considerable and, in many cases, irreparable harm. Acts of re-enchantment are ways of recalling, and bringing back to conscience and consciousness, the sacredness of all that is. Such acts seek to remember and honor the sacredness, belonging, inter- and intra-connectedness, and

I. MARVELING

agency, of both human and non-human being(s). Sharp divisions between living and non-living things are blurred or erased, distinctions between organisms and environments are shown to be a question of perspective, and value is affirmed, not as something granted by fluctuations in the market or in utility, but as a sine qua non of being itself. As a result, we are asked to show considerable care as we find our place within this shared web of life to ensure that we contribute to the greater flourishing of all life.

Given that we are living through the sixth mass extinction, much of the work of re-enchantment has been (appropriately) directed at the "natural world" around us—the oceans, the rivers, the forests, and the plants and animals and creepy-crawlies who have found their places of belonging there. However, what can sometimes be forgotten or even denied by those doing this work is that homo sapiens is and are a part of this natural world, and homo sapiens also must be re-enchanted through our actions and the ways in which we treat one another. One sees this forgetfulness and denial even in the term "Anthropocene" when it is applied to refer to the catastrophic changes that have occurred in our time. "Anthropocene" means the Human Epoch, or the geological age wherein shifts in the earth's climate and fundamental cycles are definitively influenced by humans. This is misleading. Humans lived for tens of thousands of years without disrupting these cycles and without manufacturing mass death and mass extinction. It was only after vast amounts of wealth and power were hoarded in the hands of a very few, very rich people that mass devastation occurred. We do not live in the Anthropocene, we live in the *Plousiocene—the Epoch of the Rich*, the age when the rich have shown their willingness to kill everything and anything at all, by any means at all, if it advances their profits or their profit margins even just the slightest bit. It is they, and not humanity in general or humanity as such, who are responsible for these things.

Thus, as each new person comes to my workplace seeking good company and as we introduce ourselves to one another, I often whisper to myself, "enchanté, enchanté." You are enchanting. I am enchanted by you. I am delighted to meet you.

In order to facilitate our collective re-enchantment, it is necessary to recover a sense of wonder so that we are constantly and genuinely marveling at those who choose to share life together with us. We are all marvels and wonders. To see another person as a marvel is to recognize that they are a miracle, a singularity, the one and only them that has or can or ever will exist and, although they exist for only the briefest of moments (and perhaps we only get to know them for the tiniest part of that briefest of moments), they are here, now, with us. How can this not fill us with wonder and astonishment? Therefore, do whatever it is you need to do in order to never forget that the people who come seeking help, those who are oppressed, who are scorned and abandoned by others—spat on by University students, beaten by cops, raped by drunken men, laughed at in videos shared on social media platforms—are well and truly and deeply *marvelous*. If you find this hard to believe then spend a lot of time listening, spend a lot of time learning, spend a lot of time attending to those whom others despise and learn from those who know how to communicate to them that they are marvelous.

Because there need not be anything voyeuristic, paternalistic, or sensationalistic about coming to understand that people are marvelous. Of course, each person is sensational (by which I mean that they are exciting and full of unanticipatable surprises) but this does not mean sensationalizing them (in the sense of viewing them as a source of entertainment or selfish personal gratification). Quite the opposite, in fact. We view others as marvelous because we glimpse something that is fundamental to who they are—something that no amount of suffering, violence, abuse, or oppression can ever take away from them. We see this and we honor them by celebrating it and by treating them the way that such people deserve to be treated. Each person, in other words, is *spectacular* but not a *spectacle*. Their marvelousness does not exist for us, or for our use, abuse, or gratification (although they, in all their marvelousness, also exist in relationships of shared responsibility, accountability, and connectedness). Their marvelousness is their own and, as such, deserves to be treated with circumspection, honor, tenderness, and care. This reminds us, yet again, that we are being granted a great honor and an equally great responsibility when people come to us seeking support, help, and good company.

ii. Thanking

We celebrate people in our active recognition of their intrinsic but often denied and abused marvelousness, and this recognition spontaneously gives rise to a sense of gratitude and thanksgiving. This then initiates a mutually reinforcing feedback loop between marveling and thanking.

However, because most of the vocal proponents of developing an "attitude of gratitude" (those who then use the hashtags #grateful and #blessed) tend to be exploiters and oppressors who are doing little more than gloating and publicly reveling in the wealth that they have accumulated by dispossessing others, and the privilege they experience because they are on the "#winning" side of oppression, I developed a deep distrust of those who urged us to move towards gratefulness. When people suggest that yoga or meditation or "mindfulness" are what we need to encourage in order to "improve the quality of life" of people who live in slavery, who are systematically abused, punched down, chewed up, spat out, and left for dead, not only do I discover that we feel grateful for very different things, but I also start to wonder if gratitude is appropriate at all. Consequently, I frequently found myself meditating upon the well-known words of Psalm 137 (a song especially familiar to those who participated in various uprisings against racism, slavery, and colonialism in the Caribbean):

> By the rivers of Babylon,
> There we sat down and wept,
> When we remembered Zion.
> Upon the willows in the midst of it
> We hung our harps.
> For there our captors demanded of us songs,
> And our tormentors mirth, saying,
> "Sing us one of the songs of Zion."
> How can we sing the Lord's song
> In a foreign land?

Less well-known is the conclusion of the Psalm:

> O daughter of Babylon, you devastated one,
> How blessed will be the one who repays you
> With the recompense with which you have repaid us.
> How blessed will be the one who seizes and dashes your little ones
> Against the rock. (NASB)

It is precisely those who are proclaiming their own state of blessedness, those who are constantly posting pictures of all they are grateful for—their latest vacation, their newest vehicle, the latest check they cut for a local charity, hospital, or university, their most recent social gathering where they went to see-and-be-seen—whom the Psalmist condemns and with all the heartbreak, rage, despair, and grief of those who know what it is to have their children taken, their health destroyed, their homes bulldozed, their land stolen, their bodies raped, and their lives uprooted, whom the Psalmist wishes the utmost devastation and violence upon in return. I have often thought about this cri de coeur and how it is universally filtered out of public recollections of this Psalm—hard words, hard words.[1] But if you do not understand them, if you cannot respond to this Psalm by saying, "I know that *feeling*" (regardless of whether or not you can agree with what that feeling calls for), then you really cannot claim to understand what it means to live as a member of a people who have been and are being oppressed. When tormentors demand mirth from the tormented, when captors demand songs from the captives, when oppressors demand gratitude from the oppressed, a refusal of all three of these things is necessary, appropriate, and evidence of the uprising of the spirit of Life. "You want me to be grateful? *Fuck you.*" And, while the oppressor more than likely walks away offended and confused ("*Oh. My. God. I was just trying to help!*"), feel free to flip them off as they go.

As a result of observations like these, I spent many years deeply skeptical of any kind of focus upon gratitude. Gratitude seemed to be especially evident amongst the complacent and it seemed to breed complacency and I did not want to be complacent. What I learned over time, however, is that remaining so thoroughly rooted in devastation, sorrow, anger, outrage, and pain, was, for me personally, ultimately unsustainable. After thirty years, I was completely heartbroken, overwhelmed, exhausted, and longing to die. I held on to life for the sake of my (then very young) children but I found my

---

1. Jesus wasn't wrong when he said that it is truly hard for the rich to get on the right side of history; for, in order to do so, they must dispossess themselves of their stolen wealth and land—which, as Jesus knew, is everything they owned—the very thing the rich are unwilling to do.

II. THANKING

grip was slipping. I didn't know how much longer I could hold on. My heart was breaking. My mind was breaking. My body was breaking. And it was then, through a series of events, that I rediscovered wonder. I rediscovered a sense of wonder about what it means to be alive—if only for the briefest of moments—and what it means to be a part of that which is and was and ever will be. I rediscovered a sense of many of the things I am trying to highlight in this text—beauty, inter- and intra-connectedness, mutuality, gentleness, and kindness—and I also rediscovered that beneath the language of love that I applied to so many things (my relationships with my children, with my nephews and nieces, with my brothers, with the people I knew on the street, with others involved in the struggle), gratitude was already present. I just needed to recognize it, culture it, grow it, and share it. Doing this did not mean I stopped feeling those other feelings of sorrow or rage. It means they were not the only feelings I felt.

This sharing of heartfelt gratefulness is especially important. Giving thanks to others and for others—for their company, for their choice to share their lives with us, for the wisdom, experience, and relationships they bring with them, for the ways in which they contribute to shaping our life together, and for the unique niche they have within our ecosystem—is an important element of building community spaces in a field where the language of care has been so heavily co-opted by those who are apathetic and abusive. Giving thanks to and for others is one way of both moving beyond and explicitly countering the politeness and formality that are part of the abuse that comes with professionalization and the imposition of bougie social norms into communities of people who either physically cannot or deliberately will not shape their lives around those norms.

By being thankful we immediately acknowledge to some, in the presence of others, that we favour them. Thankfulness, then, is one component of taking sides and of demonstrating where our allegiances lie. This is a very different thing than simply trying to make ourselves "accessible" so that we can professionally support people in attaining the kinds of outcomes we desire for them—because despite trending talk about being "client-centered," these are actually pre-determined priorities that we track meticulously given that we receive funding from governments and corporations to attain them and need to demonstrate that we can do this competitively in an overcrowded and underfunded market. Thankfulness celebrates who people already are and moves us into solidarity with them. Consequently, such proclamations of thanksgiving must be matched with gratefulness that, not only thinks fondly of others, but that also is ready to make itself manifest by actions that show our good will, which express our pleasure in those who we are thanking, and which, in the presence of hurt, harm, or wrongdoing, quickly move in the direction of pardon, mercy and grace.

In this regard it is interesting to note that the same Proto-Indo-European root ("*gwere-") can denote both favour, praise, and celebration (thus: *gra*titude, con*gra*tulations, *gra*ce), and also something that is heavy, weighty, or venerable (as in *gra*vity, *gra*ve, ag*gra*vate). This seems appropriate to me. All too often thanksgiving and expressions of gratitude are trivialized and commercialized and become functions we ritualistically perform, not because our hearts are in those actions, but because they are a social nicety expected of us. Giving thanks to and for others becomes a box we tick to demonstrate our good breeding. In this way, it becomes the very opposite of what it is supposed to be. It becomes a thing we do for ourselves and to show others something about ourselves. It becomes selfish.

We also see how this selfishness infects other ways of expressing thanksgiving for others when mostly older, mostly White, mostly middle- or upper-class, mostly heterosexual, mostly cisgendered, mostly men, refer to others as a "gift." To describe another person as a gift (to the world or, more pointedly, to myself) risks objectifying that person and transforming them into a thing that exists for our (or my) pleasure or benefit. Furthermore, transforming the labor, accumulated wisdom, talents, abilities, and presence of another person into a gift, which, by definition, is the kind of thing that is to be given and received free of charge, also belittles their labor, denies the need for compensation or restitution, minimizes their agency, and all-too-often contributes to the exploitation and consumption of the one who is praised as a gift or as gifted (who is, as a general rule, not an older, White, middle- or upper-class, cis-het male, because these men know they can always be well-compensated for any real or imagined contribution they make). In other words, either we take gratitude seriously—we understand that it is a weighty thing, something to be practiced with thought and care, something requiring us to treat others with *veneration*—or the chances are that we are simply serving ourselves more than others by how we go about giving thanks.

This mention of veneration leads us back to the affirmation of the sacredness of each and every person who comes to us seeking good company. This sacredness is something people always carry with them—it is a part of who they are that can never be taken from them. Therefore, thanking them for being who they are and for sharing life together with us must always be present in our interactions with them. Thus, over against the self-righteous bougie oppressors who talk about being #blessed while racialized women cut their toenails or massage their bodies, and over against old White men who think everyone who is good and beautiful and talented and true exists for their private consumption ("I'll eat you up, I love you so!"), we, even in the context of a society that uses us, abuses us, and leaves us for dead, persist in feeling grateful because—looks at us—we are all in this together, we have one another, and there is no company we would rather keep than this one.

iii. Grieving

When I began to work on this writing project, the top priority chosen by many municipalities and the local service providers who partner with them was to participate in policing people who have been deprived of housing by seeking-out and then dismantling so-called "encampments" (i.e., "tent-cities," "squats," or "urban campsites" on private or public property). Encampments have been on the rise due to the ongoing imposition of austerity measures, cuts to services, the increasingly precarious nature of formerly secure work, reductions in shelter spaces, and the ongoing ways in which wealthy individuals and corporations have been driving real estate market rates up to ever-less-affordable rates for the average person. In London, Ontario, since the city began to more closely monitor and govern "homeless populations," more people were recorded as camping in 2019 to 2020 than in any other year. However, because these campsites infringe on private property, because they purportedly effect the profit margins of downtown businesses, because they do not fit within the neoliberal model of municipal development, and because even liminal spaces must be increasingly monitored and policed, municipalities were heavily focused on tearing them down. In order to achieve this, social service providers who identified as "advocates" and "supports" of "people experiencing homelessness" were required to do what the police would have otherwise been called to do—enforce property-related municipal bylaws. Essentially, a kind-hearted social worker can achieve the desired outcomes (the removal of the encampment) in less time with less conflict than a police officer. In fact, one local agency that is regularly praised for the work they do with "the most vulnerable" developed a specific bylaw enforcement team to work closely with the police to accomplish these goals. It's a vivid illustration of the ways in which social work and policing increasingly co-constitute one another, as claims about being caring are made in relation to disciplinary, punitive, and harmful practices.

III. GRIEVING

In the early days of the COVID-19 pandemic, the very same officials, officers, and agencies who were adamant that all encampments must be removed were urging us (as concerned citizens) to buy tents for people who have been deprived of housing. Observing how homeless shelters can become hot-spots for the spread of COVID, and noting how many people who are deprived of housing have compromised immune systems and inadequate medical care, the solution put forward was *not* to then provide adequate medical care, proper medication, or housing. The solution we were told to pursue was purchasing tents (with our own money, as the city is not funding this) and donating those tents so that people who are deprived of housing can better engage in "social distancing."

What is remarkable about this is how the same people can completely reverse their position on an issue without ever acknowledging or addressing the underlying justifications they proclaimed for holding the previous position and without explaining how their new position still aligns with the values they claimed to hold before. Thus, the question looms: what exactly are the values or practices that undergird the same parties taking completely contradictory positions in different circumstances? I would suggest the following: the core value at work here is maintaining those who are deprived of housing *precisely as those who are deprived of housing* in a way that does not compromise the well-being and profits of the propertied classes. Busting encampments is a good tactic for real estate developers and neoliberal cities when gentrification is the norm. Providing tents (and not housing or medical care) is a good tactic when experiencing a pandemic and trying to maintain norms around who is or is not permitted to have housing, or a prescription for medication, or a family doctor, and whose priorities are served by the ways in which we are governed. Specifically, pride of place still goes to defending our notion of private property and ensuring we are maintaining the laws that exist in order to help the rich get richer—notably, here, by not violating the sacrosanct nature of rent and the absolute sovereignty of the property owner over their private property (including buildings left empty while people sleep outside). The pandemic threatens property relations and so, for such a time, we give out tents. However, if the pandemic were to end today, you can be sure that tomorrow these same people would go back to busting-up encampments.[1]

---

1. In fact, a few months after I wrote this chapter, the city began to drastically reduce funding for people to stay in hotel rooms, thereby forcibly depriving a number of people of housing (as shelters continue to be operating at a significantly reduced capacity, no new affordable housing has appeared, rental rates have continued to increase, and, even before COVID reduced shelter capacities, they were still nowhere close to meeting the level of need in the community). At the same time, the city returned to

However, we must be absolutely clear about the results of this. This is a death-dealing practice. It is one that continues to normalize cruelty (so that we don't even notice that we are being cruel or how cruel we are being—in fact, it makes us feel kind when we are cruel!), and one that continues to leave people to die in the most inhuman circumstances.

Let me provide a few examples of how this plays out. A couple of weeks ago, a dead newborn baby was found in a porta-potty in Vancouver's downtown eastside (porta-potties were installed as "comfort stations" since access to public washrooms has all but completely disappeared—although using the language of "comfort," rooted as that language is in notions of consolation, of soothing grief, and of cheering up or offering solace, to describe this stretches credulity and, in fact, is highly offensive). A mother had labored and given birth in the porta-potty and the newborn had not survived and so the body of the newborn was left behind and the mother, well, nobody knows what happened to her. Then, as I was writing this chapter, I received news that someone had died in a porta-potty by a campsite outside a local homeless shelter. It was reported that this person was in the porta-potty, injecting their medication and miscalculated their dose. By the time they were discovered, they were dead. In both instances, public officials—politicians, managers, medical officers of health—expressed regret but were more focused on explaining that nobody can be blamed for such things, this is nobody's fault, tragedy is a part of life, some people are living higher risk lifestyles, and, yeah, this is definitely not my department's fault and most definitely not *my* fault, and it's probably best if we all move on. It is times like these, when people die in the most dehumanizing environment possible and when people respond to those deaths with the utmost disregard for the

---

tearing down encampments. In part, this is a return to "business as usual" when it comes to oppression, but it is also necessary for the City to go after encampments lest their existence make people question claims made by the city and its partners about the number of people they "successfully housed" during COVID. In fact, those claims have been hugely exaggerated. During the pandemic, City-funded Housing Workers have been placing people in hotels. These placements were recorded in statistics as a person "successfully housed." However, because these people only usually end up staying in that hotel for two to four weeks, workers from the same program find that person a room in another hotel. This is then recorded as an additional person "successfully housed" statistic, with no mention being made that, in fact, this is the same person being recorded twice and with no mention that being "successfully housed" means being provided with temporary accommodation in a hotel. Thus, over the last few months, the same seventy-five or so people have been cycled several times between various hotel rooms, which (if that happens four times per person—a not unrealistic estimate) produces the "evidence-based" claim that the city successfully housed 300 people when, in fact, nobody has long-term housing and everyone is now looking at being deprived of housing in the next two months.

III. GRIEVING

worth of those who died (and those who are left behind), that I have to force myself not to lose my mind.

Throughout this book but especially in this section, I emphasize the importance of honoring others, of recognizing that they are marvelous, of celebrating their specialness and belovedness, of centering their dignity and worthiness, and of acknowledging who they are in their own individual uniqueness and in their inter- and intra-connectedness. This is the heart of our efforts. If we neglect these things, chances are that we are not being good company to and with others. So we do this work, and we prioritize these things, and we focus here, but we are constantly coming up against long histories of abuse, oppression, neglect, abandonment, and cruelty. Consequently, we persist, and we hope, and we refuse to cease striving, and we do our fucking damnedest to counter the histories written on the bodies of our loved ones, but kindness is rare and cruelty is common, and safe spaces are small and unsafe spaces are large, and the times we get with those who are tender-hearted is often a fraction compared to the times we have spent with those who are cold-hearted. As a result, it is not uncommon for people to disbelieve us when we try to reflect back to them the beauty, and goodness, and worthiness that we see in them. And here's the thing about that: when a city leaves someone to die in a fucking porta-potty, when they leave a human being, someone's loved one, someone's child, someone's sibling, someone's friend, someone who loved and who was loved, a sacred fucking life, to die in a porta-potty—a stench-filled plastic shit-box, buzzing with flies, with urine and feces and mud smeared across the plastic floor; a reeking fucking plastic shit-box that they were forced to use because city officials would not allow them access to a home or any other facility with a bathroom; because even during a pandemic the city decided they should just live in a squat (an "encampment"), where they tried to inject their own medication because they had nowhere safer to do so, and where they overdosed and died—and not one public official, not any single fucking one, went on record and said, "this is horrendous, this is awful, this is devastating, this is heart-breaking, and we are doing everything, everything we possibly can to ensure that it never, never, never happens again," then I think, "what can we possibly say or do to counter this?" Because, while I and a few others may try to reflect the belovedness of those whom we encounter back to them, when a city abandons people to die in a reeking fucking plastic shit-box, the most compelling message they receive is actually this: "You, at the core of your being, both inside and outside, through-and-through, are a *fucking piece of shit.*" What can we do, us little people who want to love and be loved and be good company to and with others who have been left for dead, to counter the force of this message and the sheer viciousness and utter brutality of this violence? Some days, it feels like there is nothing we can do. And I am weary, weary, weary of people trying to comfort me by saying, "you're a good worker, you do what you can, you can only do so much," when we would be able to do so much more if those offering that comfort weren't so at ease with leaving my loved ones to die in public washrooms, in bathrooms, in porta-potties, and anywhere else that people go to expel waste from their bodies. My friends and loved ones are not waste to be expelled from our political body. But, for as long as we abandon them to die alone in porta-potties where they have gone to take their medication, my loved ones are going to find it very hard to believe otherwise about themselves.

And so we *grieve*. We grieve deeply. We grieve continually. As much as there is one part of our hearts that is always saying "thank you!" there is also another part of our hearts that is always grieving. And this act of grieving is one of the ways in which we celebrate and honor those whom we have known and loved and who have known and loved us. Having had an opportunity to see the beauty, goodness, wonder, magic, and music in those whose company we have shared, how could we not grieve?

Consequently, learning the art of grieving, of honoring others by grieving the ways in which they have been hurt, betrayed, and left for dead, and learning to live our lives as we grieve without ceasing, becomes critical to our ability to be good companions. I will have more to say about this in Part Four ("Parting"), but for now it must be emphasized that grief is something that we do precisely because we honor and celebrate others. Grief and celebration go hand-in-hand and, given the brevity of each individual, we cannot have one without the other. Thus, as an old revolutionary once said, being good company to and with others means rejoicing with those who rejoice *and* mourning with those who mourn.

What makes our grief in situations like those I have described above especially difficult to carry is that, unlike the griefs that arise because we live in community with others who are mortal and who sometimes experience catastrophic accidents or unforeseeable disasters (the general griefs of finitude and temporality), this kind of grief is paired with the recognition that so much of the pain, suffering, misery, and death that we grieve is *unnecessary* and *deliberately caused*. There is no good reason for an adult to torture a child. There is no good reason for a boss to rape a worker. There is no good reason for a person to be deprived of housing. There is no good reason for a person to be left to die in a reeking fucking plastic shit-box. This is not to say that there is no reason at all for these things—it's just that the reasons are *not good* (reasons like greed, selfishness, fiscal responsibility, fear, apathy, and the valorization of cruelty all come quickly to mind). Thus, while we already struggle to bear up under and work through the grief and loss that comes

III. GRIEVING

from such unavoidable things as mortality, trying to bear up under and work through the grief and loss that comes from avoidable but extraordinarily cruel things, can be very challenging—especially when, day after day, week after week, month after month, year after year, one bears witness to the harms caused by these very things. Grief becomes a part of us. It changes us. This cannot be avoided. And so we need to learn to change with our grief in ways that fit with where we want to go. This is not always easy to do. But it is a task that is required of us precisely because of our commitment to care for and honor others. Because I have consistently observed the following: if we shut ourselves off from grieving, we also compromise our ability to care, and when we compromise our ability to care in this way, we also begin to honor others less, and this trajectory, itself, becomes a self-reinforcing feedback loop and, if we are not careful, over time, tender-hearted people who become overwhelmed by grief can become hardened and actually end up hurting or abusing those whom they once cared for.

Consequently, as we find our way to grieve without being annihilated by our grieving, we learn that we must always carry two things that, in fact, are the same thing viewed from different perspectives or at different points of time. In the one hand, we hold our wonder and gratitude and we say "wow!" and "thank you!" In the other hand, we hold our pain and loss and weep with a sorrow that is deeper than words. At all times, we learn to carry both together. In this way, we find a way to move beyond the false hope of a facile optimism, and the despair of a nihilistic pessimism, into the complexity of a love that remains, through both living and dying, enamored with the other who is known and experienced as beloved.

3. Being

While welcoming and honoring are activities that require considerable self-reflection, they are essentially other-focused. It is appropriate and important to begin with this focus upon others so that, when we think about ourselves, we do not think of ourselves in isolation but, instead, understand that our selves are constantly constituted, negotiated, formed, and transformed in and through the relationships that we have with others. By observing this, I am not trying to glorify some kind of self-deprecation and suggest that I, in and of myself, or you, in and of yourself, don't really matter. That's nonsense—and it is always abusers who want you to feel this way about yourself. Of course I, in and of myself, matter. And the same applies to you, dear reader, and everyone else, too. However what I am emphasizing is that, in all of our mattering as who we are, we are always *composite* beings. I do not and cannot exist by myself; none of us can. There are no firm and hard boundaries here. That which I refer to as "myself" and that which I refer to as "others" are constantly moving in and out and through and within and around one another. It turns out that all borders—not just borders between nations but borders between "self" and "others"—only exist on the maps where we draw them. They are what I refer to as *significant fictions*. They only exist because we say they do but, because we say they exist, these fictional entities or frames end up having a very real and material effect upon our lives, how we understand them, what does and does not appear to be realistic or possible within those lives.[1] Asserting this does not mean claiming that the self is an illusion or that there is no such thing as whatever it is we experience ourselves to be (call that the "I" or the "ego" or whatever you like). It just means that who we are is something more than what we have been taught to think. We are, each

---

1. As Michael Mann observes, when commenting on the discipline he expertly works within,"[m]ost sociologists subscribe to the maxim: 'If people define things as real, they are real *in their consequences*'" (*Fascists*, 22; emphasis added).

3. BEING

one of us, a multitude intersecting, overlapping, and blurring together with other multitudes, worlds without end.

Beginning with others and the ways in which all of us are connected and co-constituted together with others is an important corrective to the rampant marketing of individualism within our context. It is widely observed that individualism is great for expanding markets and profiteering into ever-new domains of life. But individualism is also essential to maintaining those who are oppressed within a fractured and isolated state. Solidarity becomes difficult in a world where we are taught to value ourselves only and precisely in the areas where we are different from everyone else. All too quickly, the pursuit of *personal distinction* comes to replace the fight for *collective liberation*.

It is the oldest strategy of empires who expand through militarism, theft, slavery, and colonization—*divide et impera*. Divide and rule. This is a particularly useful technique used to maintain divisions between various conquered nations and to prevent those nations from uniting in order to overthrow their imperial rulers. Thus, for example, the Romans utilized othering tactics in order, for example, to maintain divisions between Greeks, Celts, and Judeans. If the Greeks and Judeans both looked down on the Celts as uncivilized barbarians, and the Greeks and the Celts looked down on the Judeans as atheists, and the Judeans and the Celts looked down on the Greeks as perverse aesthetes, then the Romans (who actually exacerbated and encouraged all of these conflicts) could maintain their rule over all three groups and, in fact, play the public role of peacemaker and mediator between those groups. In this way, they justified their right to rule. The Romans argued that they were the ones predestined to rule the world because of their righteousness and their commitment to law and order (even though it was Roman conquest and colonization that produced and encouraged a great deal of these conflicts). All empires, both before and after, have followed this model (and, in fact, have lasted for longer or shorter times based, in part, on their ability to do this successfully).

The worldwide empire of transnational capitalism in its contemporary neoliberal iteration is no exception. In fact, capitalism has conquered and devastated more of the globe than any other empire, in part because it pushes this strategy of divide and conquer to its absolute limit. While previous empires were more exclusively and explicitly reliant on brute force (from which there was still at least some kind of outside, hidden pockets of resistance, or places to where one could flee), the life-shaping rule of capitalism is increasingly all-encompassing, all-seeing, and not only the primary thing shaping our external environment but also the primary thing shaping us as individual subjects (subjects, then, in the double sense of that word:

both as "a person" and as "one who is subjected"). Neoliberalism does not only circulate on the "macrolevel" (at the level of global arteries) through international trade agreements, the traffic of goods, speculation on property or food markets, the digitalization of money transfers, and mass migrations of people; it also circulates on the microlevel (at the level of individual capillaries) through how we brand ourselves, the dreams we aspire to fulfill, and the desires we have. At every level, neoliberalism encourages division, encourages distinctiveness, encourages fostering one's unique brand status and advancing one's brand equity or human capital over and against anyone and everyone else. Thus, in our supposedly enlightened society, where we try to convince ourselves that we have advanced beyond the ethnocentric, religious, or superstitious violence and genocide of "more primitive civilizations," we not only continue to experience (denied, or glossed over) ethnic, racial, or classist divisions between large groups like Whites who oppress Blacks, or dispossessors who plunder the dispossessed, or settlers who claim Indigenous lands as their own, we also experience divisions *within* races, *within* classes, *within* peer groups, *within* families, and even *within our own selves*. Division is everywhere. And so we are ruled.

Note that, by making this observation, I am not mourning the supposed loss of the hetero- or more recently homo-normative nuclear family, or other more or less stabilized aggregates which have been used in the past to maintain and further perpetuate the trajectory of the status quo.[2] Rather, I am calling for a recovery of the sense and practices of connectedness that encourage us to form solidarity networks that transcend our divisions and counteract the ways of connecting (or not connecting) that are currently normative (hence, for example, the rhizomatic associations so loved by Deleuze and Guattari, over against the arborescent configurations favoured by the state).[3]

With this in mind, then, and from this place of co-constituted and co-constituting connectedness, I want to examine four characteristic ways of being that I think are essential for our efforts to be good company to and with others. These are: being honest, being gentle, being affectionate (tender-hearted), and being comforting. I will examine each in more detail in the sections that follow. Each of these ways of being should be considered both as a way of being that should be definitive of the multitude that each of

---

2. Empires, it should be remembered, have always loved "Family Values" and the way these values replicate oppressive and violent hierarchies of power in domains like the household unit where it has historically been much more difficult for the eyes and the arms of the state to reach. For an examination of how that plays out in our contemporary context, see Cooper, *Family Values*.

3. See Deleuze and Guattari, *Capitalism and Schizophrenia*.

us are individually, and as a way of being that should be definitive of all of us when we are gathered together and understood collectively.

A. Honest

When oppression, colonization, the hoarding of goods through dispossession, the enforcement of housing deprivation, and the love of money more than the love of others, is definitive of the context in which people live, then truth itself becomes something that is weaponized and used against the oppressed, colonized, dispossessed, and left-for-dead. This is a necessary component of oppression if it is to be sustained over time. Oppression's material and objective reality must be masked and denied, the privilege of oppressors must be justified, the policing of deviance must appear reasonable, the imaginations of oppressed people must be limited, the victims must be blamed, and the victimizers must not only be exonerated but held up as virtuous and ideal models to emulate. Consequently, mixing together the insights of Ludwig Wittgenstein and Michel Foucault, we can say the following: in the context of oppression, truths are statements that are produced following the rules established by the language game in which the statement is made (that's Wittgenstein); but, equally important, the rules of language games are not made in vacuums but, instead, are made in order to favour the interests and goals of some people and invalidate the interests and goals of some other people (that's Foucault).[1] This, then, helps us to understand that there is no easy, one-to-one correlation between "truth"

---

1. On this point, Foucault's comments on the role played by the psychiatrist as an "expert witness" in criminal cases is especially significant. Reviewing reports prepared for the French courts by prominent psychiatrists, he observes the following: "So, these are discourses that ultimately have the power of life and death . . . From what does this power of life and death derive? From the judicial system perhaps, but these discourses also have this power by virtue of the fact that they function as discourses of truth within the judicial system . . . Discourses that can kill, discourses of truth, and the third property, discourses—you yourselves are the proof and witness of this [as Foucault had just read examples from times when expert witnesses deployed arguments that strike the modern listener as absurd]—that make one laugh. And discourses of truth that provoke laughter and have the institutional power to kill are, after all, in a society like ours, discourse that deserve some attention" (*Abnormal*, 6).

and "reality." Looking at mathematics, itself a particular kind of language game, helps to illustrate this. We say that "one plus one equals two" is *true* but we do not say that "one plus one equals two" is *real*. In fact, in reality, this is often not the case—while adding one apple to one other apple gives us two apples, adding one drop of water to one other drop of water gives us . . . one drop of water; and things can quickly get even stranger. If I add one fungus to one alga, I can end up with one lichen (thus, in reality, sometimes "1x + 1x = 2x" and sometimes "1y + 1y = 1y" and sometimes "1a + 1b = 1c!"). Furthermore, precisely because mathematics deals with the production of true statements (and not real statements), it is able to utilize all kinds of things that have no presence "in reality" (for example, negative numbers, imaginary units, and most of what is called "pure math"). This is not to say that mathematics is not useful in our day-to-day lives. It is obviously very useful for all kinds of things. It's just that the "truth" of math can, in no way, be correlated with the "reality" of our world. And the same observation applies to all language games (from philosophy, to sociology, to the data and statistics gathered by social services). As expressed in different language, then, *even truth itself is a significant fiction*—something we create but something which then dramatically influences and shapes our life together.

In the context of oppression, truth is used to justify, enforce, and further develop the trajectory of oppression. Part of this process is setting up language games so that those who are oppressed are forced to confess to certain truths. Once these truths are established, the sufferings experienced by the oppressed are reframed as the results of their own self-harming actions or as a justifiable punishment for their criminality, immorality, deviance, or non-compliance. In this way, oppression is disappeared into the environment; it becomes as natural-feeling and invisible as the air no one sees but everyone breathes.

Let's look at how this plays out in one particular environment—so-called homeless shelters. There are any number of rule violations that can occur in a homeless shelter and, once one has confessed to violating a rule, there is a punishment that is automatically attached to that violation. What matters, when meting out punishment, is the acknowledgment that the rule was broken, and what does not matter is anything related to the context or series of events that resulted in that breakage. Decisions are made in this way under the pretense of "justice" or "fairness." In fact, this ensures that people who reside in shelters are regularly punished in an unfair and unjust manner. This is so, in part, because a large number of rules that exist in shelters are oppressive, violent, and harmful to those who go to shelters seeking support. For example, a person who suffers from chronic pain but who no longer has a family doctor, may purchase medication from a street-level pharmacist and then inject that medication (in a McDonald's bathroom, in an alley, by the river or the railroad tracks), but, not wanting to litter or risk anyone else being poked by the used needle, that person may put the needle back into their backpack so that they can properly dispose of it in a sharps container at a shelter. However, once back at the shelter they may not have the immediate opportunity to dispose of the used needle and it may be found in their backpack when staff members request a bag check (having noted that the person "appears to be under the influence of [name of substance]"—although this just means that their medication is doing what it needs to do in order to support them with managing their pain). Once this discovery is made, the person will be asked to confirm that this is their bag. Once this truth is established, punishment becomes compulsory, and none of the contextual factors mentioned above will be considered. In fact, if the person claims to have brought the needle back to dispose of it properly and safely, this will almost certainly be interpreted as a sign that the person is a liar who is not yet ready to be responsible and accept the consequences of their bad decisions. Tough love, then, is posited as a solution. And, in fact, this "love" is exceptionally tough for those who are found to be in possession of needles for, while people in local shelters can end up being kicked onto the street with nowhere else to go for a week if they are found to be in possession of "drug paraphernalia," they can be (and frequently are) denied any safe, indoor space to sleep for *thirty days* if they have needles because shelters commonly classify these, not as "drug paraphernalia," but as *weapons*.[2] This ban is actually twice as long as the bans people usually receive for engaging in physical acts of violence like, for example, punching-out another resident. If the person then objects to this treatment or becomes upset by it, they are frequently red-flagged as violent and the cops will likely be called to forcibly remove them. Of course, it almost (but not quite) goes without saying that none of this is actually loving and the (usually Christian-faith-based) shelters who continue to wage a war on people who take medicine in ways that have been criminalized are active and abusive participants in oppression. What *is* loving, however, are the actions taken by shelter residents who choose to keep a stockpile of needles for others residing in the shelter so that their peers can have access to sterile medical equipment, without being at risk of being forced out onto the street. The laughably sad irony is that when these caring individuals are found out by shelter workers and subsequently kicked out, the shelter workers tend to

---

2. Prison administrators take the same view of needles and have used this to try and counteract efforts to bring harm reduction into prisons even though the very few prisons that have implemented harm-reduction practices have never seen needles used as weapons.

view them as particularly egregious rule-breakers and deeply-entrenched "addicts" ("they've got big problems, man; they had *so* many needles in their locker!") when, in fact, they are actually just particularly loving and caring individuals.

Given that this is the case, two things are required of us if we seek to be good company to and with others. First, we have a *moral obligation to lie* when a statement of facts is placed in the service of Death. Second, we have a moral obligation to be not truthful but *as honest as we know how to be* with those who are given over to Death. Both of these points need to be unpacked.

When I was a child, I was taught that lying was wrong, sinful, shameful, and a distinguishing marker of a person with poor character. I was taught that lying could be both active or passive. On the one hand, I could explicitly deny or contradict the truth by fabricating something false; on the other hand, I could just hide the truth or try to prevent it from coming out. I was taught that both of these ways of "lying" were equally wrong. However, I was taught these lessons about lying in the context of a household ruled by an abusive father and where punishment for any kind of rule infraction (regardless of how cruel or arbitrary the rule itself was) almost always resulted in physical, emotional, psychological, and moral abuse. Thus, speaking "the truth" was something that frequently resulted in abuse and that justified the abuse to make it appear as a just form of punishment motivated by love for the one being punished. As a result, lying (whether "actively" or "passively") frequently became the only way of trying to escape that abuse. However, because truth had been weaponized against me, and because I had no way of assessing the broader contextual dynamics in which this violent truth-producing process occurred, I also believed that lying was wrong and, insidiously, the more I lied to escape being abused, the more I believed I was an immoral and bad person who *deserved* to be abused. As with so many others who are oppressed, abandoned, and abused, I was trapped within a regime of truth that offered me no succor, no comfort, and no escape. If I told the truth, I was violently abused; if I lied, I reinforced the narrative (a narrative I was incapable of questioning at that time) that I deserved to be abused.

Deliverance begins to come, in part, when we deny the moral authority claimed by these death-dealing regimes of truth. Once we deny this moral authority—once we recognize that any kind of regime of truth that produces and justifies death-dealing violence against children, those who are impoverished, and any others who are oppressed, is profoundly immoral—we will start doing whatever is necessary to counter, prevent, and overthrow that violence because our commitment to Life, liberation, and mutual care runs deeper and is far more profoundly moral than any valorization of "truth for truth's sake." In this context, lying in a certain way is evidence, not of our moral depravity and our need to be further disciplined, but of exactly the opposite. Just ask the Germans who sheltered Jews during World War II. Or the Nicaraguan campesinos who hid Sandinista freedom-fighters from the American-backed death squads. Or the slaves who helped one another flee plantations in the Antebellum South. Or the shelter residents who kept six, denied seeing anything, and never ratted out their peers, when their peers needed to have a safe place to inject their medication

Thus, for those of us who share a commitment to being good company, but who work in oppressive institutions, learning the art of lying to our bosses (and some of our peers) is one of the critical ways in which we can create safer space within an otherwise unsafe system. Much like many French factory workers found all kinds of ways to monkeywrench or sabotage the production quotas of the Nazi factory owners, so also deceiving and lying to our bosses about what we know or do not know, what we witness or do not witness, and what do or do not do, can make a real life-giving difference for those whom we claim to serve (and, in fact, it is worth continually recalling that the people who come to us seeking good company, and most emphatically *not the bosses*, are the people whom we actually serve).

One example of how this plays out is the unsanctioned safer injection site that Mechele and I ran out of the bathrooms in the program we facilitated (already mentioned above in the "Working Together With" chapter). But this can play out in all kinds of other small or big ways. Sometimes, it's a little lie—like when a boss asks you to go tell someone they are being kicked out and you say, "okay," but then you go and give the person a warning about not being a heatscore and come back to the boss and say, "well, I talked to the person and instead of kicking them out we had a really good chat and I gave them a warning and I don't think it will be a problem again" (and the boss may or may not be annoyed by this but it is hard for them to change the end result and, if you do this well, it's even harder for them to know that you never intended to kick the person out at all, even though you said you would do so). Sometimes it's a bigger act of deception—like when I used to secretly host or pay for hotel rooms for youth who were deprived of housing, who were kicked out of the youth shelter where I worked in Vancouver and who had literally nowhere safe to go. Sometimes it's a more systematic act of lying—like doing one kind of work to be good company, but manipulating statistics in order to ensure that the government thinks you are doing the disciplinary, status-quo-affirming work they want you to do in order to keep funding you (although, to be fair, in a market where all parties are forced to compete for less and less financial support, *everyone* lies with their stats—program stats are an excellent example of how math produces statements that are true but not necessarily real. There are many creative and imaginative ways to do this well.

So we reject any abusive moral regime of truth that institutional and other authorities force upon those who are oppressed. We demonstrate this rejection, in part, by being willing to lie in the service of Life, but we also demonstrate this rejection by being *as honest as we know how to be* in our conversations with and among the oppressed. Thus, over against truth, which is produced by language games that are played according to the rules established by those who have the power to enforce them (even while they simultaneously try to deny this operation by naturalizing truth and trying to equate their truth with the real—i.e., they want to make truth an *ontological* category), I posit honesty as an *existential* category. Honesty is the way we feel when we consistently adhere to our values, regardless of the situation in which we find ourselves. Thus, I can affirm, along with Federico Fellini that "I'm a liar, but an honest one."[3] I honestly serve Life and seek to contribute to that which is life-affirming and life-giving at every possible turn. And, when it comes to our relationships with those who are oppressed, honesty becomes especially evident through the practices of transparency, authenticity, and deconstruction—three things that counter the Death-dealing practices of contemporary regimes of truth.

By transparency, I mean being absolutely upfront and open—not just initially but continually—about our values, our boundaries, who we are and are not, what we do and do not do, our allegiances, who we partner with, who we avoid, and who we oppose, and why we are this way and act this way. This requires vulnerability and it requires vulnerability from people who may be accustomed to being in positions where they can get away with or justify not being vulnerable (in fact, they may have been drawn to those positions in the first place because of the feeling of invulnerability they get there). Calling for this kind of behavior may appear rather unremarkable for those who have never been stuck trying to negotiate "the system," advocate for change within it, or hold its agents accountable for their actions. However, as anyone experienced in those areas can tell you, access to the information required to create change is rigidly stratified and controlled. What information agencies choose to release to the public or to concerned individuals tends to be vague, full of jargon or buzz words, replete with calls for people to keep trusting in the good intentions of the service providers and highlighting the need for patience while further research (and then further research, and then further research) is accomplished. The implicit

---

3. See Fellini, *Fellini on Fellini*, 53–54.

suggestion is that any who are overly upset or urging rapid reforms or resolutions are behaving in an unreasonable and irresponsible manner that has the potential to case great harm (listening to the head of the local police union arguing for *increases* to police funding and the *further integration* of policing into communities, as others call for defunding the police, is a solid example of what I am talking about here). Any formal or informal complaints submitted by individuals or concerned parties are treated in a similar manner. Institutions, across the board, have standard ways of responding to such occurrences: strictly control who has access to what information, placate and delay those who bring forward concerns or calls for change, and then repeat this process until people give up, go away, or (as I have seen happen on several occasions) breakdown in ways from which they never fully recover. Simply put, every single institution—from police forces to hospitals to school boards to homeless shelters to community health agencies—do their absolute damnedest to prevent any external group (including the public or the parties whom they claim to serve) from having access to the information required to hold them accountable. Because this is one of the key areas in which transparency makes us vulnerable—*it makes us open enough that others can legitimately hold us accountable to the claims we make about ourselves.* Everyone in so-called caring professions postures as though they are open to being held accountable in this way—"we are here to listen, we are here to learn, we want your feedback," they say, and "we are client-centered and recognize the expertise of those with lived experience," they add—but when it comes to feedback, complaints, grievances, challenges, or suggestions that fundamentally disrupt their perception of themselves, that jeopardize their brand status and their ability to compete for funding, that may provoke a scandal, or that interfere with the comprehensive priorities, goals, strategic action plans, and quality improvement plans that they have *already* formulated, one quickly realizes that, regardless of how sweetly they listen to you, they will not change and they will always have very good reasons not to change ("Our budget is already established for this year, but we might be able to do this next year" [spoiler: they don't do it next year]), just as they also have good reasons not to discipline abusive workers ("We spoke with other staff members who were present and, once we received a fuller picture of what happened, we are confident that we have handled the situation appropriately, although maintaining confidentiality means we can't tell you what we did or did not do in relation to that staff member who continues to be employed here"), to not lower their barriers to service ("We would love to lower our barriers to service, but we need to make sure everyone feels safe here"), and to not be liable for anything ("We had security measures in place that, if you had utilized them, even though nobody is ever trained to utilize those security measures in this way, this event would not have occurred—so, regardless of what you make of your own responsibility for your own self, we know that this was not *our* fault").

Consequently, change, when it comes, is usually forced upon these services against their will. Thus, for example, I once helped to organize a group of shelter residents who wanted to collectively advocate for better conditions in the shelter where they were staying. One of their top priorities was addressing the extraordinarily dehumanizing state of the shelter bathrooms. These bathrooms were horrendous. In fact, they were some of the grossest bathrooms I have seen anywhere (and I have seen some pretty gross bathrooms—if you remember "the worst toilet in Scotland" from Danny Boyle's *Trainspotting* [1996], you will have an idea for what they looked like). Toilets were frequently clogged and overflowing with shit and no one came to plunge or fix them. There were large streaks and splashes of blood across the walls of the showers (where it looked like more than one person had hit an artery while trying to take their medicine). The blood was left on the wall for days. Mirrors were cracked and stall doors were kicked off their hinges and were now either non-existent or could no longer be latched shut. To add injury to insult, some staff members took advantage of this to go and spy on residents while they used the bathroom stalls to try and catch them injecting their medication so they could then kick them out (some staff members even competed to see who could kick out the most people in a set amount of time). For the people staying at the shelter, the state of the bathrooms sent a very strong message to them that they did not matter, that they did not deserve to have a clean, safe, or private place to go to the bathroom, and that they were only a little higher than the shit that flowed on the floor around them. Consequently, a group of shelter residents gathered a list of signatures requesting that the bathrooms be improved, explaining their reasons for asking for this improvement, and also explaining that they expected the need for further repairs to decline as people would be more respectful of the space if they felt that the space (and those who ran it) was more respectful of them (a truism frequently overlooked by disciplinary institutions). The shelter management acknowledged receipt of the letter but noted that bathroom repairs did not fit with their budget for that fiscal year (which had just begun). They also noted that, given their need to pick between different priorities and respond to various crises as they emerged, bathroom repairs would likely not be on the list of things done the next fiscal year. The shelter residents took stock of this response, acknowledged that the shelter had set some priorities but noted that these priorities were set without consulting any shelter residents, and so they requested that shelter management reconsider their priorities. Shelter management stated that they would not do this. The shelter residents then went and took pictures of the bathrooms—of the overflowing shit, of stalls with no doors, and of the large streaks of blood that had sprayed and coagulated on the walls. They mentioned these pictures to the shelter management and also mentioned that they were willing to go public with their campaign if the shelter management still chose to not address their concern. They stated that they felt the priorities of the public, or others to whom the shelter management were, in fact, accountable, might be more in line with the priorities of the shelter residents. Suddenly everything changed. By an unexpected "stroke of good luck," the shelter management found the money to not only repair but to fully renovate their bathrooms, and work began very quickly after that. This, then, is the kind of "advocacy" work that is required in systems that claim to be transparent, fair, accountable, and reasonable but which are none of those things.

The transparency we embody must be different than this. It means not only saying, "this is who we really are" but also being *so open that power dynamics are altered* to such a degree that the people who come to a community space seeking good company actually have *real power* to ensure that those who hold that space are, in fact, behaving appropriately.

This form of transparency is also related to authenticity. Authenticity, however, is a difficult thing to talk about because of the connections it has accumulated and the affects that have sedimented around it, not only at the popular level but in various disciplines. Essentially, to proclaim something as "authentic" means to assert that it is what it appears to be. With something like a work of art, this can often (but not always) be established with some confidence ("yes, this work that looks like it was done by Van Gogh is, in fact, an authentic Van Gogh"), but all of this very rapidly becomes complicated (and heated!) when we move from discussing things like art to discussing things like people. Not only have philosophers and social theorists highlighted significant problems between any kind of one-to-one relationship between "appearance" and "reality," they have also challenged the idea that there is any kind of "real" or "authentic" self at the root of who we appear to be. When we take these ideas and add further insights from psychoanalysis—the recognition that we, ourselves, are often completely deluded about who we ourselves really are and, in fact, frequently do not know why we do what we do, feel what we feel, and desire what we desire—it isn't difficult for cynicism or surrender to set in. Each new flight from "fakeness" (or, to use Heidegger's language, from "the inauthenticity of the They-self") ends up simply opening up another market for branding.[4]

---

4. See Heidegger, *Being and Time*, 247–77.

For the anti-capitalist Left, this presents serious problems about the possibility of creating real alternatives to our contemporary situation. For the Right this produces sneering and gloating remarks like, "you pretend that you're doing something different or better, but really you're just like us" (an enduring theme in the work of Andrew Potter) but the transformation of hippies or other trending-Leftists into yuppies or entrepreneurs does nothing to disprove this claim.[5] Serious concerns are raised about the relationship between a focus upon "being your authentic self" and the rise of a narcissistic consumer culture. Even worse, we have seen how people acting authentically, *appeal to their own sincerity in order to do a great deal of harm to others*—like, for example, White women who *genuinely fear for their lives* because they are in a park or on a roadway with a Black man or boy, and who then attempt to get that Black man or boy lynched or murdered by the police.

Therefore, if we want to retain authenticity as a goal or a value, a few things are required. First, just as with honestly, we must understand authenticity to be an *existential experience* rather than as something ontological. Authenticity is feeling or affect, not a thing-that-is. Second, because authenticity is a *specific way of interpreting how we experience ourselves or others*, it can also be a misinterpretation. Emmett Till was no more a threat to Carolyn Bryant than Christian Cooper was a threat to Amy Cooper (no relation of his), although both women claimed that they authentically feared for their lives. Regardless of the truth of those claims (it seems quite likely one or both were lying), there's a good chance that many of the cops who killed unarmed black men who were running away from them also genuinely feared for their lives (in fact, given the number of instances in which they report fearing for their lives, it seems highly probable that cops are the profession with by far the highest percentage of cowards).[6] Third, because our feelings can sometimes be mistaken (although still authentic), it is important for us to check our feelings and this is part of what is contained in calls for Whites and other members of oppressive groups to "check their privilege." We need to assess the accuracy and reliability of things we authentically feel. In order to accomplish this, transparency is of critical importance. It is by being transparent with ourselves and others about what we are feeling—including and most especially feelings that we find troubling, keep secret, or don't know how to cope with, evaluate, or interpret—that allows us to determine why we feel that way, what we should subsequently do with those

---

5. See Potter, *Authenticity Hoax*; Potter and Heath, *Rebel Sell*.

6. On that note, I would like to suggest that giving guns to people who claim to be genuinely scared of everything and everyone is a really bad idea.

feelings, and if we should seek to foster other feelings instead. This work is important not because things are all about me and my feelings, but because, as the example of Emmett Till so vividly illustrates, people are regularly betrayed, brutalized, and murdered because someone claimed to *genuinely* feel some kind of way. Vulnerability is, yet again, required here. Being authentic means that we stop hiding ourselves—or at least who we believe ourselves to truly be—from others. This requires some self-acceptance but it is not a form of self-acceptance that is premised upon viewing ourselves as entirely good, justified, or correct. Rather, it is a form of critical self-acceptance that recognizes we are in the process of both becoming more truly ourselves *and* different than we are now. Thus, I must accept myself enough to be able to be authentically myself with others, but by being authentically myself with others I am opening myself up to change. Carl Rogers expresses this well: "the curious paradox is that when I accept myself as I am, then I change . . . we cannot change, we cannot move away from what we are, until we thoroughly *accept* what we are. Then change seems to come about almost unnoticed."[7] Thus, for example, the racist who cannot accept herself as racist is unable to change and become anti-racist, because she cannot or will not admit to any racism in the first place (which helps explain why Martin Luther King Jr. came to view White liberals as a greater "stumbling block in the stride towards freedom"[8] than White Conservatives). Change only becomes a possibility if she first recognizes herself as racist (and if she also believes that being racist is not a desirable thing to be).

This kind of authenticity, where we are open about who we are, where we take responsibility for who we are, and where we permit ourselves to be held accountable for who we are so that we can change, is especially important for those who wish to be good company to and with people who are oppressed. This is the case because oppression is so thorough-going that many of the ways in which we look down on, condemn, and hurt rather than help people who experience oppression are not visible to those who come from oppressor groups, regardless of how well-intentioned or woke they believe themselves to be.

Furthermore, practicing this form of authenticity is doubly important because, all too often, services expect or demand this heightened level of vulnerability and sharing from those who come to them seeking assistance. In fact, if people who come seeking help do not demonstrate this, they are often barred from receiving service or punished for their lack of transparency (labeled as "pre-contemplative" or "obstinate" or as "still needing to hit

---

7. Rogers, "This Is Me," 17.
8. King, "Letter from Brimingham Jail."

rock bottom," by the social workers and caring professionals who turn them away). Beware of demanding from others what we ourselves refuse to do! And especially beware of those who believe they have the right, authority, justification, and power to engage in this kind of unequal relationship with others. If we desire others to be authentic with us, then we must be authentic with them. When we do this, we frequently realize that parties on all sides need to make changes. And, in fact, as we make difficult changes (recognizing ways in which we have been racist or oppressive and then changing to be anti-racist and anti-oppressive), so also others begin to see that they, too, can make difficult changes. In this way, the oppressors are liberated from being oppressors and the oppressed are liberated from being oppressed.

The third critical feature of honesty is taking advantage of where one is located (if one is located within one of the so-called caring professions), in order to assist community members to engage in the ongoing act of deconstruction necessary to charting a more liberated, life-giving, and life-affirming way forward. Deconstruction provides community members with the contextual information they need to understand why services exist in the way that they do and why they talk one way but act another way. This is important work because it helps people to understand that their "failure to thrive" within those services is not so much rooted in their own (moral or other) shortcomings as it is rooted in the disciplinary and oppressive nature of the institutions themselves. Armed with this knowledge, community members become better equipped to engage with those institutions in ways that end up meeting their needs. Instead of accepting the abuse they had falsely believed that they deserved, people begin to find ways to fight back in order to wrest life from the hands of those who would hoard its abundance and leave them to die. This takes many forms and education can be ongoing. Along the way, for example, I have taught people what their rights are with police officers (although I always warn people that anyone who exhibits an awareness of their rights when interacting with cops immediately becomes more likely to be targeted by police violence), I have taught people how to "be shrewd as serpents" when meeting with prospective landlords in order to get a place (it's harder for a landlord to kick you out once you are in than it is for the landlord to stop you from coming in to begin with), I have postured as a former employer so that I can provide people with references so that they can get some income stability (in one of my better moments, I even created a fake company with a fake logo and letterhead in order to provide a very formal-looking reference letter), and I have even pretended to be people on the phone (because given how rude and uncaring government officials frequently are on the phone, the anger, developmental disability, or mental state of the person requiring assistance prevented them from being able to navigate the calls themselves). I firmly believe that all of these actions were morally required of me given the reality of oppression in which this work was taking place. Assisting others with deconstructing these dynamics also helps them to see that their own efforts to game or manipulate the system are not wrong but are, in fact, *just*.

In this way, deconstruction not only leads to resistance and liberation; it also contributes to what Paulo Freire refers to as "conscientization."[9] Conscientization, according to Freire, is a reflective and active process through which one becomes aware of the broader socioeconomic and political dynamics that create the circumstances in which one lives. "De-ideologization," as Ignacio Martín-Baró refers to it, is an important part of this—people are taught the reality of their experiences, they are taught that the feeling they have of being wronged is accurate, they are taught that they are not crazy or immoral or lazy for feeling this way.[10] Those who claimed to want to help did not help. All too often, self-proclaimed helpers actually hindered them and prevented them from gaining freedom from oppression. But conscientization is also more than de-ideologization. Through conscientization, one discovers oneself as a person with political agency and power and the ability to engage within broader socio-economic and political dynamics in a way that makes a difference. Thus, for example, through conscientization, those who have been impoverished go from viewing themselves as failures, as sick, or as lazy, to viewing themselves as oppressed and they then begin to organize themselves to work towards liberation. Honestly deconstructing our own workplaces, and the broader socioeconomic and political dynamics in which we live and work, is a critical contribution to this.

---

9. See Freire, *Pedagogy of the Oppressed*, 87–124.
10. See Martín-Baró, *Writings for a Liberation Psychology*, 31.

B. Gentle

Sometimes, when the young people I worked with in Vancouver did not return to where they were expected to spend the night, I would go out to the alleyways, strolls, dive bars, speakeasies, after-hours clubs, and single-room occupancy hotels to see if I could find them. Many nights I did not find anyone, although I got to know others in the community this way. Some nights, I did find the person or people I was looking for. It meant a lot to them to know that someone was thinking about them, that someone cared about them, that someone was willing to go out into the night (and god knows where else) in order to try and find them. For some young people, simply having someone find them in an alleyway, sit with them awhile, and then walk back to the housing program with them, became a transformative life event. Many nights, if things were quiet, I did this when I was working. My coworkers would cover for me. The youth would never rat me out. If my bosses knew what I was doing, they would have fired me.[1]

One night when I was out looking for youth who had not returned as expected to the residential youth program in Vancouver, I was in a high traffic alleyway behind the Carnegie Centre—a hub for street-level pharmacists, people who are seeking medication, and debt collectors seeking debtors. I was talking with a group of three or four entrepreneurs whom I had gotten to know. Everyone was alert (everyone is always alert in such places, at such times, even if they appear not to be), but the vibe was mostly relaxed. The mood shifted when another young man arrived. He was very

---

1. I, too, had my life transformed in this way. When my parents forcibly deprived me of housing, with the knowledge and complicity of other adults and the leaders of their church, I found myself frequently experiencing so much internal turmoil, self-loathing, and a sense of dis-ease, that even when friends invited me to stay at their places, I often quietly slipped away—especially if other friends were around and hanging out as a group—and walked the streets all night. There was one friend who always noticed this and he would find me and, rather than trying to talk me into going back or anything else, he would quietly walk with me. My friend doing this was basically the one and only thing that others said or did at this time that genuinely made me feel loved.

angry. Someone had disrespected him and he was intent on getting revenge. He made threats. He was not the kind of man to make threats and not follow through on them. Everyone's guard went up. I saw the little shifts in body language and affect that occur when people go from alert but chilling to being ready for anything while appearing relaxed (a hand lingering at the edge of a pocket, a slight shift to a more staggered stance, a fist clenched around a lighter, someone yawning, someone scratching their lowered chin). Observing these changes, I said the following: "David [not his real name], I know you're really upset. Would you like a hug?" David looked me in the face, everyone froze, and for a second it was as if time stood still. Then he said, "yes," and he hugged me and I hugged him, and I could feel everyone start breathing again and there, in an alleyway at the heart of the heart of the downtown eastside, two young men hugged, while a group of good fellows looked on and nobody laughed, and nobody cracked a joke, and everyone knew that something very serious and also very good was taking place. And then we went back to bantering and smoking and, after flicking my butt away, I went back to work.

I tell this story not in order to boast (or suggest that everyone should go around offering hugs to entrepreneurs in alleyways late at night!) but to share lessons I have learned along the way, and one of the most important lessons I have learned is this: people, all people, everyone, but especially those who are suffering and oppressed, must be treated with gentleness.

I have spent a lot of years thinking about why people, caring people or, at the very least, people who desire to be caring, are so frequently cruel, brutal, and unkind to those who come to them seeking support. It is such a common occurrence and yet such a blatant contradiction between the ways in which agencies market themselves and the ways in which most people genuinely desire to be, that I was initially shocked and puzzled by this. Eventually I realized the following: *the greatest obstacle to gentleness is fear*, and most people in so-called caring professions are actually afraid of those whom they claim to serve. Of course, if you spend any amount of time working in an environment where people who are oppressed come seeking help, you will eventually see someone acting aggressively, threateningly, or violently. Fear is a normal reaction to witnessing or experiencing such things. However, because workers generally lack the lenses to understand how oppressive environments and institutions dehumanize and harm those who come to them seeking good company, and because they then fail to understand that people who are dehumanized and harmed in *the very places where they were promised that they would be understood and supported* can often react to this betrayal and hurt with anger (and who wouldn't feel anger after experiencing this?), workers and workplaces end up developing fear-based cultures that say they do what they do in order to keep everyone safe but which, in fact, normalize cruelty.[2] This, in turn, creates its own feedback loop—the more we treat people with cruelty, the more people will respond with (righteous) anger rooted in a very real sense of betrayal.

It is gentleness that disrupts this feedback loop and creates its own alternative, equally self-reinforcing cycle. But, given the ways in which we have been brought up within cultures of fear, if we want to learn how to be gentle, we must be courageous. It takes courage to respond to anger with gentleness, to listen to a person who is threatening in order to hear their broken-heartedness, and to then respond with comfort and care rather than with defensiveness. But this courage is not foolhardy. It is neither blind nor stupid. Rather, it is rooted in the belief—the proof of which I have seen over and over and over again—that people are not monsters, that gentleness is a balm to many wounds, and that we are all much safer if we treat one another with the strategic vulnerability gentleness requires rather than rushing to expel, punish, or hide from each other.[3]

Over and over again, I have witnessed the truth of St. Francis de Sales's assertion that "nothing is so strong as gentleness, not so gentle as real strength." I hesitate to describe gentleness in this way, because I worry about how those enmeshed within patriarchal cultures (especially cisgendered men) rush away from anything that seems "soft" or "vulnerable" or "tender" and seek to overcode even the simplest acts of lovingkindness with the language of toughness.[4] Sometimes it's really great for soft to just be soft, for vulnerable to just be vulnerable, for tender to just be tender. But, yes, sometimes it does require strength for us to continue to live out our commitment to things like gentleness, especially in situations where that feels really scary or risky. What is important here is *distinguishing between strength and toxic masculinity*. Toxic masculinity is about presenting oneself as invulnerable, it's about appearing to be bigger, faster, stronger, more competent, and more lethal (if it comes to that), then the next guy. Consequently, it is frequently paired with outbursts of violence that target more vulnerable, oppressed, or

2. Recall, again, my friend who was left to die like a dog on the concrete steps outside a shelter because the workers were afraid to let him in.

3. Note that I *not* offering this as advice to those who are experiencing intimate-partner violence or abuse of any kind. Rather, this advice has more to do with how those who hold space—especially those who are paid to hold space—also have the responsibility to work through situations of conflict and threats of violence that arise as a result of the persistent oppression and abuse of those who come to those spaces seeking good company. I will have more to say about this in the section below called "Battered Company."

4. Like Mark Driscoll, the MMA-loving American pastor who emphasized the killer abs of Jesus and declared that "I cannot worship a guy I can beat up."

physically weak people (i.e., people I can harm with little or no risk of them harming me), so that those who may be able to cause harm to me think twice about doing so.

Toxic masculinity, in fact, is one of the ways in which we—especially cisgendered men—are encouraged to live within our culture of fear. It is an approach that, unlike gentleness, accepts the lessons we are taught about being afraid. It views every fear as well-founded—whereas gentleness actively questions them all. Do I really need to fear Muslims? Do I really need to fear people who are impoverished? Do I really need to fear Indigenous people? Do I really need to fear Black children? Do I really need to be afraid of the dark, of spiders, or of open spaces? In this active questioning, gentleness discovers that almost all of our fears are unfounded. Asking questions like these is part of the reason why people who are gentle are almost always more courageous than people who perform toxic masculinity. This is why a good community support worker or a volunteer at a drop-in for sex workers is exponentially more courageous than all the cops who claim to fear for their lives every time someone plays a video game too loudly or sleeps or puts their hands-up or doesn't put their hands up or does what they say or doesn't do what they say (to pick just a few, well-known recent examples when cops killed people). It simply makes no sense whatsoever to have fear determine how you treat those whom you claim to serve. In fact, if we fear those whom we say we care about, this is often evidence that our caring is insincere—it is a story we are telling ourselves about ourselves, not something that others will experience as meaningful. This is well captured in 1 John 4:18: "There is no fear in love; but perfect love casts out all fear." That's a bold statement (after all, who among us can claim to love perfectly?), but I have often reflected on it when I have felt afraid and it has helped me to assess what to do with my fear and what I must do to try and ensure that I am loving others well.

Thus, for example, in the work that I and many other loved ones have done, we have consistently gone into situations that others have been taught to fear, but we have found that acting gently, seeking to understand, and demonstrating real care consistently bring about peaceful and mutually satisfying resolutions. These are the very situations that the cops say they need full body armor, militarized SWAT teams, and lethal force (or the threat thereof) in order to respond to with any semblance of safety. Again: cops are also one of the most fearful groups of people I have ever encountered. Because they give themselves over to their fears rather than question the legitimacy of them, they end up doing a very great deal of harm ("I feared for my life," says the cop who shot and killed the unarmed Black child who is running away from him). As for me and my friends, sure, we've been through

B. GENTLE

some trying situations and sometimes we have been hurt emotionally or psychologically by what we have encountered, witnessed, or participated within, but not one of us has ever sustained any life-threatening physical injury. Our lives have been changed by this work, there is no doubt about that, but our lives have never been taken and, just as importantly, *we have not taken any lives when we felt afraid*. We have gained the strength to do this—both individually and collectively—because—both individually and collectively—we have never stopped being gentle with those whom others have treated violently. In return, those whom others have treated violently and who, therefore, do not necessarily have many reasons to be kind to others, have never stopped being gentle with us (although, of course, if all goes well, this "us-and-them" very quickly becomes a "we"). And this, in turn, makes our community, the "we" that we are all becoming together, not toxically masculine but very strong.

We are gentle people, even in situations that are distressing because our commitment to certain things and people is something that we hold more deeply than any fear-based reaction we might have. This, in fact, is what it means to be courageous—to continue to adhere to your values even when you are in situations where you feel afraid. The scarier the situation, and the more you persist in living out your values (when other avenues *feel* safer or more comfortable or less distressing), the more courageous you are. Thus, for example, courage is demonstrated in an unwavering commitment to do no harm to others and to, in fact, welcome and honor others, even if you perceive (rightly or wrongly—and, in my line of work, it is almost always wrongly) that others might possibly harm you.

What, then, does it mean to be gentle? To be gentle means to be very careful in how we treat others, not because we are afraid of what they might to do us, but because we are concerned about what we might (perhaps inadvertently) do to them. Gentleness means recognizing that people are incredibly valuable (literally priceless—i.e., existing outside the domain of monetization) but they are also incredibly fragile, and so we show the utmost care in our interactions with them. Further, given the realities of our world, being gentle means recognizing that almost everyone—and especially those who are oppressed—are carrying more than they can reasonably be expected to bear. Oppression is a heavy thing. The Rastas describe it well when they refer to it as a downpression. It pushes you down and down and down, and, if it cannot be stopped, it will one day push you down enough times or with enough force that you will never get up again. Because of this downpression, people are tired, people are hurting, people are sad, and people are struggling to not believe life-denying lies about themselves (and not succeeding all that often or all that well). Consequently, it is of the utmost importance that we be gentle. We just don't know, on any given day, in any given life, what a person is going through.

Observing this does not mean we are somehow responsible for another person's actions if we unintentionally do something that they find upsetting, but it does mean that we have *a responsibility to try* to create the kind of world where it is *easier* for people to be kind. *Gentleness is acting in such a way that this kind of world becomes possible.* Force, coercion, violence, or the threat thereof can produce all kinds of people with all kinds of habits but they almost all and always fail to produce people who are kind or the sort of world where kindness is more likely to feel easy and natural. This, then, speaks to the second relationship between gentleness and strength captured in the earlier quotation from St. Francis de Sales. Not only does gentleness require and produce strength in those who practice it; gentleness is far stronger than most other strategies we are encouraged to develop in our efforts to make the world a better place. Gentleness succeeds, in fact *only gentleness can succeed*, in many of the places where state-imposed violence is proposed as the solution but where it actually fails, time after time after time.

Finally, the strength of gentleness is revealed when we consider that the trillions spent on weapons, the exponential increase of "counter-terrorism" measures, the ever more invasive forms of surveillance and data capture that we accept and take for granted, and the ongoing expansion of policing have not made any kind of discernable difference in terms of producing a more live-able world for the vast majority of human and non-human beings or in terms of producing people more dedicated to kindness and the common good. But, as I have witnessed, time after time, gentleness is able to do this far more frequently, far more efficiently, and in far more seemingly hopeless conditions, than anything else.

C. Affectionate (Tender-hearted)

At SafeSpace London, prior to the COVID-19 outbreak, sex-working cis- or trans-women, non-binary folx, and people who are gender-nonconforming would gather together within a small but comfortable, confidential, and secure drop-in space in order to visit and prepare themselves for work (SafeSpace is run by current and former sex workers and their accomplices). Sex workers would access the space in order to connect with one another, in order to get some basic supplies either for home—some food for family members, some clothing or a birthday gift for a child—or for work—harm-reduction equipment, something sexy to wear, or a rocking pair of heels—and in order to visit with friends or chosen family members. Unlike most social services, SafeSpace made people genuinely feel welcomed and honored ("this is the first place I've ever felt truly at home," and "I actually *belong* here" are common sentiments expressed by the exceptionally devoted volunteer base). SafeSpace is also unique because a lot of what people shared in the space was a safe form of affectionate touch. People cuddled on the couch. They held hands. They touched in those brief but tender ways that people enthusiastically consent to when they feel safe—especially when they may have been touched in different, less caring, or even violent ways by others.[1] After COVID hit, all of this

---

1. Note that, by making this statement, I'm not saying that there is a one-to-one correlation between sex work and violence. I firmly believe in the legitimacy of sex work as work and, as in any field, I believe that some workers legitimately enjoy their work more or less than some other workers. However, because of the criminalization of sex work, sex workers are forced into work conditions that make them much more vulnerable to experiencing violence from the hands of misogynistic men like cops or bad dates (i.e., because they are oppressed, they are exposed to violence). Extensive and conclusive research exists in this regard and speaks to the critical importance of distinguishing between sex work and human sex trafficking—something that many governments and services—even Violence Against Women services—often will not do. As a result, they end up further harming both those who do sex work and those who are trafficked for sexual purposes (for more on this, see for example Oudshoorn, "Sex Work Is Real Work").

changed. People were no longer able to enter the space. Instead, they could only wait outside the door to receive some food, clothing, or other supplies before being asked to leave so that others could be served and social distancing could be maintained. Given the number of services that were closing and turning people away—especially during the first two months of the pandemic—SafeSpace also responded to the greater need in the community and began to distribute similar aid to others. SafeSpace began to aid *anyone* in need—from impoverished families to men deprived of housing. As a result, SafeSpace received a fair bit of praise and an increase in (time-limited, emergency) funding, but the pandemic changed the dynamics of the support offered and the safety experienced by sex-working cis- and trans-women, non-binary folx, and people who are gender-nonconforming. To support SafeSpace with meeting some new challenges (notably, an increased presence of men who were acting in an aggressive and explicitly threatening manner), I spent some time volunteering at the space. This was the first time a male volunteer had been present there and, although it helped in some ways, it also made some sex workers very uncomfortable. One of the things this illustrates is that while we all often have to make changes to accommodate less-ideal circumstances in crisis situations, even seemingly small changes have an exponentially more harmful affect on those who are more oppressed and isolated. If everyone gets pushed down just a little more, those who are already on the edge of the cliff, get pushed off. To provide another example, my friend Jodi mentioned that, before the pandemic hit, she had spent several months slowly building a trusting relationship with a sex worker who accessed the space. The week before everything changed, the sex worker reached out and gave Jodi a hug before leaving the space and, as with any hug that is just the right thing at just the right moment, it was a brief but wonderful moment. A week later, after COVID hit and new protocols were put in place, that sex worker returned, saw my friend Jodi and, with tears in her eyes, said, "You were my last hug." They cried together, two meters apart. Thus, while those of us with loved ones may be inconvenienced by social distancing, that's a very different thing from suddenly not experiencing *any* kind of safe, affectionate touch from *anyone* for an extended period of time.

    I have often thought that the loss of loving and tender touch experienced by people who are oppressed is one of the most hope- and humanity-destroying elements of that experience. I have witnessed this longing for safe, affectionate touch in many of the men I have known who were deprived of housing. This is a large part of the reason why hairdressers and barbers who volunteer at drop-in programs or shelters are often the most popular volunteers. People line-up out the door for a haircut not so much because

C. AFFECTIONATE (TENDER-HEARTED)

they need a haircut (many people would try to come back week after week after week) but because here, for maybe the first time in a very long time, is a person who will touch them in a way that feels good, in a way that confirms that they are not eyesores or a blight upon the community but just regular human beings, in a way disconnected from any kind of abuse or exploitation, and in a way that lets them know that they deserve to be pampered and cared for. Here is someone who will touch them in a way in which they want to be touched and who, by doing this, lets them know that they are not, in fact, *untouchable*. There is nothing sexual about this. It's simply that this platonic form of touch—like the hugs and cuddles at SafeSpace—communicates something that is almost universally lacking (but which is just as universally needed) in the ways in which oppressed people are treated almost everywhere. It communicates *affection*. And it does so in a way that is instantly effective. Anyone who has known a child who cried because they fell and physically hurt themselves, who then hugged that child and saw the tears turn into smiles, knows about this powerful and nearly instantaneous effectiveness. Affection, when it is experienced, is so strong that it offers reprieve and healing not only from emotional and mental distress—it also has the ability to soothe physical pain! Part of what makes this incredible is that *affection is able to accomplish this regardless of whether or not people feel like they deserve it*. A person whose body is treated as beloved will experience themselves as beloved even if they believe that they are unlovely and unlovable. The way we feel after we enthusiastically consent to being hugged by a safe and loving person is the evidence of this. It turns out that in some ways—and this is one of them—adults are no different than children.

When I first came to this conclusion, I began to work as a "snuggle therapist," offering people platonic, affectionate touch in a therapeutic setting (with rigorous pre-screening, contract signing, and boundaries firmly in place). Because this kind of work is unusual, my business went viral in the local media when it launched. I saw myself on the front page of the local paper and thought, "hmmm, I wonder how the tough guys I've been working with are going to feel about this?" I was expecting them to tease me or, perhaps, make some kind of homo-antagonistic remarks. But they did none of these things. Instead, we had very intimate conversations about their own longings to be held in ways that made them know themselves as beloved. The guy who ran the block ended up being my biggest fan. "Dan!" he would call to me, "Come meet my friends and tell them about your business!" This was often my introduction to some of the people who would never otherwise speak with social workers, and it provided me with an "in" I would not have otherwise had with a lot of people whose lives had been criminalized and who lived by strict codes related to what kind of person one does or does not talk to. One of the results of this was that one of this man's employees—a fellow often deployed when sudden and brutal acts of violence were called for—ended up crying in a chair next to me because he longed to believe that he deserved to be loved and held tenderly, the way I held my "snuggle therapy" clients.[2]

But, of course, affection is not exclusively limited to the domain of touch. There are many other ways to show affection. Affection is related to affect—the emotional tone we establish in our relationships, build into our culture, and structure into our spaces. When our affect is affectionate it means that we are communicating to others—in our words and actions, in how we speak and *the ways in which we do what we do*—that we are attracted to them or that we are fond of them. Again, this attraction is not sexual. It just means that we demonstrate a genuine desire to be in their company. And fondness? Fondness refers to being tender, to getting down to very simple things like helping a person get another cup of coffee if they are tweaking and accidentally smash their mug on the floor instead of responding with anger or a lecture about not disturbing others or messing up the space (and providing this help in a way that makes it out to be no trouble or no big deal at all—"I was going to get myself a coffee anyway, so I might as well get you one" and so on). Fondness, etymologically, also contains some notions of folly or operating by a different logic than that of cold-hard-objectivity and, of course, if we are to love well in a world defined by all the greed, pragmatism, looting, and abandonment I have already described, then those who are most financially and ideologically invested in that system will inevitably think of us as at least a little (if not a lot) mentally ill.

To say that fondness requires us to act more simply or get back to some of the very basic things, recalling what adults and children continue to have in common, does not mean that we are ever belittling in our interactions with others. All too often, social workers attempting to be affectionate end up being condescending or patronizing (all while continuing to think that they are being loving and noble). We are not Mother Teresas on a mission

---

2. I think the fact that people were paying me $80/hour to cuddle with them in a non-sexual way also made them think I had discovered a really sweet hustle and a hustler always respects a good hustle (game recognizes game, as the saying goes). This may have been a factor in their response—although, of course, I was not trying to hustle anyone and I still firmly believe in the power of platonic, affectionate touch, and the need for us—especially men in our culture—to find safe ways to share this with one another. That said, "snuggle therapy" is not an accredited form of therapy, and there are definitely people in the scene trying to make a quick buck or others who are not well equipped to deal with the kinds of emotions and topics of conversation that arise in an intimate setting where a person feels safe and loved. Because of this, I strongly suggest that anyone exploring hiring a snuggle therapist do thorough research beforehand.

C. AFFECTIONATE (TENDER-HEARTED)

from God to "save those poor slum dwellers over there" (apparently by teaching them to accept their poverty and not have abortions, which seemed to be the gist of Mother Teresa's work). Fuck that shit. Our acts of affection arise because we love people as they are, where they are, right here, right now, and we are tender with them in the same way that our lovers, chosen family, and friends are tender with us.

Consequently, it is of the utmost importance to ensure that we remain in or continually move more deeply into a state of tender-heartedness as we pursue the goal of being good company to and with others. Many things will challenge us. The examples of others, the barriers and lack of care that are normalized, enforced, and treated as "best practices" in other so-called caring professions, the disappointments we experience, the way that being tender-hearted means that we get hurt sometimes, and the desire to not get hurt anymore all unite to try and convince us to harden ourselves. Recently, my friend Samantha and I were discussing this as she moved into being a professional counselor and was worried about how her current "delicate" state in relation to processing some of her own traumas might affect her work in a negative way. After talking it through, we came to the conclusion that being delicate—and *maintaining oneself as delicate*—was actually a much better place to work from than a state of total healing, wholeness, or wellness (in this regard, it is interesting to note that the world "delicate" contains both the idea of something alluring or delightful, as in a "delicacy," and the notion of something fragile or sensitive). Rather than viewing strength as that which makes us no longer delicate, we concluded that it is better to *show strength by remaining delicate in ways that are helpful and not harmful to others*. The key is not ceasing to love, rage, grieve and hurt alongside of others; the key is learning to sustain ourselves *as* loving, *as* raging, *as* grieving, and *as* hurting people in a community where we all seek to carve out a more life-giving and life-affirming way of doing community than what we find in our death-dealing society. Tracking all the ways in which we continue or cease to show small acts of fondness and affection is one way of monitoring ourselves to see if we are doing this well.

D. Kind

During his conversation with "a lady of little faith" in *The Brothers Karamazov*, Father Zossima says something that I have often thought about over the years. As I began to awaken to the all-encompassing aspects of oppression, colonization, dispossession, toxic masculinity, and the abuse of power that exist in our society, I also began to try and point these things out to people who benefited from them—mostly friends, biofamily members, members from my (then) faith community, my workplace, or the institute of so-called "higher education" where I was studying and volunteering. No matter how I tried, regardless of what angle I took, or the rhetorical devices I deployed (from being very factual and objective and reasonable, to being very sensitive, to being very emotional, to being very confrontational—I tried them all), it seemed that simply having these matters on the table for discussion, especially in relationship to ourselves and not as things that exist "somewhere out there," would inevitably produce anger, hurt feelings, defensiveness, and hypervigilance, which all combined to produce various ways of (justifiably, in their opinion) questioning my character, taking great offense at my words, or using any other tactic that could be deployed to not actually have to confront the matter at hand. Consequently, I often found myself reflecting upon Father Zossima's assertion that "love in action is a harsh and dreadful thing compared with love in dreams."[1] At that time, before I knew just how cruel oppressors, dispossessors, patriarchs, and bosses were capable of being when their stolen and blood-stained privileges were challenged in *any* way (or exposed for what they truly are), it certainly did seem to me that, no matter how loving I tried to be, I still ended up hurting people. In this context, during those years, even though I was trying to point out the ways in which people were harming or outright abusing those whom they claimed to love, and even though I was trying to do that in the most sensitive, respectful, and gentle

1. Dostoevsky, *Brothers Karamazov*, 66.

ways I could find, it still felt like this love, in action, was a harsh and dreadful thing compared to what I was told loving would be. I didn't want to hurt people—but I did. I didn't want to upset people—but I did. I didn't want to lose friends or lose the respect of people I respected—but I did. It turns out that there is no way for Moses (or anyone else seeking liberation from oppression) to say "Let my people go!" (or "let us go!") without deeply hurting the feelings of Pharaoh and his court.

But note the reversal that occurs here—it is the expression of loving care that is interpreted as being harsh and dreadful, rather than the environment that makes those who identify oppression appear to be unloving. This was vividly illustrated to me on one occasion, about twenty years ago, when I organized resistance to a fundraising event my alma mater had organized. As a part of that event, they hired George W. Bush to be the keynote speaker. I helped campaign on campus, leaflet and post information about the various war crimes George W. Bush committed, about the human price paid by those who suffered because of those crimes, and about Bush's persistent refusal to take accountability or acknowledge any wrong-doing. Bush was a *thoroughly unapologetic war criminal*, who was directly responsible for the deaths of tens of thousands of people (and he still is—although people tend to forget this in the age of Trump when they speak nostalgically about him and the "intersectional" paintings he does). But when I spoke about this with students on campus (most of whom were cis-het, middleclass, White Conservative Christians), I was accused of being unloving, unforgiving, and harsh. "I'm not going to sign the petition to cancel the event," said one student, "because *I choose love*."

Thus, I learned that in our invitations to oppressors, wherein we offer them the opportunity to change, to be better, to live in a better world (for the demand, "Let my people go!" is just as much an offer of liberation to Pharaoh as it is to the Hebrew slaves; Pharaoh, in his own way, is thoroughly dehumanized by his vampiric existence within the overarching context of oppression), the love that we show both them and others will always be experienced as harsh and dreadful as long as people are invested in oppressive systems.

Of course, this is only half the story. For the Hebrew slaves, and other oppressed folx, the demand that oppressors cease oppressing, will almost certainly be experienced as both wonderful (instead of dreadful) and kind (instead of harsh). That's the thing about loving in the context of oppression—it requires us to take sides. And while we may desire to "love everyone" or, perhaps, be inspired to even want to try and "love our enemies," the first thing that people like me need to realize is that George W. Bush and his friends aren't our enemies—as a cis-het, middleclass, White man colonizing stolen land, I, and those like me, have materially benefited from the things Bush & Co. did. Bush and his friends never harmed me or my loved ones or filled our environment with toxic waste, as they did by coating their ammunitions with depleted uranium in Iraq (one of their war crimes) so we do not get rare forms of cancer or have children born with all kinds of horrendous deformations (no skin, missing organs, some organs on the outside instead of the inside, unrecognizable briefly living sacks of tissue, and so on). For people like me, loving our enemies means looking at who we are harming—who we are *actually treating as enemies*, regardless of the feelings, sensitivities, or alliances we claim to have—and then stopping that harm. In other words, for those rooted in oppressor groups, loving enemies first and foremost means *putting an end to oppression so that we are no longer harming others*.[2] Does this sound harsh or dreadful? I don't know. I guess it depends on how invested you are in things like White supremacy, taking little or no responsibility for yourself while convincing yourself that you are a good person, or valuing property and profit margins more than people.

In this regard, I have been thinking about several of the old stories about Jesus of Nazareth. After touring much of his homeland in the aftermath of Roman conquest and colonization (what liberal Canadians who have oh-so-nobly reconciled themselves with colonization would refer to as the "traditional territories" of Jesus's ethnic minority within the multicultural mosaic of the Roman Empire), after visiting village after village, city after city, crowd after crowd, Jesus is said to feel "moved in the very core of his being." The Greek word used here is "splagchnizomai," and, in an onomatopoeic manner, it literally refers to Jesus being moved in his bowels—a term used to describe when someone is deeply moved with compassion. Jesus is said to have felt this way because he saw the crowds as those who were so heavily *plundered* and *mangled* that they appeared to be *flayed alive* (the Greek word here is "eskulmenoi"). The crowds appeared as those who had been forcibly *thrown down* by others (the meaning of "eppimmenoi"), and were now lying mortally wounded on the ground. Their situation reminded him of what happens to sheep who are left without a shepherd while wolves and jackals are prowling nearby and vultures are circling overhead.[3] In a

---

2. Note, then, how this reverses the more common ways in which Christians use the call to "love your enemies" to encourage people who are abused—notably in families dominated by abusive patriarchs, but more generally as well—to accept the abuse and continually forgive their abusers, even as they continue to be abused. Loving enemies is not about being oh-so-sweet and polite with those who rape, beat, exploit, or abandon us but, rather, is about ensuring that we are not participating in the rapes, beatings, exploitation, or abandonment of anyone.

3. See Matt 9:35–36. Predominant English translations tend to water this down and instead of speaking of the crowds as those who are "plundered" and "wounded," and

similar manner, the more I watched and listened to others living within our context, the more I attended to the voices and faces and lives of those in our crowded cities—from Toronto, to Vancouver, to London—the more I saw how deeply wounded all of us are. Even those who benefit from oppression in some ways all too often end up plundered, mangled, and thrown down (sometimes it just takes a little longer for them to fall).

Furthermore, the more I, myself, was overwhelmed by my own woundedness, my own losses, my own faults, the ways I was wronged and did wrong, the more I came to value kindness. Kindness, I eventually concluded, is one of the most underrated virtues today. I think we tend to look down on it—we say smart and pretty things about "empathy" and "compassion" and "listening to learn," and being "client-centered," and utilizing "evidence-informed best practices"—and along the way kindness is forgotten or infantilized. It is almost as if it is childish to talk about the importance of being kind, as if we need to somehow move beyond talking about such things once we are adults. As if kindness is too simplistic and we, in our greater maturity, intelligence, and attention to complexity and nuance, have moved beyond it. That's nonsense. And it's harmful. As I have observed over the years, those who neglect kindness or who never come to practice or master it to begin with, are almost always also those who are cruel, despite proclaiming their commitment to being compassionate, those who are unable to identify with those whom they claim to support, despite proclamations about being empathetic, and those who enforce their own (highly self-serving) agenda, despite proclamations about "listening to learn."

One of the key ways in which we demonstrate kindness is by not handing people over to harmful processes, bosses, authorities, or institutions (even if such harm is justified or considered a moral duty according to the rule of law). At times, kindness means refusing to rat people out. Kindness means refusing to betray our commitment to the well-being of anyone just because we feel uncomfortable or frightened. Kindness means not talking to cops. Kindness means not acting as if the wolves are the answer to the sheep's problems. And if someone falls in with jackals, calling in the pigs isn't going to stop them from being devoured (after all, sixteen hungry pigs can go through two hundred pounds of bone, flesh, and muscle in about eight minutes).

Note, also, how this approach to kindness, informed as it is by the dynamics of oppression, directly counteracts how liberal pacifists engage

---

oppressed (leading the reader to immediately wonder about who is doing that plundering, wounding, and oppressing), English translators tend to depoliticize the Greek and use the words "distressed" and "weary," which are much more ambiguous. After all, you can be "distressed" and "weary" without someone else making you that way.

in "activism" in order to try and brand themselves as "nice people" who are "woke" and "on the right side of all the things." Bougie liberal pacifists, like wannabe-White-savior Chris Hedges, have long taken issue with oppressed people and their accomplices who deploy less-legal tactics or engage in more discomfiting activities like targeted acts of property destruction. Hedges & Co. don't think such actions are very nice. Thus, in 2012 during the Occupy uprising, Hedges declared Black bloc participants to be a "cancer in Occupy."[4] He further describes Black bloc participants as "petty," "repellent," "grotesque," and then later as spoiled adolescents and feral (i.e. not civilized, hardly human) creatures. They are, in Hedges's words, "criminal" members of an "absolutis[t] sect," and they undercut the moral authority of the nice people—people like him—who are law-abiding and don't fight back against cops or rapists or anyone ever at all. Because, apparently, it's not very nice or kind to defend yourself when your life and the lives of your loved ones are on the line. As a result of statements made by people like Hedges, so-called nonviolent peace activists would turn other less-nonviolent activists over to the police during some Occupy protests that involved a diversity of tactics. Sometimes, these pacifists would literally *forcibly restrain* non-pacifists until the police could capture them. Other times, they would attack Black bloc participants in order to *forcibly demask* them and expose their identities. While this appears to be a flagrant violation of their own values—assaulting people because they are not nonviolent enough to meet your standards is one of the more nonsensical things I've seen in recent years—what it makes apparent is that their commitment is not so much to ending oppression as it is about making themselves distinct from "those unkind, violent people over there." In this regard, all forms of violence are said to be equal—the rape victim who fights back against the rapist is, apparently, as evil and unkind as the rapist who attempts to rape her.

Thus, it becomes clear that liberal niceness is anything but kind and anything but just or liberating. In fact, as David Graeber makes very clear in his response to Hedges, such liberal niceness actually causes life-destroying harm to people who are oppressed and who are trying to resist oppression.[5] Graeber highlights how Hedges's "misinformation . . . really can get people killed," and goes on to highlight how Hedges's hyperbolic and dehumanizing rhetoric parallels and mirrors the language used by oppressor States when they wish to attack or eliminate those who get in their way. Recent events have only confirmed Graeber's fears. White liberal "activists" have

---

4. See Hedges, "Cancer in Occupy."

5. See Graeber, "Concerning the Violent Peace-Police." Graeber's premature death is a major loss to all of us.

exposed the identities of Black people who have engaged in acts of property destruction during the Black Lives Matter uprising and, as a result, these people are now being charged and are literally looking at spending the rest of their lives in prison.[6] So much, then, for the moral paucity of bourgeois liberal understandings of what it means to be kind.

But, sure, of course it's nice to *desire* to be kind to everyone. And, sure, of course we try to use *the least amount of violence possible* in order to pursue liberation from oppression (although, thinking about Moses and the Hebrew slaves once again, sometimes the very least amount of violence possible ends up being rather a lot more than we would like). In desiring the end of oppression, we not only advocate for the liberation of the oppressed, we are also advocating and working towards the liberation of the oppressors—we just recognize that calling for this tends to sound lovely to the oppressed and hurts the feelings of the oppressors. And, yeah, if wealth were equitably distributed to all, the uber-rich will probably end up feeling impoverished. Oh well. Given what oppressors actually deserve, given how they have actually harmed others, *only* hurting their feelings and leaving them with the same amount of wealth as everyone else, is actually an incredibly kind, gracious, and forgiving act.

Again, for whatever they are worth, the old stories about Jesus help to illustrate this. If you examine those with whom Jesus is exceedingly tender and those with whom Jesus is exceedingly harsh, you realize two things. When people who have been impoverished and oppressed come to him, he proclaims their sins to be forgiven—he declares that they are counted amongst God's elect (a status that the Romans and other wannabe imperial rulers tended to apply exclusively to themselves), that there is nothing wrong with them, and that God is on their side—even if those people never express any kind of repentance for anything. Such people need not repent because, in fact, they haven't done anything wrong. Rather, they are the ones who have been wronged. However, when people come to Jesus who participate in the oppression of others, who materially benefit from those dynamics, and who intend to continue to do so, there is no talk of forgiveness. There is a lot of rage, a lot of "woe to you" statements, and a lot of talk about how God fucking hates them for what they are doing. It turns out that even "gentle Jesus meek and mild" understood the limits and failings of liberal approaches to kindness. But, that said, if any oppressor wished to jump ship, betray their own faction, sell their belongings and give the money back to those whom they impoverished, commit treason and pursue a mutually

---

6. See this important piece by Peter Gelderloos, "Amplifying the Ecological Resistance."

liberating solidarity with the oppressed, Jesus and those who gathered with him were the first to openly embrace and welcome them. And that, too, is a marvelous act of kindness.

E. Comforting

Recently, I have been studying Inuit *Qaujimajatuqangit*—what Inuit people have known to be true for a very long time (colloquially referred to as Inuit "laws," or "traditions," or "spirituality," or "principles for living," although "IQ," as it is commonly referred to, is more and other than both the sum and the difference of these things). IQ has four "big things that must be followed" (*maligarjuat*—which the *Qallunaat* [White people] tend to inadequately refer to as "laws"—which are also sometimes referred to as *piqujarjuat*, "the things one should or must do to have a successful outcome or a good life, or there will be consequences").[1] Stated in a much simplified way, the four big things are as follows: (1) maintaining harmony; (2) working together for the common good in a way that is not motivated by a desire for personal advancement; (3) living in respectful relationships with every other living being; and (4) planning and preparing for the future, whatever that might end up being. Each of these is described in great detail—in fact, each is really indistinguishable from the detail used to describe them—and many other "smaller" practices or principles are incorporated into the "big things." Thus, for example, *aajiiqatigiingniq* (working together to address that which threatens social harmony and balance) is mentioned alongside of *parnangniq tuavinnginirlu* (careful and unrushed planning), and *tunnganarniq* (being kind-hearted and caring). Taken together, IQ describes a beautiful way of being in and of the world. If followed properly, it is the process by which people are made into human beings—i.e., *inunnguiniq*, "making a human being who will be able to help others with a good heart."[2] As such, it is no wonder that, as with many of the Indigenous cultures that have not yet been exterminated by the death-march of civilization, children and the raising of children, are at the center of IQ.

---

1. On this and what follows, see Karetak et al., *Inuit Qaujimajatuqangit*, 1–19.
2. Karetak et al., *Inuit Qaujimajatuqangit*, 112.

However, as I was reading what various elders had to say about these things, I was unsettled by the following words from Atuat Akittiq:

> Our parents guided us to be human beings. It's our turn to do the same ... When we see someone sad or lonely, it is our responsibility to cheer them up in our own little ways. When I see someone sad, I try to think of ways to help them and cheer them up ... I would tell them that I need their help to do something, rather than saying that I'm doing this for them. Our young people need to learn to cheer someone up. Who knows, it might turn out to be a turning point for someone in need ...
>
> Some people would be so thankful just to know that someone cared about them.[3]

Initially, I skimmed over this passage, finding it mildly irritating and disconnected from the lessons learned by those who spend a lot of time with hurting people—namely, that urging people to cheer up ("have you tried choosing happiness?" or "maybe you should focus on the positive?") can be tone-policing at best and, at worst, a heartless form of abuse that only further isolates and harms those who are already hurting.

Furthermore, while professional social service workers have progressed from saying things like, "don't worry, God has a wonderful plan for your life," I find that the industry that has developed around Empathy™ only gets us so far.[4] When *all* a person does is communicate empathy through the various controls, mannerisms, and affects that they have been taught—they don't rush to offer solutions, they ensure they don't react in a judgmental manner as people share their pain, they attend to "micro-expressions," and utilize "active listening" skills to show that they are "genuinely engaged"—then often a person either only ends up offering a very temporary sense of relief or, in fact, creates false hope that this temporary relief—the feeling of being heard after not being heard for so long—will end up turning into something longer lasting when, in fact, it does not. (Such displays of Empathy™ are often followed by statements like this: "I've listened to you very nicely and for much longer than the time allotted to you, now go away.")

---

3. Karetak et al., *Inuit Qaujimajatuqangit*, 100–101. See also the umbrella terms used by Mark Kalluak (*iliqqusiq*—the usual pattern of behavior or being—and *silatuniq*—the ability to think and behave wisely—and *illqqusitugat*—the usual pattern of Inuit life); Karetak et al., *Inuit Qaujimajatuqangit*, 41.

4. Although, it should be noted that workers at Christian faith-based charities do still say things like, "God has a wonderful plan for your life." Just recently, during a wave of overdose deaths, a friend of mine who was grieving the deaths of his loved ones was told by his Christian boss that maybe he just needed to "find God" and then he would feel better.

E. COMFORTING

So, I paused to reconsider Atuat Akittiq's words. I've learned that both small children and elders often say things that those of us in the in-between stages of life think are silly or over-simplistic (almost to the point of being harmful, naïve, or stupid at times) but, if we stop and reflect upon what they say, there is actually often a great deal of wisdom in their words. And as I was thinking about how small children react to the pain of other children, I realized that, like Akittiq, they would gather together to try and cheer up the child who was hurting. I also realized that I was projecting my own past hurts, biases, and experiences (or inexperiences!) into the words Akittiq used. I don't think Akittiq is advising us to offer the false, othering, and harmful platitudes that I mentioned above. I think she is highlighting just how important it is for us to try to *comfort those who are afflicted*, and ease the pain, anger, distress, fear, and loneliness of those who are hurting.

The word comfort refers to the act of cheering up, consoling, or soothing another person who is experiencing grief or trouble. Tracing the word back through the Old French (*conforter*) and Late Latin (*confortare*), we also see that it is rooted, not so much in an act of easing distress as it is rooted in acts that *strengthen the person who is distressed*. Thus, the intensive prefix (*com-*, which means "with" or "together" or "in association" and carries an intensive force) is paired with the Latin root (*fortis*—i.e., strong), suggesting that, more literally, "to comfort" means *to be together with someone in a way that much-strengthens them*. Stated less awkwardly, we can say that comforting is a way of being in relationships with others that makes people stronger and more able to both survive and thrive in whatever circumstances they go through in life. The lesson here is that unless our active, nonjudgmental, and empathetic listening is paired with actions that strengthen a person (or help that person to recall, rediscover, or see for the first time the strengths they already possess) then we are sorry comforters (and all too often, at the end of the day, empathy training in caring professions mostly just teaches people how to better pretend to be what they are not).

Having said that, it is important to still emphasize that sometimes being comforting means only being able to offer a brief moment of respite, a few hours of peace, and a temporary cessation of pain. The reality of our present situation is that oppression is so ubiquitous and relentless that we often feel helpless before it, unsure of what we can to do abolish it, unsure of where we can find liberation and long-lasting peace. In such a context, all-too-brief and fleeting moments of comfort become critical to our ongoing survival, even if they do not put an end to our pain. A hug shared before we disperse into the alleyways to escape the cops, a safe space to go after a bad date, someone to be close with to ride out a bad trip or to ensure we don't overdose on a medication we purchased from a new supplier—all of these things do not put an end to our struggle but they do help us to live to fight another day. We may not be able to get out of the deep end, but that doesn't mean we should belittle the spaces where we are able to come up for air. Brief moments of respite may not win the war for us, but they do help us to survive. And this is of the utmost importance.

As I was thinking about these things and thinking about Atuat Akittiq's words, I realized that maintaining a spirit of *playfulness* is one of the critical elements of emancipatory community building. Invitations to play are, perhaps, the most frequent way in which children offer to cheer up other children. One of the key ways in which communities of good company distinguish themselves from so-called caring professionals is because playfulness is present within them. In fact, while this may be surprising to those who know me only through my writing, if you speak with people who are oppressed and with whom I have tried to be good company, I think you would discover they all emphasize my humour, my contagious laugh, and the ways in which people "just feel better" after we spend some time together (and I, too, feel better in their company). It turns out, that pausing to actually try and listen to Atuat Akittiq and learn from her, has helped me understand just how much "cheering [people] up in our own little ways," is an essential factor in our work. To quote another source, in our communities we boldly proclaim the following: "Join us, so that you may experience peace; because, yes, out there in that world you will experience oppression but, *be of good cheer*, together, here and now, in this company, we have overcome that world and made another world possible."[5]

Playfulness is essential to this. Through play we both build and affirm camaraderie. Through play we become *people* in the company of other *people*, we strip away pretensions, we encourage rule-breaking (for, as a former friend once told me, things like silliness and having a laugh are fundamentally at odds with the seriousness required to always "toe the line"). In play, we liberate ourselves from oppression—we overcome the world as it is presented to us. Play overthrows the dehumanizing pragmatism that annihilates the possibility of community emerging in institutional services. Play asserts that, "no, I'm not here in order to work towards this or that measurable outcome; I'm here because I need to have a place where we all can feel good about ourselves and where we can have a good time." Therefore, in the community space facilitated by my friend Mechele and I, we took time to engage in playful activities with people. Instead of running groups (where we could firmly control the conversation, stat who attended, and then run those numbers back to funders), we would do things like sit down at the

---

5. My rendition of John 16:33.

tables with people, joke and laugh and drink coffee, play a game of bridge or euchre, or work through a crossword puzzle together. Sometimes, other social workers or mental health workers or shelter workers or bosses would pass through our space and they would either reprimand us or mock us for doing these things—"I wish I got paid to play cards," some would say. "Aren't you supposed to be doing something useful?" a boss would ask—never realizing that maybe this was part of the reason why people who yelled at them or smashed up their spaces, treated one another with kindness and care in our space.

However, as more and more services closed their doors, moved out of the downtown core to make room for neoliberal real estate developers who specialize in plundering impoverished communities, or raised their barriers to service, more and more people in truly dire circumstances came to us seeking good company and support with urgent crises. We asked for further support from the organization funding our program but this was denied and, as a result, we lost the ability to set aside time to foster playfulness and camaraderie in the community, and this, I think, was when our efforts became doomed and we transitioned from being proactive to being reactive. Gradually, the culture shifted and ultimately the funding for the program was canceled altogether leaving more than two hundred and twenty people a day left with literally no place to go—leading directly to the massive increase of "urban campers" that this city has seen since then. However, if we are to be good company to and with others, playfulness and all the other ways in which we go about providing comfort—comforting and being comforted, too—cannot be sacrificed.

4. Parting

The English word "transient" derives from the Latin word *transientem* which refers to "passing over" or "passing away." Thus, transience refers to something impermanent, something non-durable, and, ultimately, it refers to something that is destined to die soon. However, as neoliberal municipalities have increasingly focused on managing populations (rather than resolving the root causes of socioeconomic woes, which, of course, would require a massive redistribution of stolen wealth), the term "transient" has often been applied to people who are forcibly deprived of housing (i.e., "people experiencing homelessness"). Thus, in the pertinent academic literature, we quickly finds papers with titles like the following: "The Impact of Transient Populations on Recycling Behavior in a Densely Populated Urban Environment"; "One Size Doesn't Fit All: Applying Flexibility to the Primary Care Behavioral Health Model with Transient Populations— A Report"; and, in relation one city's 2020 population census, we find the following section: "How Will Homeless People and Transient Populations be Counted."[1] Neoliberal city managers use this language, in part, to signal that they are more sensitive than their Conservative (or Neoconservative)

---

1. Such "homeless counts," as they are commonly referred to by city managers, briefly became increasingly frequent across Turtle Island and became something of a marker for cities as they assessed whether or not their efforts to "cure homelessness" were efficacious. However, because the overwhelming majority of the people counted were staying in homeless shelters (where they are much easier to find and count than those who were "sleeping rough," staying in "encampments," or "couch-surfing"), the end result of this was often a push to reduce the number of available shelter beds as this would produce a lower "homeless count." This lower count was interpreted and celebrated as a sign of success (and used to justify further cuts to shelter services) when, in reality, more people were just forced to sleep in abandoned buildings or parks, or were forced to return to an abuser. After Ontario transitioned from a liberal to conservative government (and precisely when the number of people deprived of housing and shelter began to grow exponentially), homeless counts were abandoned altogether.

forebears: "We don't talk about 'hobos' or 'tramps' or 'drifters,' we talk about 'people experiencing homelessness and transient populations.'"

And yet anyone familiar with the history of racial capitalism, settler colonialism, and the mass dispossession that has played-out across Turtle Island might suspect that neoliberalism is giving away more than it intends to when it uses this language. After all, as the forced march of "progress," swept westward across the continent, and the Canadian and American occupations were consolidated into internationally recognized nation States, Indigenous peoples who had been a part of these territories for thousands of years were suddenly declared to be transient—they were doomed to "extinction" (a word frequently substituted for what is more properly referred to as genocide when applied to the acts of national groups; that is to say, when one group of people annihilates another group of people, this is called genocide—we only call this "extinction" when referring to non-human things like plants or animals . . . or, apparently, Indigenous peoples). White Europeans argued that Indigenous people lacked the moral and physical constitution to survive within a "civilized" world. As a result, they were repeatedly said to be passing through and passing away (i.e., they were "transientem").

The same logic applies to the ways in which Whites talked about Black people after the American Civil War. The so-called "Great Emancipator" himself did not believe that Black slaves could survive in America after slavery. In fact, Abraham Lincoln opposed slavery, not because he felt that it violated the fundamental human rights of Black people, but because he thought it depressed wages for White workers. Slavery needed to be ended, from Lincoln's perspective, not so that Black people could be free and equal, but so that Black people, including Black veterans who fought on behalf of the Union, could be shipped off the continent (something Lincoln continued to recommend up until his death) so that they didn't all just die out—as they inevitably would (in his estimation).[2]

Transients, in other words, are people who are supposed to fuck off and die. And if they demonstrate their incivility and ingratitude by refusing to either fuck off or die, and if dominant populations are unable to force them to do either, then they become a *problem* (or, in the parlance of city managers, a *"priority population"*) to be *managed*.

There is a double-edged lie about permanence embedded into this language. First, by relegating Indigenous peoples to a state of transience, colonizers attempted to claim a right to the lands they colonized as if those lands were the colonizers' permanent homes. Neoliberal property hoarders (commonly referred to as "real estate developers") engage in a similar game.

2. See Johnson, *Broken Heart of America*, 161–62.

First they impoverish certain communities, then they drive up rents, buy up buildings that are left empty (and protected by security guards to ensure that they stay empty), create food deserts, refuse to rent or sell to social services (and drive out already existing community spaces and social services), dispossess people of their homes, supports, and shared public spaces, and then label those people as transients so that they can be forced to migrate elsewhere (if they don't just up and die) so that wealth-hoarders and other dispossessors can move in and be left undisturbed in what they now claim to be their "forever homes."

The other edge to this lie is the way in which oppressors desperately trying to convince themselves that impermanence, brevity, and dying are things that happen to other people (sick people, poor people, Black people, Indigenous people), and not to them. Forcing other people to die early, die young, die in poverty, die before they should, and making the kind of world where death is dealt generously and forcefully to others, helps to reinforce this belief and the relief some people experience by clinging to it. But it's a lie. Life is short. This person I am now, this body I am now, this being that I am now, I will be for only the briefest of moments. And then I will die and this person, this body, this being will no longer be and, before you know it, there will be no one to mourn or celebrate or even remember this at all. And you don't have to zoom out too far to realize that not only is this true of each of us as individuals, but it is true of us as a species. We're just passing through. In a moment, we'll be gone.[3]

This recognition leads to the fourth and final part of this book. Along with welcoming, parting bookends how we go about sharing life together. Friendships ebb and flow, people come and go, everyone moves through different seasons in life and, especially in communities of oppressed people, many other forms of departure—disappearances, murders, sudden deaths, and even, as a last resort, exiling people from the community, or leaving the community ourselves—are things that we must reckon with constantly. This ebb and flow of arrivals and departures is part of any community, and learning to part from others as well and as thoughtfully as we strive to welcome others is essential to our efforts to be good company to and with others.

---

3. Although, of course, having said this, I want to be explicit that this argument should not be twisted and redeployed to argue against claims that Indigenous peoples have to territories (or, rather claims those territories have on Indigenous peoples) based on the fact that they have been a part of these territories for far longer than the Europeans who have colonized them. Nor, of course, should this be used to justify abandoning some people to a state of enforced transience due to dispossession, violence, greed, and apathy.

4. PARTING

This is so, in part, because as I argued above, every member of a community fills a unique niche within that community, makes a unique contribution to that community, and offers what only they can uniquely offer to the community. Communities, in this sense, are like tightly-woven ecosystems, which, when they are thriving, exist in such a way that all members play a critical role to the overall well-being of the ecosystem itself. Consequently, the departure or loss of any member ends up leaving a wound in the ecosystem. If a community or ecosystem is to survive this kind of loss and continue to thrive, then relationships must change, dynamics will shift, and things cannot continue as they did before. This is why the loss of one person also means the loss of the whole—the whole that existed before, of which that person was a part, ceases to exist when that person is gone. A new whole must be created and in this new whole, as we will see, there is still a space for the person who has departed, but now this space—a space which continues to be a part of the inter- and intra-connectedness that contributes to our mutual thriving—is marked by an absence or, as we will see, a non-material presence.

If, then, we greet others by showing them that they are "well come" and "well met," then in the ways in which you go about parting from others we genuinely try to wish them a "good bye" and express our desire that they "fare well." Given the realities of oppression, this is not always easy to do—in fact, sometimes it may not even be a possibility at all (and so, like individual people, communities also learn to live with scars and wounds that never fully heal)—but, as with everything else, we do the little we can, for the brief amount of time that we have to do it. And then we don't anymore.

A. Murdered and Disappeared

The first person I knew who was murdered was a teenager who was shot at the corner of Yonge and Gould, just a few steps away from the Eaton Centre in the heart of Toronto. His blood filled the cracks in the sidewalk before overflowing the curb, filling the gutter, and draining into a nearby sewer. He died there on the concrete. It was the middle of the day, and the tourists who scattered when the shots were first fired quickly went back to shopping as the police tape went up, his body was shipped to the morgue, and the fire department washed away what was left of him.

But, as I think about things now, I'm not so sure about this timeline. By the time this teenager was killed, I had already known several people who had died by suicide. In some cases (maybe not all cases, but very many of them), I think suicide is actually the outworking of a murder that, instead of being instantly completed, is planted inside a person's body and slowly grows there until it finally hatches. Amanda Todd, for example, died after she hung herself on October 10, 2012. She was fifteen years old. But if you watch the video she posted on YouTube the month before she died, and learn about her history and what she experienced, I think it is more accurate to say that Amanda Todd was murdered by those who cruelly and relentlessly bullied her, sexually exploited and shamed her (in a process that began when she was still a pre-teen) and, ultimately, drove her to kill herself.[1] Amanda Todd may have put the rope around her own neck, but

---

1. Amanda Todd's video went viral: see TheSomebodytoknow, "My Story." If you want to know more, further online research will reveal the extent of the cruelty she faced (but *major* content warning if you choose to Google in that direction). After the man who sexually exploited her and convinced Amanda to send him topless pictures of her when she was in grade seven (i.e., when she was twelve years old) sent those pictures to her peers in multiple high schools (Todd moved schools because of this but the man kept tracking her down and making the pictures known at each new school), and after being physically beaten by peers for agreeing to have sex with a young man who already had a girlfriend but who also wanted to have sex with her, Amanda Todd drank bleach but did not die as a result. Consequently, cyberbullies made many different kinds of

that doesn't mean she wasn't murdered. The same logic, I think, applies to most of my loved ones (and a good many others as well), whose deaths are presented as the "unavoidable tragic consequences" of "the choice they made" to live "high risk" lives. My friend died on a mattress in a rooming house because the hospital kicked him out when he had a spinal infection and a blood infection and was in a considerable amount of pain because the hospital would not provide him with any kind of medication for pain; and so he was kicked out of the hospital for finding his own way to treat his pain. He died on that dirty fucking mattress in that dirty fucking room—he wasn't the victim of "tragic circumstances" that arose due to his "poor life choices." He was killed by the murderous policies and procedures of the hospital and by the killers who enforced those policies and procedures fully aware that he could die if he was not receiving intravenous antibiotics in the hospital under the supervision of a doctor. The same applies to my friend who died curled up like a dog on the front steps of the shelter that would not provide him with a bed to sleep in (after he, too, had been kicked out of the hospital despite a recent and massive head trauma sustained when he fell headfirst onto concrete from the second floor of the same shelter). His death wasn't a "sad but mostly unavoidable tragedy" wherein "nobody (but he himself) could be blamed." He was murdered by the hospital staff members who decided to kick him out. He was murdered by the security guards who enforced that decision. He was murdered by the shelter staff members who decided not to let him into the shelter because he was "behaving erratically." He was murdered. Repeat that over and over again until you understand it, until you feel it, until you cry and rage and cry some more. He was murdered. Repeat it until part of you is also murdered and part of you is also left to die in a rooming house or on the front steps of a shelter. Or in a fucking porta-potty. He was murdered.

But, of course people who are oppressed can engage in horrific acts of lateral violence and can treat others in the same ways in which oppressors have treated them. The teenager I knew who bled out from a gunshot wound in Toronto died because of that lateral violence, and he is far from being

---

memes mocking her for this (and, even after she hung herself, they continued to do so with, for example, one Facebook page called "Life's a bleach" posting a picture of a silhouette of a hanging girl with the caption: "TODDING"). It is hard to look at these images. They are astoundingly cruel. In a similar manner, Rehtaeh Parsons suicided after she was gang-raped and the video of the rape was distributed to her peers who then responded by bullying her. However, critical exacerbating factors that drove Rehtaeh to suicide were the physical violence she experienced at the hands of healthcare professionals when she went to the hospital and the utter lack of interest the police had in prosecuting her case. For more on this appalling story, see Rama Rau's documentary *No Place to Hide* (2015).

the only person I know who has died because of that. I think, for example, of an older man I knew who was stabbed to death over a five-dollar debt, and another man who was punched once in the face over a small debt, who fell over and hit the back of his head and, before anybody even knew what had happened, he was dead. But it is important for us to remember that, despite all the attention these murders receive in the media, on cop-loving TV show after cop-loving TV show, the number of murders produced by lateral violence is miniscule in comparison to the number of murders that occur based upon the ways in which we structure our life together. Far more people are being killed simply because we have created and enforced certain rules than the number of people being killed by any wannabe gangsters. Let me mention just one more example of this. The *fifteen thousand, three hundred and ninety-three* people who are known to have died in opiate overdoses in Canadian-occupied territories between January 2016 and December 2019 did not simply "die tragically due to their high-risk lifestyles" (although roughly 90 percent of these overdoses were deemed to be accidental). These people were actually murder victims—all fifteen thousand, three hundred and ninety-three of them. They were murdered by those who create and then enforce laws that criminalize certain kinds of medication or (far more frequently) certain ways of taking or acquiring otherwise legal medications (most opiates are legal if attained from the "right person" under the "right circumstances" and used in the "right way"). All of this helps explain why I believe that our current way of structuring life together is actually *perverse*. I am not exaggerating when I say that we live in a socio-economic and juridico-political system that is fundamentally death-serving and death-dealing. The proper name for those who create and enforce this system is *murderers* and the proper name for those who are killed or left for dead by this system is *murdered*—and in this regard, it bears repeating that more people on Turtle Island are murdered by *cops* (those who are heavily armed and situated on the frontlines of enforcing this death-serving and death-dealing system) than by any other profession of people (regardless of whether or not their profession is considered legal).

Living in the company of the oppressed and left-for-dead means that you end up with a lot of murdered friends and companions. Not only this— you also end up with a lot of friends and companions who get disappeared or "go missing." Most of those who are disappeared or who "go missing" are hardly even noticed or, if they are noticed, those who have the ability to find them usually don't care enough to put in any effort to do so. For example, sex workers started "disappearing" from Vancouver's downtown eastside in the early 1980s. This continued for the next *twenty years* and, although other sex workers and members of that community expressed deep

A. MURDERED AND DISAPPEARED

concerns about the disappearances, the Vancouver police regularly treated these concerns in a mockingly dismissive manner. They emphasized that sex workers, especially low track sex workers like those found in the downtown eastside were a *transient* group, they moved around a lot, maybe they were out of town, maybe they were in rehab, maybe they were in jail, maybe they went back to the rez given that a lot of the disappeared women were Indigenous ("A large number of missing sex workers," they repeated, "is really no cause for concern. Get over it already. Seriously, who cares?"). The police continued to repeat assertions like these even after they were tipped off that Robert "Willy" Pickton, a pig farmer in nearby Port Coquitlam who regularly hosted parties for outlaw bikers on his farm (known as "Piggy's Palace") was kidnapping, raping, and murdering sex workers from the downtown eastside. It took another *six years* of sex-working women "going missing" before the police did some more thorough follow-up on these claims. This despite the fact that Pickton had already been charged in 1997 for kidnapping, raping, forcibly confining, and attempting to murder a sex worker (those charges were stayed since the victim in that case was a sex worker who had "drug addiction issues" and so was considered "too unstable" to be a reliable witness). Eventually, of course, we all learned that Pickton had murdered about fifty women and fed them to his pigs in order to disappear them as completely as possible. Consequently, in 2010, in response to relentless pressure applied by the families and friends of the murdered and disappeared, the Vancouver Police issued a statement saying, "Oops, sorry about that."[2]

However, the Vancouver Police are far from unique in this regard. There are numerous other police forces in Canadian-occupied territories, especially the RCMP, the Ontario Provincial Police, and the Sûreté du Québec, who are busily circling the wagons to defend themselves and try to make the public think they cared about things like missing and murdered women because it turns out that what happened on a smaller scale in Vancouver's downtown eastside had actually played out on a much larger scale across the entire Canadian occupation where thousands of Indigenous women and girls have "gone missing" or been disappeared, over several decades, and the Canadian state (and its agents of so-called "law enforcement") never did much of anything about that (not only that but, in Québec, along the Highway of Tears in northern British Columbia, and a few other places, it seems highly probable that the cops themselves were the ones using their cop status to actively disappear, rape, or murder a number of those Indigenous women and girls).

2. See Oppal, *Forsaken*.

Living in the company of the oppressed and left-for-dead means that you end up with a lot of missing or disappeared friends and companions. My loved ones have been disappeared and disappearing for a long time. Referring to this as "going missing" is an interesting way of framing things since it makes the missing person the one who is responsible for their own disappearance. They are the subject of the verb (i.e., Tina [the subject] has gone [the verb] missing). Thus, for example, as Malcolm Payne argues in *The British Journal of Social Work*, "going missing is one of a range of choices which people in difficulties may make, depending on their approach to problems in their lives and the availability of opportunities."[3] The missing person is blamed for the fact that they are missing. But, in fact, all too often the missing person is missing not because they "chose to go missing" but because someone took them, someone disappeared them, or someone forced them, in the words of many a cop, to "move along" (or, as Joseph DeAngelo, the police officer who was also the mass murderer and serial rapist known as the Golden State Killer, said to one of his victims: "You'll be silent forever, and I'll be gone in the shadows"). It turns out that what is missing is not so much the person who was disappeared or murdered (or both), but, in fact, any kind of interest by the police to investigate themselves, or any kind of care or concern by members of the general public for those who we have been taught are trash. So it goes with transients destined to fuck off and die any day now.

But living as a friend and companion of those who are oppressed, abandoned, and left for dead (in bureaucratese: "priority populations" marked by their "vulnerability to dying tragically" or their annoying habit of "going missing"), means that we have to learn to live *through* these experiences, recognize how they mark us collectively and as individuals, and learn *how to be good company*, not only to and with the living, but *to and with the dead, the murdered, and the disappeared*. This is hard to do. In the next two sections, I will first explore some of the ways in which we can live through the experience of "not knowing," and then look at how we can go about commemorating the dead, murdered, and disappeared.

---

3. See Payne, "Understanding 'Going Missing.'"

i. Not Knowing

For many years, I worked in a program that was visited by a petite, middle-aged woman who was regularly "sleeping rough" (i.e., sleeping outside) and who pushed her belongings around in a shopping cart. She didn't say much to us or anyone else, but there were a few people who looked out for her and, if left to her own devices and feeling threatened, she was able to scream a scream that sounded like the sound cannon deployed by riot cops. It was surprisingly effective. There were several other members of this community who came around more frequently and there were many more who came around less frequently, but for some years she came and went and came and went, until she became an "old-timer" and one of "the regulars." I don't know when we all saw her last, but one day we realized it had been quite a while since we had seen her. "Odd," I remember thinking, "I hope she's okay," and then I was off to do some more crisis work with people who were waiting for me. To be honest, I didn't think too much more about it—there was so much to do and I, too, was going through a fair bit of turmoil, suffering, grief, and loss. Then, some more time passed and one day one of the men who used to look out for this woman came by to say he hadn't seen her anywhere, he couldn't find her anywhere, nobody had seen her or heard from her, and, as it turned out, she had probably been missing for over two years. Some of us spent some time trying to track her down but we got nowhere. Nobody else was interested in looking. The cops just laughed at the idea of us filing a Missing Person Report—"You want us to look for a *transient* who hasn't been seen in over two years? This is a joke, right? You can't be serious." And then, when they learned we were serious, they stopped laughing and told us to fuck off and stop wasting their time.

I have no idea what became of this woman and I worry that she wasn't okay and that things did not end well. A number of other women—especially those who are deprived of housing, those who are Indigenous, and those who are engaged in street-level sex work, or some combination of all those factors—have also been "going missing" in recent years. Friends of mine are still looking for them, but to no avail. And still other women from the same groups have had very close calls with men who tried to murder and disappear them. In fact, to the surprise of most of the world, it turns out this place where I live and work, Baketigweyaang (London, Ontario, as the Canadians call it), actually had the highest per capita number of active serial killers operating at the same time on Turtle Island in the mid-twentieth century. Three were caught ("the Chambermaid Slayer," "the Mad Slasher," and "the Balcony Strangler"), but at least one, maybe two (or more if they had accomplices) got away (four or more serial killers operating when the population of the city was only around two hundred thousand people!).[1] When "vulnerable" (i.e., oppressed and abandoned) women "go missing" (i.e., are disappeared), people have good reason to worry here even if the cops are unconcerned.

However, when you have friends and loved ones who have been disappeared or who you expected to continue seeing and then you suddenly and unexpectedly no longer see, with no word of goodbye, no signs of an upcoming departure, and no reappearance, you are plunged into a state of *not knowing*. Whereas you once knew how to contact your friend or loved one, whereas you once expected to see them very soon, whereas you once could confirm that they are okay or, at least, getting by, now you do not know how to contact them, you do not know if or when you will see them again, and you cannot confirm if they are okay or, in fact, if they are dead or alive. Not knowing is experienced as a mixture of fear, anxiety, helplessness, and uncertainty as to whether or not one should feel hopeful that their friend's situation suddenly improved and they left without looking back, or feel grief because their friend has been murdered and may now be lying in an unmarked grave or, as happened to fifteen-year-old Tina Fontaine, wrapped in plastic and a duvet cover, weighed down with rocks, and thrown into a river.

This state of not knowing is one that persists. It is open-ended, and all-too-often lacks closure. We do not know what has happened to many of our friends and, in all likelihood, despite our best efforts, we will *never* know. As such, we do not get to experience the relief that comes with discovering our friends are okay, or the working through of grief that occurs when we are able to bury our dead. Therefore, if we are to endure over time in our efforts to be good company to and with others, we need to find ways to carry this experience of not knowing within ourselves without either hardening our hearts or being overwhelmed by it.

---

1. See Arntfield, *Murder City*; also Brown, *Forest City Killer*.

I. NOT KNOWING

If we harden our hearts, we close ourselves off to intimacy and mutuality with others. Having loved and lost, we can choose to not love so boldly, so vulnerably, or so deeply next time. Having been wounded by the sudden absence of a loved one, we may choose to try and not permit ourselves to risk being wounded in that way again. Instead, we try to make ourselves hard. As a result, we can become more task- than people-oriented. We might still do good work and offer meaningful support but now we do it as a job. Not only this but, maybe we only do this job because we feel we do not have enough transferable job skills to move to another field of work and, hey, we've got bills to pay and kids to feed. So we do the work but we pull our heart back from the work. We become closed off. And, as a result, spaces of mutual sharing, care, and vulnerability, become increasingly like any other social service environment. But, "hey, look, I'm still helping," we tell ourselves, and so we miss the ways in which our efforts to preserve ourselves can end up damaging and fundamentally reorienting the community as a whole.

The reason why people harden their hearts in this way is to prevent themselves from being overwhelmed. People pull back from mutual care and vulnerability because they feel like they just *cannot* take it anymore. They notice themselves doing other things to cope with the painful mixture of feelings that comes with not knowing—they drink more, they engage their partners less, they become less kind with their children, they take more and more pills in order to sleep at night and function in the day. They are overwhelmed. "I need to survive," they think, "I need to be able to still be a good partner," they continue, "and I need to still be able to care for my kids." If they don't do something or change something, they will, in fact, be entirely overwhelmed.

Often those involved in this work have become lost in the comfort various substances offer. Often, they are unable to maintain intimate partnerships outside of work. Often, they have limited contact with their children. Often, they suicide. My brother, Josh, who was once a paramedic in Toronto before he went on long-term disability due to complex post-traumatic stress disorder, has often told me about the high rates of suicide among paramedics and what it is like to be haunted by the ghosts of the children they could not save and the memories of parents who begged them to do so. Those of us who seek to be good company to and with those who are oppressed also know what it is to become this kind of repository of sorrow. Few of us, over the long haul, have not at least considered killing ourselves; few of us, over the long haul, are not haunted.

Thus, we must chart a course between the Scylla of hard-heartedness and the Charybdis of being overwhelmed. This is no small task and, as I have observed over the years, few of us (perhaps none of us?) can find the way through on our own. Especially here, we need to help one another. Specifically, we need to find ways to help one another remain in the state of not knowing *without being destroyed and without becoming destructive*. Different individuals and different communities find different ways to do this but, a lot of this is captured in the ways in which communities engage in acts of commemoration related to by the dead and the disappeared. Therefore, I will now look at commemorating in more detail.

ii. Commemorating

When we engage in the act of commemoration, we call something or someone to mind. Rather than simply allowing our memory to ebb and flow as it will, we actively work to bring someone or something to remembrance, we re-mind ourselves of that person or thing, and, in this and other acts, we perpetuate the memory of that person or thing. Commemoration is often accomplished through memorialization. There are many ways in which we do this—from participating in solemn events and rituals, to posting notices or plaques, to erecting statues or gravestones, to fondly, playfully, or sorrowfully sharing stories of loved ones on dates that remind us of them. Whatever the act, each moment of memorialization communicates that the person or thing we are calling to mind is memorable—someone or something excellent, deserving of being called to mind. Thus, when we are parting, commemoration continues the work we began when we remembered others as a way of acknowledging them when we welcomed them (Section 1.B.iv, above) and when we went on to honor them by celebrating them through acts of marveling, thanking, and grieving (Sections 2.D-ii and D.iii, above). Commemoration, then, is how we continue to celebrate, grieve, and be good company to and with those who are no longer present with us—or, more specifically, those whose presence is now experienced as *a present absence among us*.

The dead, departed, and disappeared are not simply gone, as if they were never here, as if their companionship was only a thing that occurred in the past. The dead, departed, and disappeared are still with us—in part, because we ourselves were co-constituted by and with them and so part of them remains as part of us now; in part, because there is a void left behind where they used to be among us (and this is both true in our communal spaces—an empty chair where they used to sit, a bench they never sleep on anymore, and so on—as it is true of our internal spaces—as any lover who has felt as though their heart was ripped out when their beloved departed can testify); and also, in part, because they have left their mark upon us both physically (perhaps through a quote they left on the wall, or a piece of art or a poem they gave to us) and non-physically (because, after they shared their story with us, there are certain sights and smells and sounds we will now always experience through the lenses they provided).

However, when we think about the presence of the past in the present, we often think about this as something ominous. This is often the case with both trauma and the ways in which violence becomes structured into systems. Thus, for example, when speaking about race relations in the American occupation of Turtle Island, one of Obama's speech writers quotes Faulkner: "The past is never dead. It's not even past." Or, as Philip Baker Hall's character in *Magnolia* asserts, "We may be through with the past, but the past ain't through with us." He makes this statement in the context of a film that demonstrates how the "sins of the fathers" continue to cause affliction in the lives of their (adult) children. As a result, in our collective imaginary, the past is frequently a thing that *haunts* us. On the one hand, this is not surprising, given how much our collective existence here on Turtle Island is premised upon the practice and concomitant denial of genocidal violence but, on the other hand, we often also experience this as individuals. Thus, for example, the paramedics I already mentioned who suicide because they are haunted by the ghosts (something more than memories, something less than corporal bodies) of the children they could not save.[1] In this way, those of us who have come to know and love many who are now dead, murdered, departed, or disappeared may find ourselves increasingly haunted by the presence of their absence. It turns out that the dead, much like the living, clamor for our attention.

Commemorating is one way for us to go about being good company to and with the dead while also continuing to be good company to and with the living. If I spend too much time with my dead, if I constantly dwell on them, seek out the places that remind me of them and am endlessly filled with sorrow and anger and rage about all the ways in which their deaths were brought about because of oppression and apathy, there is a good chance that I, too, will depart the company of the living to join the dead. Therefore, commemorating becomes the means by which I can both carry and bury my dead.

Let me provide an example of this. Approximately seven years ago, and then over a period of several years, I got to know many middle-aged men

---

[1]. I still recall one afternoon in Vancouver when I took a nap on my couch and dreamed that I was napping on that couch and, while I was napping, the ghost of a young woman I worked with and cared deeply about walked passed my window weeping and weeping and weeping.

II. COMMEMORATING

who had spent most of their lives using alcohol to soothe their pain and cope with their traumas (pain and traumas caused by things like residential schools, or abusive parents, or the loss of loved ones, or being systematically targeted, oppressed, and abused by authority figures, or some combination of all of the above plus more). Many of these men, due to their extreme impoverishment and dispossession by all the carceral and "caring" institutions of the State, also found themselves drinking alcohol products that were not intended for consumption (mouthwash and hand sanitizer being the most prominent examples). I became good friends with many of these men and, in fact, started a support group for men who drank alcohol products not intended for consumption that was deliberately *not* a recovery group operating with the goal of abstinence in mind (there were plenty of other groups like that in town and they weren't doing much of anything for these fellows). Instead, the group was intended to be a time of mutual care, when people could share tips or suggestions related to harm reduction or ways in which they could look out for each other, and when people could just be acknowledged, honored, valued, and cared for as people in the company of other people.[2]

Today, all but one of these men are dead. Several of them died painful deaths and lived out their last days feeling utterly rejected, alone, uncared for, and unnoticed. They died like stray dogs struck by cars and left to eventually bleed out or die from dehydration or exposure in a ditch beside the road. They died like they were nothing and nobody and worthless. Eventually their bodies were collected—from a squat, from a bed in a shelter, from a doorway—and taken to the morgue. Some were claimed by family members. Many were not. And that was it. That was all. That was them.

Thinking about these men and all they suffered—along with so many others whom I have also known—can fill me with despair. It can darken my vision. It can make me want to do reckless, hurtful things. It can make me want to die. And so I have created the following ritual for myself: once a year, I buy a few beers—the kind of beers these fellows liked to drink when they didn't have to pinch pennies and find ways to get as drunk as fast as possible with as little cost as possible—and I go down to the river where they liked to drink and I cheers them and I pour some out for them and I have a drink myself with them and tell them about the last year and what is going on and how we still miss them so much and how we wish them well

---

2. Although my employer eventually canceled the group and told me to stop running it because the attendance was too low to justify that use of my time and it didn't produce the stat-able outcomes they were interested in producing to secure funding—after all, the men in the group weren't going on to find secure employment or stable housing; they were just going away from the group feeling a little less alone.

and hope they are finally at peace and that their pain has ended and their traumas have healed and I say thank you very much for everything, for being who you were, for doing the best you could, and we love you and miss you and I'll see you next year. In this way, I mourn them, I celebrate them, I honor them, and I am good company to and with them, while also being able to continue to strive to be good company to and with the living. In this way, in fact, I have learned to be *well-haunted*. For, if you look at the roots of the word "haunt" you will discover that it only means "a place frequently visited," something that is done habitually, and also the act of *going or bringing home*. Of course these men (and others) haunt me. We are homes to one another and, for those who have been forcibly deprived of housing this is no small thing. We become one another's "forever homes" and commemorating is one of the ways in which we acknowledge this. So, to slightly alter the words of Mother Jones, I pray *with* the dead and fight like hell *with* the living.[3] This is what works for me; this is how I can stay balanced.

What works for each of us will not always be the same—but all of us have to find a way to achieve some kind of balance in this area (even if we more-or-less regularly have to make adjustments to maintain that balance) or we will not survive. This is just as true of us as groups as it is of us as individuals. Hence, for example, the annual march in Vancouver's downtown eastside that takes place on February 14 (Valentine's Day according to the Hallmark calendar) to commemorate the lives of women who have been murdered or been disappeared in that neighborhood. Or, to pick another example, the annual march in London, Ontario, which calls to mind women who have been disappeared in this community (an event organized by the friends of Shelley Desrochers, who has been disappeared since 2016) as well as commemorating, naming, and remembering, all those who were murdered in the custody of the local police or the local maximum-security jail. *Co*-mmemoration is a thing that we do *together* as we grieve and celebrate and bury and carry our dead.

But the act is different when we commemorate those who have been disappeared and who now exist, from our perspective, in some kind of limbo between the living and the dead. Here, commemorating means continuing to seek them out, continuing to look for them, and continuing to hold a place for them at the table (perhaps literally, perhaps metaphorically). It means persisting in the state of not knowing I described above without giving up, despairing entirely, or losing your ability to not only search and fight but to also live and feel delight. In fact, *learning to still hold on to this feeling*

---

3. The original wording is "pray for the dead and fight like hell for the living" and it appears in her autobiography. See, Jones, *Autobiography of Mother Jones*, 40–41.

of delight-in-living, and what I have previously discussed as thanksgiving and wonder, is *especially important for us even in the midst of ongoing grieving and not-knowing.*

In fact, the grief we experience due to the murders and forced disappearances of our loves ones can last our whole lives. Here, in our culture that claims to be in denial about death but which actually assigns death and dying to Others who are either said to deserve it—like those who have been criminalized and colonized—or who are said to not matter enough to care about—like those bombed, impoverished, poisoned and dispossessed in faraway lands—and in a culture driven by the immediate gratification of consumers and the high productivity of workers, grief has been pathologized. We have been taught that it is only permissible to grieve in certain ways (nothing too exuberant and certainly nothing disruptive), or for certain lengths of time (at most, in social services, our corporate benefit packages grant us three days leave from work only when an immediate family member dies, and then we are expected to return to regular duties), and if we find ourselves grieving something contextual—like the ongoing existence of oppression, like abusive labor policies, like death-dealing police forces—we are told we need to "focus on the positive" and that we will "catch more flies with honey than with vinegar." All in all, happiness, peace of mind, and a pleasure-filled existence become the mandated norms for us (regardless of how realistic those norms actually are). As a result, those of us who refuse to be comforted (for as long as oppression exists), those of us who refuse to abort our dead before our grieving is completed (which often takes more than three business days for immediate family members but also for friends and acquaintances whose deaths are not covered in our benefits), and those of us who grieve in ways that others find offensive, unhelpful, or just a little too uncalled for ("*Fuck* the police!" we scream as we grieve in the presence of those who have raped, abused, and murdered our loved ones), may actually find ourselves feeling guilty if our grief lessens or if we also feel things like joy or gratitude or delight. This is even more true when we grieve those who have been universally abandoned, neglected, cast down, and ignored to the point of being forgotten. "If my grief lessens," we say to ourselves, "if I am somehow less devastated by your absence, am I not becoming like those who never cared for you at all?" In other words, we often feel like we dishonor those whom we have loved and lost if we, somehow, are not always overwhelmed by the grief we feel when we lost them.

But this is not the case. After all, our loved ones who are now only present as an absence would not want us to live the rest of our lives overwhelmed by grief, devastated by mourning, and vulnerable to being targeted, oppressed and exploited in all the ways they were. They want us to still find joy, delight, wonder, and thanksgiving in life. Of course they do. So we work through our grief, *not so that we can eliminate it but so that we can carry it well.* And we say thank you *so that* we can mourn, and we mourn *so that* we can say thank you, and this is exactly what we do in our acts of commemoration. In this way we avoid the false dichotomy between a death-dealing despair that drives us to suicide (or to a long slow death at the hands of alcohol or an employer who encourages us to work endless overtime) and an equally death-dealing optimism that forces us to say everything is okay, over and over, no matter what and, hey, not only can we profit from this but, in fact, our margin of profit will increase every year no matter what, we promise, and isn't that great, and I'm so happy, I'm so happy all the time.

B. Battered Company
(Destructive Companions)

U p until this point, I have focused on things like being welcoming, kind, gentle, patient, tender-hearted, creative, and thoughtful, with the intent of helping us to collectively work to be good company to and with one another. However, anyone who has stepped into these waters knows how troubled they can be, how difficult this work is, how complicated and intertwined and really fucking fucked up everything actually is. Those who have become jaded, wounded, or otherwise marked by their efforts might, in fact, accuse me of being too idealistic—as if what I am weaving is a sometimes dark but ultimately dangerously unrealistic, over-simplified, and romanticized fairy tale that presents us with a beautiful fantasy that can never be realized in the muck and turmoil and mess of our day-to-day life. In response to this, I wish to say two things.

First, I wish to remind this imaginary critic (and the very real reader) that I am writing what I write based on more than twenty years of lived experience trying to work these things out in environments that others (like my imagined critic, perhaps) continually write off as too challenging, dangerous, unworkable, or hopeless. If I then still sound like a romantic, it's because I love my people, the homes we have made for ourselves, and the life we have created together. I am not a detached observer. I am neither an academic, drawing conclusions about best practice based upon double-blind studies and the latest, most cutting-edge ethnographic research, nor am I a boss in some corporate non-profit, manipulating stats to show how we successfully met the goals established in our strategic action plan so that we can get the money that others would put to better use. I am a lover who has never stopped falling ever more in love, not because I am blind to the mess and fuckery and violence and tragedy and massive obstacles we face, but because I can't stop seeing the wonder, the goodness, the strength, the wisdom, and the incredible sacredness that is found both in individuals who have been oppressed and abandoned by others, and in the ways in which these same people can rise up and live, snatching life out of the jaws of death, or creating it out of nothing. I am not ashamed to proclaim this love. I am proud to love and be loved in this way, in these places, with these people. If that seems too idealistic, too unrealistic to you, then perhaps you need to ask yourself who or what taught you to love in the way that you do.

Second, I will also say this: to suggest that fairy tales are things that we leave behind as we become adults and move from fantasy to reality, to suggest that "real life" is fundamentally different than the worlds we encounter in fairy tales, is itself a fantasy. This is *the fantasy of objectivity*, of factuality, of the at-handedness of reality, and of scientism as expressed at the height of modernity's hubris (although science as it currently exists—especially in the domains of physics, biology, organic chemistry, botany, ecology, cosmology, and even maths [notably pure maths]—has moved well beyond these fantasies, neoliberal economists, developers, and population managers, as well as social-service coordinators, community-health researchers, and many within the psy disciplines still appear stuck in the triumphalistic but not actually all that intelligent European past). As I already described above, we have seen some of the ways in which this fantasy drains not only the world (this river delta, this forest, this marshland, this tree) of any kind of essential lifeforce or sacredness, it also reduces all of us to financialized pragmata—*things* defined by *usefulness* and the *dollar-value* that can be assigned to them. This fantasy is more gruesome than any fairy tale, no matter how far removed those tales are from contemporary sentiments. We see the death-dealing and death-serving consequences of our belief in it all around us, every day. Indeed, from this perspective, some of the beings that we may have treated as *priceless* (this ecosystem, this lifeform, this person, you, me) can now, depending on the circumstances, be considered genuinely *worthless* and be disposed of as such (some people really, truly, actually and factually are *human waste* according to this logic). What a terrible fantasy! What a horrifying fairy tale the vision of reality that has been imposed upon us has proven to be.

But, of course, the terror and the horror are only felt by some. If you are a powerful White man, an engorged capitalist, a rapist cop, or the kind of person who gets rich or hard because of these things, then this is precisely the kind of fairy tale you love. So it turns out that we are, all of us, now living out the fantasies of the most violent people amongst us. And part of the way in which people who delight in serving Death make their fantasies a reality is by convincing us that it is the only reality possible, it is the realest real, and every other vision of what can or could be, is a dream had by children

B. BATTERED COMPANY (DESTRUCTIVE COMPANIONS)

who must inevitably awaken to "the truth" about "the way things are" as they "mature" and become adults. Unfortunately, the truth about the way things are, which we come to accept or resign ourselves to as we age, is so appalling and so unlivable that trying to live within it makes a good many of us go insane—depression, anxiety, nervousness, changes in appetite, narcissism, psychosis, dissociation, loss of sleep, inability to concentrate, memory loss, orgasming too infrequently or too frequently, suicidal or homicidal ideation, fucking madness—these are all symptoms of efforts, conscious or not, to reframe an unlivable reality in order to try and live within it (or in order to resist it). As a result, the management of madness has become one of the biggest hustles going today. Madness, it should be noted, is the term preferred by those who push back against their own pathologization. The more common term used is "mental illness" but, really, neither of these terms quite captures what we are dealing with when it comes to *mental harm*. "Madness" refers to ways of being that resist capture within the status quo and ways of being that are not compliant with the norms of the status quo. "Mental illness" refers to something that (despite lip service paid to psychosocial models) is rooted within the biochemical networks of an individual's brain. *Mental harm* refers to ways in which oppression, impoverishment, neglect, and abuse damage a person in their mind, consciousness, and spirit, as well as in their body because, of course, all of these things are connected.[1]

All that to say this: if you think the ways of sharing life together that I am describing sound like an unrealistic fairy tale, then good! We need a little less of the so-called "realism" we have been taught and a little more of a sense of wonder, creativity, surprise, and openness, longing, desire or faith in the possibility that maybe, who knows but maybe, what we have been taught is impossible might actually be possible, if not today then tomorrow, if not tomorrow then the next day. Because maybe, who knows but maybe, the person to whom you have been entrusted for care (your social worker, your community cop, your uncle, your stepmother, the rulers themselves,

---

1. Thus, while I affirm Ignacio Martín-Baró's affirmation that, far from suffering en masse from "full-blown pathologies," those who are impoverished actually survive that impoverishment because of their "ingenuity, creativity, and energy" (see Martín-Baró, *Writings for a Liberation Psychology*, 90), I also want to recognize that, in my context, solidarity, relationships of mutuality and reciprocity, hope for a better world, and a devotion to building resistance to that which is, as one also builds an alternative society within the shell of the old one, are all largely absent. When this is the case, people become much more vulnerable to being mentally harmed because, in various ways, all of those things help shield us from mental injuries. For more on Mad Studies see, for example, Burstow, *Psychiatry and the Business of Madness*; Burstow et al., *Psychiatry Disrupted*; and LeFrancois et al., *Mad Matters*.

or the senior with candy who comes to your aid when you are lost in the woods), doesn't actually have your best interests at heart. Maybe they actually want to disappear you, or enslave you, or prevent you from breaking out of the role they have assigned to you—from cleaning the cinders in the fireplace, to looking good on the arm of a man, to working hard today and then working harder tomorrow, or to fattening you up for the family dinner. In other words, in one way or another, maybe all they actually want is to despoil and devour you like a werewolf or a wealthy White man. But maybe, who knows but maybe, there are options available to you that they cannot imagine, there are paths to liberation that they cannot see, there are impossible possibilities accessible only to you and not to them—magic and fairies and secret doorways and unexpected allegiances and the uprising of the left-for-dead and the fragility of power and the vulnerability of those who tower over others because they might just be cut down at their roots—like giants on beanstalks, or kid-eaters leaning into open ovens, or those who set out to do great harm but reap, for themselves, what they have sown for others.

However, and this is an important transition point, relating back to the objections raised by my imagined critic, having noted both of these things, it is nonetheless true that things are messy. Things are incredibly complicated and we are trying to built life rafts in stormy seas. Things really are "really fucking fucked up." Not only this but, as I have already begun to suggest in my remarks about fairy tales, there are, indeed, people to whom our communities are not open. In fact, there are *people against whom we must defend our communities*. Cops and real estate developers are the most obvious examples but, of course, we must also defend ourselves against the priorities and values of potential funders, and the influence of moralizing do-gooders, self-aggrandizing philanthrocapitalists, missionaries seeking converts, and White saviors. However, all of these threats are essentially *external* to our communities (even if, due to a lack of other options, we are sometimes forced to gather in spaces they own, surveil, manage and, to the best of their limited abilities, rule over). A much harder fact to face is the observation that sometimes we must defend ourselves against *members of our own communities*.

Sometimes, and this is a great tragedy, people who have been treated cruelly also become cruel in ways that kindness cannot quickly or easily counteract. Sometimes, people who have been preyed upon also become predators who will go on to mirror the actions of bosses, cops, and other abusers, and who will see inclusivity and welcome as things to be exploited to their own advantage. Some cis-men, for example (given that it is overwhelmingly although not exclusively cis-men who act this way), no matter

B. BATTERED COMPANY (DESTRUCTIVE COMPANIONS)

where they are situated in the context of oppression, dispossession, impoverishment, and abandonment, will continue to seek out women or children whom they can abuse in order to, well, in order to achieve any number of things that rapists, batterers, and abusers seek when they inflict harm upon others (a feeling of power, a way to process their own trauma, jouissance, whatever). Sometimes, in other words, people need more support to be good company than the support we can offer. If we then still welcome them into our communities, we put others at risk, for without that additional support (whatever it may be, however much time it might take to become effective), these people will hurt others, and will have a destructive influence upon the community as a whole.

Therefore, no matter how welcoming or kind we aspire to be, it is still necessary for us to recognize our limits and recognize that a refusal to implement boundaries places the most oppressed at risk of experiencing harm even in spaces we desire to designate as safe (or safer). We need to recognize and accept that a refusal or inability put these boundaries in place actually makes us *un*welcoming and *un*kind—in the sense that, if we do not recognize our personal and communal limits or establish boundaries, we actually *undo* our own efforts to be welcoming and kind. In order to do this in a way that is meaningful and effective, this also means occasionally using some kind of force or coercion in order to make people adhere to these limits and boundaries against their own will. Those of us who are kind-hearted, empathetic, and gracious may especially struggle with this but if we do not use some kind of force to impose the will of the community upon those who wish to violate the community or harm an individual member of the community (for example, a violent man who wishes to enter a communal space in order to drag out an ex-partner who has fled from him), then we are permitting violence and men of violence to destroy everything we are trying to build together.

And yet this, too, is an incredibly difficult thing to do well. After all, as already mentioned, these threats do not arise from outside—they arise from within. They come from community members we know and love, they come from those who are oppressed, they come from people who are sometimes admired by others in the community, or from people who also contribute in some very meaningful ways—but they are threats nonetheless. We must address them and deal with them well, but we must seek to do so in ways that do not further the oppression and harm already experienced by the men (and occasionally others) who persist in acting in destructive ways. Therefore, in the three sections that follow I will examine this topic as it relates to three things: establishing alternate courts of justice, restoring ecosystem thriving, and exiling.

i. Alternate Courts of Justice

Justice, in our context, it not only blind—it is ruthless. Over the years, as I have witnessed people who have been impoverished, colonized, and abandoned confronted with the full force of the law, while others with wealth and power are free to overtly engage in any number of activities that are considered crimes when performed by others (from employers who steal wages from workers, to banks who rob low income earners of their houses, to real estate developers who dispossess the already poor and then force them to migrate elsewhere, to social workers knocking back line after line of coke at their work parties), I have come to the conclusion that, in our context, *you get as much justice as you can pay for*. The so-called justice system, in other words, is not so much about "fairness" or "giving people what they deserve" or creating a well-ordered way of living together with one another, as it is about normalizing and enforcing oppression and, more generally, as it is about allowing the agents of the state to claim that they, and they alone, have an exclusive right to use violence in a way that is considered moral or good. This is why those who are on the receiving end of justice—along with their friends and travel companions—often do not refer to the "justice system" and, instead, refer to the "injustice system," or the "juridico-discursive model of power," or the "carceral state."[1] Justice language is *affective* language deployed within the discourse of Western "civilization" to make living as law-abiding citizens something that is *morally compelling* but, for as long as laws are death-dealing and exist in order to favor the property of some over the lives of other, then *justice itself is immoral*. True justice (if we feel like the language of "justice" is something worth holding

---

1. The term "the injustice system" is commonly deployed in communities of struggle, but see also Smith, *The Injustice System*. On "juridico-discursive . . . ," see Foucault, *History of Sexuality*, and any number of others who have engaged with his work; on "the carceral state," see again Foucault, *Discipline and Punish*, but also, for some examples of those who have expanded this analysis, Chase, *Caging Borders and Carceral States*; Oliver, *Carceral Humanitarianism*, and also Wang, *Carceral Capitalism*.

I. ALTERNATE COURTS OF JUSTICE

on to), then actually *requires us to break the law* and, beyond that, it requires us to refuse to treat the justice system or the agents of the state as a default or preferable option when it comes to resolving issues of violence that arise within our own communities. If the so-called "justice system" is one of the most powerful tools deployed to maintain oppression, then we cannot hope to get to a liberated space if we rely on the agents of that system to resolve our conflicts.

Here, we need to be careful because criminalized groups of people (prisoners, outlaw bikers, other organizations that engage in coordinated activities that are criminalized) often mirror, replicate, or even exaggerate the violence, abuse, brutality, and ruthlessness that is practiced by mainstream agents of "justice." Within various subcultures (which brand themselves as "countercultures"), oppressive systems of debt and indebtedness are created, sexual violence is used as threat and punishment, and capital punishment is also deployed. Here, as in mainstream society, the rule of law that operates and the punishments imposed by alternate courts of justice are just as death-dealing and just as death-serving as any state-imposed justice system. Therefore, a first and important lesson for those of us who are seeking alternatives to the current moral and legal ordering of our society is that we must not rush to valorize, romanticize, or *indiscriminately* affirm and support whatever alternative codes of conduct or moral systems already exist "on the street" simply because they present themselves as an alternative to the injustice of our status quo. Many of these options are also unjust. They may provide an alternative, but it's a pretty terrible one (like giving our master a razor to cut us with instead of a whip to whip us with and thinking that this somehow makes us free).

Over against the so-called justice system and the ways in which its violence, ruthlessness, and commitment to serving death are mirrored in some criminalized organizations, two other justice-based models for community transformation have been gaining some traction in social services and in communities of oppressed people themselves. The first is an Indigenous model that has been popularized and adapted by mostly White prison reformers, Mennonite peace activists, or prison abolitionists and it goes by the name of restorative justice. The second, transformative justice, is an independent development that has arisen under the leadership of mostly Black women who are, themselves, members of impoverished communities in the territories occupied by the United States, as a response to the injustice system. It critically engages with restorative justice, frequently overlapping with it but also criticizing it and differentiating itself from it in important ways.

Restorative justice, as my brother Judah explains, employs a needs-based response to crime.[2] Crimes create harm, harms produce needs, justice (in this model) works towards meeting those needs, and, when it is most successful, it brings about healing. Furthermore, not only does restorative justice differ from the justice system in prioritizing the needs of people who are victims of crimes (the justice system prioritizes the punishment of people classified as offenders and the satisfaction, not of the people harmed, but of *the law itself*), it also takes a more comprehensive approach and examines the contexts in which crimes occur (although, perhaps, the correlation it makes between "crime" and "harm" should be questioned, given the ways in which we have already seen how the process of criminalization itself is what drives the production of harm in many cases). Thus, it asks not only about the needs of the person harmed, but also about the needs of the person who committed the offense, and the needs of the community. Healing (rather than the punishment of those who offend) becomes something that is directed at people who have been harmed first and foremost, but also at people who cause harm, and at the community more broadly.

However, while restorative justice's professed orientation around the needs of the person harmed are admirable, in practice the model has been criticized for actually centering people who offend and their needs. Recalling that much of the popularization of this model came from prison reformers or abolitionists who were advocating on behalf of offenders (who were—usually very appropriately—seen as victims of the injustice system of the State), it is fair to say that this took place more regularly twenty-five years ago than it does now. However, the model also only works where the person who causes harm is willing to admit to their guilt and is then also willing to participate in some kind of mediation or resolution process. This presents a pretty narrow window for work. This window is only further narrowed when we recognize that not all people who have been harmed will want to participate in this process as well. Not only this but restorative justice can face serious limits because of its choice to (sometimes) operate within systems and institutions that are hostile towards structural criticisms (prison officials, for example, are not particularly inclined to listen to criticisms of how criminalization, rather than certain crimes, is the major source of harm and about how prisons, themselves, are a huge source of harm and actually produce criminality itself). In other words, although a good many practitioners of restorative justice have strong feelings about the fundamentally abusive, oppressive, and colonizing role played by the police, the courts,

---

2. On this and what follows regarding restorative justice, see Oudshoorn, *Little Book of Restorative Justice for Sexual Abuse*, 24–26; and also Oudshoorn, *Trauma-Informed Youth Justice in Canada*, 155–79.

I. ALTERNATE COURTS OF JUSTICE

and the prisons, they make a strategic choice to mute themselves so that they can still operate in partnership with those institutions, hoping to accomplish some good by doing so (I say this not to criticize them—I wish them all the best and only worry that they will find those environments too overwhelming and their partners too cruel, and I worry about what that will do to them and their devotion to others). However, in practice, this means that restorative justice can end up being fairly closely wed to the paradigms, perspectives, and overall worldview of the so-called criminal justice system itself, even though practitioners push back against that as best as they are able. As with even the slightest change or the tiniest reform, the institutional changes brought about by restorative justice practitioners—like being able to do their work within prisons—only came after considerable work, against great opposition, despite chronic underfunding, and the ever-present risk of job termination; in fact, the mainstreaming of restorative justice in some Canadian prisons is an excellent example of the sort of ambiguity and hybridity produced by struggles against oppression; here, reformers are trying to coopt systems and systems are trying to coopt reformers and both things are happening simultaneously in complex ways.

Alongside of restorative justice, and sometimes in critical conversation with it, members of impoverished Black communities, especially Black women, began to develop their own alternative model of justice. Having seen the ways in which the deeply racist prison industrial complex devastated Black communities in the American occupation of Turtle Island, practitioners of transformative justice are committed abolitionists. As Mariame Kaba and Shira Hassan state in their aptly titled *Fumbling Towards Repair*, "Prison Industrial Complex (PIC) abolition is a political vision with the goal of eliminating imprisonment, policing, and surveillance, and creating lasting alternatives to punishment and imprisonment."[3] However, there is no denying that some people in prisons have done very harmful things and, in transformative justice, there is no desire to give rapists, abusers, or other (usually) men of violence, a "get out of jail free card" so that they can continue to harm others. Transformative justice, then, is continually developed when we, as communities, decide that the police and prisons are just not a good or viable way to solve our problems together. According to Kaba and Hassan, transformative justice is defined as follows: "Transformative justice (TJ) seeks to provide people who experience violence with immediate safety and long-term healing and reparations while holding people who commit violence accountable within and by their communities."[4] This

---

3. Kaba and Hassan, *Fumbling Towards Repair*, 13.
4. Kaba and Hassan, *Fumbling Towards Repair*, 21.

model then exists, as Erica Meiner points out, "in an uncomfortable alliance with the more established and recognized practice of restorative justice."[5] While restorative justice is primarily apolitical and sometimes does (but also sometimes doesn't) align with the state, transformative justice is explicitly political and actively working to accomplish its goals outside of the structures of the state.[6] While doing this, it pursues the following goals: 1. survivor safety, healing, and agency; 2. accountability and transformation of those who abuse or cause harm; 3. community response and accountability; and 4. transformation of the community and social conditions that create and perpetuate violence—systems of oppression, exploitation, domination, and state violence.[7] Thus, the focus falls much more heavily both on the well-being of the survivor (note the absence of victim language here) as well as on the need for accountability not only in relation to those who abuse or cause harm (note the absence of offender language) but also in relation to the community as a whole. Here, the politics of transformative justice comes to the fore. We are not looking at simply helping a few individuals to heal in relation to a seemingly "one-off event." We are working to create transformed communities where such "one-off events" are *less likely to occur* and, when they do occur, are handled in a much better way *within and by the community itself*. This is not a model that wants to tweak the system a little bit here and there in order to meet the needs of a few people. This is a model that requires us to systematically overhaul how we share life together, beginning from the understanding of the ways in which we, collectively, share in the production of abuse or harm.

Here, I believe it is of the utmost importance that we attend once again to the words of Cyrée Jarelle Johnson already quoted above (in the section about Inter- and Intra-Connectedness). Johnson states the following:

> Personally, I believe the accountability model is a conservative and confessional one. It stops at the level of admitting to the violence—an important step but only the first one . . . This model forgets that *abuse thrives in silence and isolation, and that can only occur when a community turns away from great injustice.* Thus, whole communities are implicated in all instances of child sexual abuse. I don't need anyone to confess their guilt publicly—I already know who harmed me, and in many cases, so does

---

5. Quoted in Kaba and Hassan, *Fumbling Towards Repair*, 22.
6. As per Shira, quoted in Kaba and Hassan, *Fumbling Toward Repair*, 22.
7. Kaba and Hassan, *Fumbling Towards Repair*, 21.

I. ALTERNATE COURTS OF JUSTICE

everyone else. *I need a community where everyone recognizes the role they played in the violation.*[8]

Yet, as we have seen already—from public health officials who say "not our fault" in response to news of a man dying in a porta-potty, to social services saying "we're on the right side already" in response to challenges from the Black Lives Matter uprising, to police officers emphasizing that they only used lethal force because they "feared for their lives," to funders emphasizing the need for services to produce measurable outcomes to demonstrate their utility, to city managers working hand-in-glove with real-estate developers to produce "a more livable city" (by which, of course, they mean a city where the impoverished have been removed from public spaces, where public spaces have been privatized, and where the wealthy can work and play and enjoy themselves without discomfort or fear)—the way of structuring life together that dominates our contemporary society is one that is premised upon *the denial of any shared responsibility* and *the refusal to be held accountable* (especially if those doing the accounting are situated on the bottom or outside of the hierarchies of power that dominate us). Furthermore, as I have personally learned over and over again, if we try to direct this emphasis on responsibility and accountability back upon ourselves and the organizations in which we work, we will always be treated as problematical, troublesome, or "not a nice team player." In fact, there is a good chance that we will be disciplined, punished, or terminated from our positions, if we persist in this work, no matter how monumental our efforts to be sensitive and use a "soft touch" when bringing these matters into focus. Thus, as Sarah Schulman aptly observes, a great deal of the "pain, destruction, waste, and neglect" that we or others experience in life occurs because of "our resistance to facing and resolving problems," which, Schulman goes on to say, "is overwhelmingly a refusal to change how we see ourselves in order to be accountable."[9] However, Schulman also quickly clarifies that such openness to accountability, and willingness to face and resolve problems, must necessarily be a feature of our *collective* life together. She writes: "At the center of my vision is the recognition that above all, it is the community surrounding a conflict that is the source of its resolution. The community holds the crucial responsibility to resist overreaction . . . and to offer alternatives of understanding and complexity."[10]

---

8. Kaba and Hassan, *Fumbling Towards Repair*, 58; emphases added. Thus, while the old saying that "it takes a village to raise a child" is certainly true, it is equally true that it takes a village to *abandon* a child.

9. Schulman, *Conflict Is Not Abuse*, 20.

10. Schulman, *Conflict Is Not Abuse*, 20.

Therefore, as suggested by the title of Kaba and Hassan's book, to engage in communal acts of transformative justice (a transformed model of justice, a form of justice that requires *all of us to be transformed*) is extraordinarily difficult and messy work, especially given that we don't have recourse to the overwhelming brute force of the State, and given that we often lack models to help us know how to work this out on the ground. We fumble towards repair and, even if we do so with the utmost caution, people still get hurt, people still get misled, and people still end up feeling betrayed, let down, or retraumatized.

Over time, I have come to the conclusion that learning to deal with internal conflicts well is, perhaps, the most difficult intra-community work that we do. I am still learning as I go. I am still dissatisfied with how well communities I have been a part of forming have learned how to do this. I am still dissatisfied with how well *I* have learned how to do this. This is partly why, in this section, I spend time highlighting other models. We need to be attentive to them and learn from them. They may be fumbling, too, but a good many of them have learned a lot more than we have and are further down the road—the road they made by walking—than we are. Therefore, in the next two sections, I will look at two outcomes (one more ideal, one less ideal) that can occur when we, as communities, attempt to implement our own court of justice, live by our own standards, and not appeal to the racist, classist, colonialist violence of the agents of the State to enforce our norms.

However, before describing those things, there is one last thing I wish to emphasize. Here, perhaps more so than any other area, it is essential that we only attempt to engage in this kind of effort if we are, in fact, thoroughly *members of the community in which we work and are recognized as such by the other community members*. This is work that only insiders can do. This is well illustrated in the documentary *The Interrupters*, which looks at how formerly high-ranking gang members in Chicago now work to mediate and resolve gang violence there.[11] They broker ceasefires, arrange deals, and work to peacefully resolve conflicts, precisely and *only* because they have the respect, recognition, and credibility within the gangs to do this work. Therefore, we can only dare to think that we have the right or ability or smarts needed to engage in this kind of work if others in the community

---

11. See, *The Interrupters* (2011), directed by Steve James. Highly recommended! "Violence Interrupters" are one part of the CeaseFire anti-violence model that was developed in Chicago until funding was cut in 2013 and the Chicago Police—who already did not want to work with former gang members in the CeaseFire program—got their wish and more punitive "anti-gang" (i.e., anti-Black) laws were implemented. CeaseFire was one local implementation of the "Cure Violence" model developed by Gary Slutkin—for more detail, see here: https://cvg.org/who-we-are/.

I. ALTERNATE COURTS OF JUSTICE

have affirmed this about us. Short of that kind of trust, rapport, respect, and mutuality existing, there is a good chance our efforts in this regard will be experienced as another form of colonizing, evangelizing, or policing (and there is a good chance that, if we insist on doing this work despite these warnings, we will do more harm than good). Consequently, if you do not exist in the community in this way, if community members have not come to you to ask you to help with this work, you need to do what you can to develop communal spaces and cultures so that this work can be done, and to build up those who are *already* doing it or who *can* do it. In other words, step aside. Take a supporting role. Get out of the way, and support those who are already doing a good thing to do it to the best of their abilities.

ii. Restoring Ecosystem Thriving

Broadly speaking, the injustice system doles out punishment in order to satisfy the law (which, itself, is in the service of Death, given its rootedness in imperialism, colonialism, racial capitalism, and, ultimately, the creation and justification of hierarchies of power and wealth between individuals and groups). "Street justice" and "prison justice" frequently mimic and reinforce these dynamics, even if they create courts of justice that exist outside the structures of the state. Restorative justice and transformative justice offer alternatives that focus not on punishment but on healing. For both, this shift of focus to healing is gained from looking at Indigenous politics the ways in which Indigenous peoples (from the Quechua and the Mayan, to the Tseil-Waututh and Anishinaabe, to the Sami and the Yakut, to the Maasai and the San, to the Hmong and the Rohingya, to the Māori and the Koori) go about doing justice in their communities.

However, two things should be noted here. First, a focus upon healing can very easily fit into the ways in which the medical model is currently deployed in order to justify the use of force upon the bodies and communities of those who are considered "in the way" or "problematical" for the goals of neoliberal capitalism and those who profit from it. I have spent a considerable amount of time criticizing that in this book, and I am concerned that, in our contemporary context, we are not well-equipped to speak of (or understand) "healing." Such language, and such a focus, must be treated with a caution and care (and, I think, the need for transformative justice to arise in response to restorative justice, and criticisms of transformative justice that have arisen by those who are immersed within it, affirm this point).

Second, to say that "Indigenous peoples" can be put together into a single whole that shares a single value is overly simplistic. I have named only a very, very few. In Canadian-occupied territories alone, there are at least 634 known sovereign Indigenous peoples. Globally, thousands of independent nations of Indigenous peoples account for 6 percent of the world

II. RESTORING ECOSYSTEM THRIVING

population (but, it should be noted, 15 percent of those who have been most impoverished around the world). While there are some similarities between groups, each group also has elements that are unique to them and specific to their context.

For example, the Inuit Qaujimajatuqangit (IQ; already mentioned in the section on Comforting), does not speak so much of "healing" as it speaks about "making able human beings," "working together for the common good," "living in respectful relationships with all beings" (including past and future generations of beings), and, in situations of conflict, *restoring harmony*. Punishment is not generally a part of this—experience showed that those who violated the IQ would face natural consequences that were undesirable—but the focus on the wholeness, wellness, and balance *of individuals as members of a group* and *of the group itself* was a major priority.[1] This leads to the guiding principle of *aajiqatigiingniq* ("working together to deal with threats to social harmony and balance"), which Rhoda Karetak describes as follows:

> The purpose of the *aajiiqatigiingniq* system was to ensure that *inuutsiargniq* (wellness) was continually supported by the community. *Aajiqatigiingniq* is related to *parnangniq tuavinngin-nirlu* (carefully planning without rushing) . . . it was a careful and thoughtful process used to seek solutions when there were issues facing a person or family, or which impacted negatively on the community. The process was not employed lightly. Negative habits or behaviours were always quickly and strongly confronted as soon as they were noticed. If a person did not change their behaviour, then community caregivers—usually Elders and people significant to the person doing wrong—would gather to set a plan in motion to correct the wrongdoing. We used to bring the people to account and we helped them to understand the consequences of their behaviours for everyone. As well, there was support provided for the person to correct the behaviour. Each person in the *aajiiqatigiingniq* process had a role to play in supporting the individual to improve. *Aajiiqatigiingniq* was intended as a process to restore the individual to well-being and to being a productive, caring member of the community.[2]

Atuat Akittiq describes the process in this way:

> In the past, people who broke the laws [that is, the IQ] of the Inuit would be counselled by their own people. I am sure the

---

1. See Karetak et al., *Inuit Qaujimajatuqangit*, 3–5.
2. Quoted in Karetak et al., *Inuit Qaujimajatuqangit*, 11–12.

> Elders wanted to counsel anyone who was caught breaking the law more than once, to find out why they kept repeating something that was not accepted. The person might not completely stop what they had been doing right away, but they would get warnings and also support to change. There were no policemen, so the accused would not end up going to jail, but Elders would ask the parties involved to confess a wrongdoing, forgive each other and move on ...
>
> In my parents' day when an accused person needed to be brought back into harmony, the council of Elders would gather around the accused and counsel the person. All the people involved would be asked to speak—and the accused as well. The expectations were set for how to live well, and the Elders offered support for the person to meet these expectations in the future. After that, they all forgave each other and everyone moved on to live in harmony with each other ... Some people changed for the better and others remained unchanged. A person who would not conform might be removed from the family or group for everyone's safety.[3]

"Without harmony," Joe Karetak and Frank Tester go on to say, "Inuit—and all people—are individually and collectively out of balance. Violence and mistrust replace a common purpose with self-interest, driving individuals to step on the person beside them."[4] Mark Kalluak summarizes this as follows:

> Life means being in harmony with people, land and all living things, and respecting them. Life is more enjoyable when we follow these expectations. Being happy was encouraged by our Elders. Living harmoniously and helping our fellow human beings was the way to maintain happiness.[5]

Thus, not so much "healing" (which we tend to subsume under the category of "health") as the restoration of harmony that produces both individual and collective wellness (which, again, should not be immediately correlated with "health"), so that people can pursue a common goal, are at the center of how Inuit peoples resolve conflicts.

However, some of the discomfort raised about restorative justice as it was practiced twenty years ago, may be relevant. There is the concern

---

3. Karetak et al., *Inuit Qaujimajatuqangit*, 125; I will have more to say on this removal in the next section, "Exiling."

4. Karetak et al., *Inuit Qaujimajatuqangit*, 12.

5. Karetak et al., *Inuit Qaujimajatuqangit*, 43.

II. RESTORING ECOSYSTEM THRIVING

that the needs of the person who caused the harm may be prioritized over the needs of the person harmed; there is the concern that a person may be asked to forgive when forgiveness is not what they desire (forgiveness was mentioned by Atuat Akittiq above—thankfully, restorative justice as a practice has moved away from its earlier focus on forgiveness as a one-size-fits-all cure) and there is the concern that the restoration of harmony may require people to go back to relationships that are not desirable, rather than reorganizing communal space so that relationships and the ways in which people are inter- or intra-connected can be transformed. I am not sufficiently knowledgeable about IQ and Inuit ways of doing justice, as those have actually played out over time in various Inuit communities, to know how substantial these concerns are (in fact, it may be that none of these concerns are legitimate—for example, addressing the needs of a person who has caused harm does not necessarily require us to neglect or not prioritize the needs of the person harmed, having forgiveness be a topic of conversation does not necessarily mean that people are being forced to forgive when they do not want to be forgiving, and restoring harmony does not necessarily mean that a person go back to a potentially harmful or now fundamentally upsetting and unsafe situation). These are just things that I wonder when I consider the descriptions provided above—and I wonder these things, not so much because I worry about IQ (I do not worry about IQ at all—it would be absurd for me, a colonizer living outside of the artic, to do so) but because I worry about how well-intentioned do-gooders in my context might poach from IQ and use it in ways that it should not be used, to produce outcomes it should not produce.

However, given my own context, I have very mixed feelings about centering the notion of "harmony" or "restoring harmony" when we seek to address conflicts and respond to people who act destructively. The theme of harmony is all too often deployed in my context as a tool used to defend a harmful status quo—"don't rock the boat," "kill 'em with kindness," "you catch more flies with honey than with vinegar," and all that bullshit (I mean, who said I wanted to catch any flies??). Here, again, the criticism is not of IQ or of how Inuit peoples have gone about structuring life together as it is about romanticizing others, and thinking we can take what we like from their romanticized cultures, without attending sufficiently to our own culture, and expect the kinds of results we romantically imagine others always attaining.

For myself, the paradigm that I find most useful is not "health and healing," or "crime and punishment," or "restoring harmony," or, in fact, anything that includes the word "justice" in its name. Rather, as I have thought about all these models, I have concluded that the model that most accurately expresses what I think we are all trying to accomplish when we deal with conflicts and with destructive companions is *the restoration of thriving to ecosystems that have been injured and the restoration of thriving to individuals who have been injured within those ecosystems*. Furthermore, or rather, at the same time, given that each individual fills a unique niche within an ecosystem and contributes in unique way to the thriving of the whole, we cannot separate these two things, and must understand them as intra-connected components of a single task—the task of *contributing to thriving* (about which I will say more in the conclusion about "Loving and Raging in the Mean Time"). Focusing on the thriving of individuals as members of a community, and how this relates to the thriving of the whole community, while *simultaneously* focusing on the thriving of the community and how this relates to the thriving of the individual members of that community, is what I believe should guide our work when navigating conflicts and working with destructive companions. To me, in my context, this seems to be a safer and clearer way to speak about what others have said in other contexts about things like restoring harmony, individual and collective healing or wellness, and working together towards a common goal.

This carries several implications (two of which I will explore here). First of all, it means that we do not see any conflict or opposition between the needs of a person who has been harmed, the need to prevent harm from occurring and, most especially, prevent the most oppressed, abandoned, and marginalized members of our communities from being exposed to potential harm, *and* the needs of the community as a whole. When we prioritize the needs of those who have been harmed and those who are most at risk of experiencing ongoing or future harm, we are doing the very best work for *the community itself*, because, of course (and it bears repeating), each person has their unique niche and role within the community and the community cannot be what it is and cannot fully thrive if any person is being harmed within it or by it—"an injury to one, is an injury to all."[6] This means, for example, that if a charismatic spokesperson within our community ends up being an abuser of their intimate partner or their children, or whomever else, we do not sacrifice the well-being or needs of those who were abused because we are afraid of the repercussions for the community if it becomes known that this person is an abuser or if this person is no longer a spokesperson for the community. Those who protect abusers out of some imagined commitment to "the greater good" or "our collective well-being" are simply operating from a misconception of what constitutes "the greater

---

6. A slogan popularized by the Industrial Workers of the World and credited to David C. Coates. See Haywood, *Autobiography of Big Bill Haywood*, 186.

good" or "our collective well-being." It is not good for any of us or for our community as a whole if we permit people to get away with abusing others simply because of the niche they currently fill or the role that they play. We are fundamentally mistaken if we think we can get where we want to go if we sacrifice some of the most vulnerable and oppressed members of the community along the way. Doing so actually demonstrates that we are going in the entirely wrong direction. This is where those who are fond of Nelson Mandela's statement that "a nation should not be judged by how it treats its highest citizens, but it's lowest ones," are entirely correct.[7]

The insights of anarchist anthropologists paired with everything we are now learning about ecological developmental biological evolution and the co-constituting dynamic and blurred boundaries between organisms and environments are highly relevant here. Getting by and getting ahead isn't about "survival of the fittest" wherein only the strongest or most ruthlessly self-interested survive—it's about *all of us collaboratively working together* to make sure that we do our utmost *to leave nobody behind, push nobody down, and leave nobody out* as we strive to get to where we want to go *together*. If you think you have to sacrifice the most vulnerable to get there, you're wrong. Any such sacrifice is proof that you are, in fact, going in an entirely different direction despite where you say you desire to go.

Secondly, this also means that those who harm others—and who refuse to take responsibility for themselves but who continue to look for opportunities to inflict harm on others still have a unique niche they fill within our communities and roles that only they can fulfill in the way that they fulfill them. This means that, when trying to address harms and confront destructive companions, we are operating from the premise that, in fact, *they are still our companions*. They are still members of our community. They are still people who, although they are destructive in some ways, are also creative and contributing to our mutual thriving in other ways. Consequently, we neither seek to return harm-for-harm, nor do we rush to turn such people over to the disciplinary forces of the State (who will certainly inflict great harm upon them and who will almost certainly ensure that the people handed over to them become thoroughly entrenched in an ever-deepening cycle of harming-and-being-harmed). Instead, as with transformative and

7. Mandela, *Long Walk to Freedom*. Often neglected in the more bougie and liberal appropriations of Mandela's work (after all, Mandela was committed to the use of illegal, revolutionary violence and terror in the pursuit of liberation), is the opening portion of this quotation: "No one truly knows a nation until one has been inside its jails" and then the more famous sentence follows. Thus, Mandela is asking us to not only evaluate ourselves and our politics from the perspective of, say, a homeless fourteen-year-old girl, but from the perspective of *those whom we feel most justified in abusing*, abandoning, and leaving for dead.

restorative justice practitioners, as well as many Indigenous models of addressing harm, we seek to assist the person in taking responsibility for their own actions, we seek to hold them accountable and ensure they take accountability for themselves, and then we seek to implement whatever changes are necessary to meet the needs of the person or people harmed and the needs of the person who has caused the harm so that that person is meaningfully supported to *stop engaging in harm*. Sometimes this is easy to do, sometimes it is very difficult to do, and sometimes it is impossible (a theme I will pick up in the next section, "Exiling"). Here, this can be understood as "restoring harmony" so long as that work is not, in any way, taken to mean returning to the status quo that existed when the harm was taking place. After all, sometimes the best way to restore harmony between people is to ensure that they have space from one another (for example, the best way for my ex-wife and me to restore harmony with one another was for us to stop being married to each other) and sometimes the best way to restore harmony within a community is to significantly reorient the ways in which that community is structured. In other words, while communities will always have certain boundaries and certain defining features, it is also necessary that communities possess the kind of fluidity necessary to continually reduce the possibility for harm, to continually address harms that do occur, and to continually contribute to the establishment of a feedback loop built around thriving.

However, recognizing the presence of destructive companions also raises the question of how open our communities can or should be. On the one hand, it reminds those of us who seek to create spaces that are safe(r), welcoming, and useful to those who have been excluded from essentially all other communities or public spaces that we cannot put some community members in harms way just because we want to be welcoming to everyone who comes to us seeking good company. On the other hand, it speaks to the need for some spaces to be more exclusive. Sex workers really do need "sex worker only" spaces. Those who identify as female (cis and trans) who are fleeing from domestic violence really do need spaces free of those who identify as male (cis and trans). And those who identify as male really do benefit from (cis and trans) male-only groups related to taking responsibility for harming others. It is important to maintain and recognize the value of *variously bounded communities within one overarching community*. Each ecosystem, after all, is itself a part of a network of other ecosystems and, much like individuals within an ecosystem, each ecosystem will thrive to a far greater degree if the overall network exists and is thriving. We need to work and network to both ensure that there is a space for everyone and that

II. RESTORING ECOSYSTEM THRIVING

there are some spaces for certain people and not for others. When this is the case, we can truly thrive together.

However, recognizing our own boundaries and the limits we have to impose on openness, can be challenging for those of us who are working to carve out a safe place for and with people who have been denied access to all other (safe or not-at-all safe) places. In particular, when the reality of our context is that some people have literally nowhere else they can go that is safe, and when these same people then persist in acting in ways that are destructive to others and to the community itself, in the community spaces we help to hold and maintain, we sometimes feel obligated to continue to hold space for these people—even in the absence of any taking-of-responsibility, or any commitment to change that is demonstrated in real change taking place, or any willingness to be accountable for anything at all—because we do not want to cast these destructive companions out into a world where no safe or good options are available to them. As a result, other community members are placed in harm's way and, sometimes, very real, lasting, and devastating harms follow. Thus, even the most welcoming, kind, gentle, affectionate, and comforting communities must still turn away some community members who come to them seeking good company. It is this theme that will be explored in more detail now.

iii. Exiling

I spent much of the first half of my life trying to figure out how to have a relationship with my father. After he forcibly deprived me of housing when I was a youth, I decided to forgive him (although, with the support of his church elders, I was actually the one forced to apologize to him—for secretly skipping school and forging notes to get out of class—before he would speak to me again). But, as I went through my twenties, I found it difficult to maintain a relationship with him. It seemed that what I desired to receive from him as a father—love and support and attentiveness and care—was not forthcoming. Instead, I found myself using up large amounts of my own energy trying to meet his emotional needs. And I put in this work while he simultaneously found ways to subtly belittle, mock, cut down, or lie about my experiences, my achievements, and any recollection of the ways in which he abused his children when they were young. I found my interactions with him were often exhausting and distressing—both because I sought what he would not give me and because what he did give to me was a continuation of the abuse I had already experienced in much more physical and terrifying ways as an infant, as a child, and as a teenager. Then, around the time my son was born, my father began to threaten both me and my family (because I had started talking publicly about some of the abuse I had experienced from him). At that point, I decided to cut off all contact with him and, in fact, I did not see him or speak with him for the next seven years. However, at the age of thirty-six, I found myself once again living in the same city as him. I debated on whether or not I should contact him and decided to do so. At this time, I found that I was able to manage my feelings about our interactions much better because I had entirely given up on expecting him to meet any of my emotional needs or care for me in any way that felt meaningful to me. However, I found much of his behaviors were still the same—still the same narcissistic focus upon himself, still the same micro-aggressions, and still the same self-justification (no matter

III. EXILING

how contradictory his stories were they always led to the same conclusion "any harm I caused, if I caused harm, and I probably didn't really, and other people have been harmed a whole lot more than my kids were harmed and they turned out just fine, *is not my fault!*"). This did not hurt me as much as it did in the past because I genuinely expected nothing else from him at this point, but it also made me question what point or purpose was being served by me continuing to have an active relationship with him. This questioning only deepened over the next couple of years as I began to recover memories of sexual abuse I had experienced as a small child.[1] I decided to tell my dad about these memories and gave him the opportunity to take responsibility for himself so that we could have a more genuine relationship with each other. Alternatively, if he did not wish to do that, I gave him the option of denying any responsibility and choosing to end our relationship with one another. He chose the latter option. Since then, I have not had any contact with my father and I have no plans of seeing him again while he is alive.

In the past, when I have talked about the loss of my father in my life (a loss that goes back to the very beginning of my life, given that my father was rarely anything but a source of terror and pain to me when I was young), I have often referred to this as a sort of amputation. Undoubtedly, my father has lived his life as a wounded man. He was abused and traumatized in many ways as a child and, despite the patience and long-suffering of those around him, he never did the work necessary to heal and ensure that he did not pass his pain and trauma on to the next generation. Perhaps he could not. Perhaps he chose not to. Either way, the end result was the same. My father is wounded and he cannot or will not do what he needs to do in order to stop harming and exploiting and using up the people closest to him. My father, in other words, became like a gangrenous limb upon my body, and no treatment, no matter how patient, no matter how painful to the rest of the body, no matter how creative, no matter how successful with other gangrenous limbs, succeeded in preventing the rot from spreading. In such an instance, the gangrenous limb must be removed from the body so that the rest of the body does not die. The rest of the body will then live but it will always live with the absence of that limb (and, at least in this context, I can attest to the reality of phantom-limb syndrome, where you still feel the limb, it's pain, it's presence, even though it is no longer visibly present). However, I have also learned that, once we get passed ableist biases and preconceptions, it is entirely possible to live a happy, healthy, whole, and sometimes even a better life (sometimes even a much, much better life) with one less limb. Not only this but sometimes I imagine that the gangrenous

---

1. I explore this in some detail in my novel, *Magnificent Work*.

limb, itself, actually has no desire to harm or kill the rest of the body—or, if it is so wounded and so focused on it's own attachment to the body regardless of if that kills the whole body including itself, then I imagine that there was a time when it was younger, perhaps before it became as wounded as it ended up becoming, that it hoped or wished to not harm others in the ways it had been harmed.

However, I have moved away from thinking with the help of this simile. I have grown to distrust any kind of enframing or narrative or storytelling that, somehow, someway, equates people with disease and then uses that equation to do something to those people that those people wish was not done to them. We saw the almost limitless violent potential of this kind of language used in multiple genocides and ethnic or political cleansings in the twentieth century—notably but far from exclusively in fascist-occupied territories in the middle of the century, wherein others, like Jews or Roma or Socialists or Communists were painted as a disease that needed to be destroyed in order to make society pure and healthy—and, having collectively failed to learn our lesson, we still see the ways in which communities of people "flagged as public health concerns," are then confronted with the full force of the State. It is best, I decided, to drop the metaphor and speak plainly. Thus reworded, the conclusion is as follows: my father appears to be incapable of being in a relationship with me that does nothing but cause me harm and, based on the evidence accumulated over three-and-one-half decades, it appears that there is nothing that can be done to change this. Therefore, for my own well-being, it is necessary that I no longer have contact with my father.

This is a real loss to me. It creates an absence in my life.[2] I mourn that absence and loss but I also recognize that the life I live now is fuller and better than it would have been if I had persisted in returning to be abused over and over again by him. I also like to think that this is what is best for my father—surely it is better for him not to be able to cause harm to me, surely that is also not good for him—but I'm not so sure about that. I'm cautious about the self-comfort and self-justification involved in claiming that. Maybe it's not better for him—he certainly would say that it is hurtful to him—but it is necessary nonetheless. Be that as it may, I do know that, even though I have no contact with him, I do not actively wish harm upon him and I also recognize that, in other environments and in other relationships,

---

2. I would have liked to have had an honest, gentle, tender-hearted, kind and comforting father, but I never did. So, in a way, the absence of my father as the father I desire to have goes back to when I was born, and I just finally and fully accepted this at the point when I respected his choice to not take responsibility for himself and to leave him to himself.

III. EXILING

he is capable of being a better man (his students, for example, always spoke very highly of his talent and of his charisma as a teacher). As much as he is able without hurting others, I hope that he is happy. Cutting off contact with my father is essentially what is necessary for my own thriving and, in fact, *the kindest thing I can think to do* for and with him, given the lack of real alternatives. And, really, at the end of the day, if oppressors are dehumanized by their participation in oppression (and I believe that they are), then *removing my father from an environment where he has the ability to oppress is actually a part of his liberation* from the context of oppression just as it is also a part of mine.[3]

But this is the point I want to make by telling this story about my relationship with my father: there will also be members in our communities who are like my father. There will be those who cannot or will not (who can say?) change their ways. There will be those who continue to seek to cause harm to others or who continue to deny they are responsible for causing the harms that they cause (and who, therefore, continue to cause those harms). And there will be those whom we have to remove from the community (sometimes for a short time, sometimes for a long time), because the community and individual members therein, will not be able to thrive—in fact, they will do the opposite of thriving; they will suffer, wither, and either transform into something much less than they could have been or die altogether—for as long as such destructive companions are permitted to be present as *destructive companions*.

At this point, liberals who are uncomfortable with the ways in which I have criticized them thus far may feel like they can turn the tables on me. In fact, by calling for the necessity of exiling some people from our communities, some critics may wish to suggest that I am no different than those whom I have so strongly criticized throughout this book—I'm still including some, abandoning others, working with some and not working with others, and, although I posture as if I am oh-so-kind-hearted and caring, I am actually just the same as them. Generally, when you criticize people with power for their hypocrisy, they are delighted when they feel like the can throw the same charge back in your face—it makes them feel like they can, once again, avoid acknowledging their own guilt or shame. They use the counter-charge of my supposed hypocrisy as an excuse to not actually engage with the substance of the criticisms I have raised. So they sneer, and

---

3. Even though, as I mentioned earlier, oppressors tend to see those who offer them liberation from their participation in oppression as cruel, insensitive, or mean-spirited, whereas the oppressed tend to have very different feelings about opportunities for liberation from the context of oppression—because, obviously, the former benefit a great deal from that context while the latter suffer a great deal from the same.

they hiss, and they laugh and high five, and then go home and take a Trazadone or a Zopiclone so that they can continue to sleep the sleep of the just.

Perhaps not surprisingly, my father provides one of the most obvious examples of how this argument can be deployed. To paraphrase from memory, when I was cutting off contact with him the first time, he said something like the following to me:

> How can you claim to care so much about people who are suffering and abandoned by others, and yet choose to hurt me? You're a liar, Dan, and you're lying to yourself about the kind of person you are. You're not a good person. If you were who you say you are, you wouldn't do this to me.

Now, of course, all of this neglects my father's adamant refusal to take responsibility for himself, his inability to accept any means of being held accountable, the ongoing harm that he did to me, and the fact that, for more than thirty years, I did try to work this out by every other avenue I could imagine. It's a fairly straightforward example of a man who persistently harms others who tries to paint himself as the victim of those whom he has harmed when they choose to withdraw from his company.

However, individuals, institutions, and agencies who respond to those of us working to build life-giving and life-affirming community spaces by saying, "You exclude people, too!" use that as a reason to not listen to criticisms that are raised about more death-dealing and death-serving arrangements. To refuse to recognize the legitimacy of the police, to work towards decarceration, to resist those who normalize the violence of oppression and pathologize the dispossessed, and to try and move towards the kind of world where we recognize the specialness (belovedness), worthiness, and inter- and intra-connectedness of *all* people does not mean that there are not times when, *here and now*, in *this place*, with *these people*, boundaries must be maintained, and some people may not be permitted into the community space or may be required to leave it. Suggesting otherwise would be like thinking we could invite David Grossman to come and teach our local cops to be better killers (this is his speciality—he is a police trainer with expertise in what he refers to as "killology") while also simultaneously, in the same room, hosting a meeting for survivors of police violence.[4]

---

4. For more on Grossman, the culture of killing that exists in American policing, and to witness officers being told that "when they go home after killing someone, they will have the best sex of their lives" (my paraphrase) check out *Do Not Resist* (2016) directed by Craig Atkinson. Here, to use slightly different language, we see an idolatry of power and violence that ultimately enthrones and worships Death. Policing, in other words, is a motherfucking death-cult.

III. EXILING

However, the way liberals and other participants within the carceral state want to paraphrase what some of us have to say about exiling persistently destructive companions who will not take responsibility for their actions and who refuse to be held accountable at times, is that, okay, we (the liberals) exclude people at times, but you (the radicals or whatever) do the same thing, and so, really, we're all just doing the same thing—you (the radicals or whatever) just want to try and feel superior but you're not. So, as with abusers, the complexity of the argument is vastly over-simplified (to the point where a different argument is presented), and then the focus is shifted to negative conclusions about the character of the people making the argument, and in this way the status quo is justified, the enforcers of the status quo are relieved, and we all continue merrily on our way to devastation.

What this entirely overlooks is that there are vastly different ways of excluding or including people, vastly different reasons for doing so, vastly different manners of going about enforcing boundaries (when force of some kind is necessary), and vastly different trajectories being pursued that, in fact, *make exclusionary acts more or less frequent as we follow those trajectories*. The trajectory of the status quo creates a feedback loop that requires ever more exclusion (which is why we also see a continual rise in surveillance technology, security industries, and the militarization of the police), whereas the trajectory I am proposing creates a feedback loop that makes exclusion less and less likely to be necessary (even if we never get to a point where nobody is ever excluded from anywhere or anything—which, if you think about it, is not actually a desirable outcome, for, as I mentioned earlier, some spaces that exclusively serve specific groups of people will always be necessary).

Thus, as I have looked around at how communities that existed prior to policing worked with their most destructive companions, and as I have looked at models developed within contemporary communities that will not make recourse to the police to solve (or, rather, worsen) their problems, I have come to the conclusion that, sometimes, exile is the best that we can do. "To exile" means "to banish, expel, or drive off." Etymologically, it contains overtones of wandering and of one who is both taken out and, at the same time, one who walks out on their own. To exile a person, then, is to refuse to admit that person into our community space, or to send that person out from our community space (likely against their will, likely requiring at least some kind of force—for example, physically placing yourself in front of a door so that a person cannot open it to enter a space). Exile, then, is an enforced banishment. We must call it what it is, instead of masking our actions with some kind of feel-good language (for example, referring to forcibly preventing a person from accessing mental health services as a "step away") so that we feel better about ourselves—the truth is that sometimes we have to do things that don't make us feel good about ourselves and we need to be honest about that. In fact, if we sugar-coat what we are doing, then we may be inclined to do it more indiscriminately. We need to hold on to our discomfort with this, in part, to make sure that we are only acting in this way when it is absolutely necessary (and, in fact, I think a lot of social services use feel-good language to refer to this kind of action precisely because they banish people all the time for the most unreasonable reasons). So, okay, sometimes we must banish people and cast them out into exile. Sometimes this is only for a very short period of time to create some distance and help people to cool down; sometimes, when all else has failed, it is for the foreseeable future or until such a time as some kind of dramatic change takes place in either the life of the individual or the life of the community (this can be a very long time—perhaps, even the rest of a person's life).

However, as I have circled around this idea over the years, I was concerned that exiling people from our community spaces may cause harm to other community spaces. If we exile persistently destructive companions, do we contribute to the potential harm experienced by others elsewhere? Are we playing the same game as the Catholic church played when it passed around pedophile priests, or that social services still play when they pass around workers who sexually abuse program participants?[5] I wish the answer to this was a hard-and-fast "no." But, unfortunately, I think the answer is more complicated. If we do things well, then I think we can say, "hopefully not." If we think others are at risk, to the best of our abilities, we will

---

5. In the Catholic church, this was a deliberately planned-out strategy created by higher-ups, including Joseph Ratzinger, who became Pope Benedict, in order to protect the church from scandal (even though it continued to expose thousands of children to ongoing sexual abuse). In contemporary social services, the concern to avoid scandal is also present. Given that agencies are competing with one another for very limited funding dollars, any scandal related to an agency could significantly affect their ability to continue to run their programs and so, when workers are confronted about being sexual abusers, the agency has a very strong desire to keep the reason for that person's dismissal a secret. Consequently, if the person who sexually abused others is smart (and if they have been abusing people for awhile in more than one agency they usually know how to play this game), they will agree to sign a non-disclosure agreement about why they were dismissed and they will also request (and receive) a severance package and a generic reference letter that they can then use to go and attain a position at another social service where they will continue to sexually abuse others. I have seen this play out many times in multiple cities. It is one example of what we mean when we talk about rape culture as a structural thing—i.e., we have structured our services and funding-models in such a way as to make outcomes like these extremely likely. I'm still waiting for the investigative journalists who will break this story wide open. There's a Pulitzer waiting for them.

III. EXILING

warn them.[6] We have no desire, as my brother Judah said when reflecting on these things with me, "to punt someone elsewhere to prey on others." And, as Cyrée Jarelle Johnson reminds us, community members are also contributing factors in abuse. This means that, although we are not responsible for the actions taken by men of violence (unless we are those men of violence), we do have a responsibility related to *the knowledge we possess* and *how we share that knowledge* to be good neighbors to other communities, groups, or individuals within our broader network of ecosystems. In fact, a lot of community-based groups already do this thoughtful, preventative work (for example, sex workers who find ways to post or provide information to other sex workers about bad dates so that those other sex workers know what to watch out for). Furthermore, we are not providing others with the means of accessing or gaining trust in other spaces to continue abusing vulnerable people (as the Catholic Church did and social services still do). Therefore, while we need to reject the form of victim-blaming that says we (those who exile a destructive companion) are responsible for the harmful and destructive actions that this person then might engage in elsewhere (a strategy deployed by violent men for ever: "the cold dinner you had out for me is what made me hit you," says the abusive partner; "the short skirt you wore to the club is what made me rape you," says the rapist; "you're poor because you're lazy," says the hoarder of wealth), we do need to consider other individuals and communities when we exile people from ours. This is complicated territory to navigate, only further complicated by the legal and professional contexts in which a lot of this work takes place (which contributes to social services "punting people elsewhere to prey on others"), and I wish I had more confidence in our ability to do this well every time but, yes, we truly are "fumbling towards repair."

That fact of the matter is that, even if it leaves a hole in our community, even if it fundamentally alters how we all learn to fight and thrive and flourish together, even if it is difficult and, worst of all, even if we are uncertain as to where a person might go and even if exiling a person from

---

6. Although, on this point, the personal safety of the person who may consider issuing the warning is a significant factor. For example, a woman who was abused by a man, who then flees from that man and then finds out that, shortly thereafter, that man is dating another woman, may consider warning that other woman about the man's behavior but she is not required to do so in ways that will jeopardize her safety—just as she is also neither responsible for the actions taken by the man in his relationship with the other woman, nor is she responsible for that man in any way after leaving him (i.e., she doesn't have to keep tabs on him for the rest of her life so that she can warn every woman he flirts with about him). My point, in this paragraph, is focused on when and how *communities* go about *exiling* people, which should not be confused with when and how *individuals* go about *fleeing* those who abuse and batter them.

our community requires some kind of use of force and results in someone feeling hurt, or let down, or betrayed (after all, there is no doubt that people who persist or rejoice in being destructive to others do, in fact, feel hurt when those others say, "you can't do that anymore," and "I don't want to see you anymore"), there *are* times when we must say to those who came to us seeking good company, perhaps even those who contributed in significant ways to the goodness of the company we experience together: "You are no longer welcome here. You cannot come here any more." Accepting this is hard, and implementing it is even harder, but if we do not do this work then it is only a matter of time before our communities themselves are destroyed and the most oppressed and vulnerable members are annihilated.

C. Leaving

Midway through László Krasznahorkai's novel, *Baron Wenckheim's Homecoming*, the eponymous baron is processing a good many matters of the heart and trying to understand how his memory of the past can be made to fit with his experiences in the present. Alas, he does so while walking down a railway track in a wooded area in the dark of night, blissfully unaware of other circumstances that point forebodingly towards the imminence of tragedy. The baron wrestles with his thoughts, he thinks and he feels, and he feels and he thinks, until he finally arrives at enlightenment—he has resolved the past with the present and, no longer adrift, he knows what he must do next. His course of action is clear and it's not too late to correct his big mistake. The narrator then drily concludes: "And in his great fervor, it would have been better if he had been paying attention."[1]

I laughed when I read that line, not simply because it is a bon mot, but also because when I look back at various times in my life, I feel like this remark also applies to me—in my great fervor, it would have been better if I had been paying attention. Specifically, it would have been better if I had been paying attention to how my great fervor was directly contributing to me missing the cues or signals or warning signs that were all trying to say, "if you continue to rush in this direction, you will experience a very intimate and painful disaster." Sometimes, it turns out, we need to *not* rush where we want to go. In fact, sometimes we need to *not go* where we want to go and sometimes, even, we need to allow ourselves to be led where we *do not want to go*. Part of what this means is that sometimes we have to leave communities we love and have helped to grow. Thus, while the partings I have explored up until now all relate to the departure—the murder, the forced disappearance, or even the exiling—of others, we also need to think carefully about and prepare for our own departures.

---

1. Krasznahorkai, *Baron Wenckheim's Homecoming*, 378.

Over the years, I have observed that especially devoted people—people who fully dive into the work of being good company to and with others, people who are not afraid to take responsibility for themselves, for what they have inherited from their ancestors, and for future generations, people who are especially considerate and tender-hearted—experience a great deal of difficultly in recognizing or accepting when the time has come for them to part ways with those whom they love and those who love them. I know this feeling well. I have often stayed longer than I could bear under the authority of abusive employers because I could not bring myself to part from those whom I had gotten to know because they came to us seeking good company. I stayed longer than I should have because of this devotion (because of my "great fervor"), and as a result I have wounds that I still carry to this day. There have been long-term consequences and repercussions. I become distressed more easily in certain kinds of situations. I have nightmares more frequently. I feel tired more quickly and it takes me longer to recover from distressing conflict situations. Whereas I used to be able to manage my discomfort, fear, and anxiety much more readily and easily, sometimes they now plunge me into a downward spiral that can last for weeks at a time.[2]

Because this is the truth of things: people change, circumstances change, unexpected opportunities arise, unexpected tragedies strike us down, some of us become more resilient over time, some of us become less so, some of us heal exceptionally quickly, some of us take a lot longer, some of us can do a lot in a short time and then nothing at all, some of us can do a little for a long time, some of us are very lucky, and others of us not so much (just ask my dear friend Stanislav about that). Therefore, if we are to be good company to and with others and also with ourselves, and if we are to truly celebrate life and contribute to its flourishing in whatever way we can, then we must recognize these elements of ourselves and others. We can't hold ourselves hostage to being who we have been up until now or doing what we have done until now, and we can't hold others hostage in this way either. In fact, even when we fully desire to be who we have been or do what we have done, those options are not always available to us. Injury, trauma, the sustained experience of oppression and abuse, these things do not just hurt us bodily or mentally. They also take possibilities and futures away from us. They change us and they change who we have the possibility of becoming. If we have good companions and a bit of luck, there can still end up being

---

2. Thankfully, I have found a medication that helped me manage this result, not of mental illness per se, but of being abused and oppressed for several years. As with so many others labeled "mentally ill" what I experienced was not so much illness as a wound or injury that was inflicted upon me. Some wounds last a short time, some wounds last a long time, some wounds last a lifetime.

C. LEAVING

marvelous options available to us, but these options are *different than they otherwise would have been*. For example, being forcibly deprived of housing by my parents fundamentally changed who I was and who I could become but, lo and behold, it also introduced me to the best people in the world and set me on a trajectory I would not trade for anything else.

Therefore, the ebb and flow of companions, including companions who choose to part with us, and including ourselves when we choose to part from others, is also another fundamental element of being together with others that we must learn to negotiate well. Sometimes we part with others because we have to, and sometimes we part with others because we want to. Parting will be something we choose to do at some point with loved ones, with a beloved community, and with loyal and faithful companions who have journeyed with us on the way. In the three sections that follow, I will explore three components related to this. They are: suffering, convalescing, and choosing when to stay and when to go.

i. Suffering

The work I am seeking to describe in this book is, like this book itself, a labor of love. As such, it is something I am passionate about. Learning to be good company to and with others, in all the ways I have described above, is my passion.

In contemporary English, the word "passion" refers to feelings of intensely strong emotion and, in particular, emotions related to admiration and desire. But there is an older meaning that underlies our contemporary usage. In Latin, the word "passionem" refers to suffering and, in particular, suffering that must be endured, experienced, and *worked all the way through to the end*. Hence, for example, those who talk about the execution of Jesus of Nazareth as "the passion of the Christ." Originally a way of talking about suffering that one must endure, the notions of intense emotions, feelings, and desires, became associated with passion when the Latin word *passio* was used to translate the Greek *pathos* (pathos relates to both suffering and feeling emotions—although, originally, these feelings tended to be oriented around pity, grief, and sorrow) sometime in the fourteenth century. From there, the modern usage of the word developed between the 1630s and the 1730s. I think we arrive at a much richer understanding of passion, how it affects us and what we do with it, if we hold together both the newer and the older meanings of the word. Yes, there are very strong emotions that stick to our passions—our passions move us and sway us and incline us to act in ways we would not act if we were taking a more detached, impersonal (fiscally responsible?) approach to things. Sometimes these strong and sticky emotions can result in great acts of violence—as with so-called "crimes of passion."[1] But, more often, passion drives us to strive to do the very best we can possibly do in relation to those people and things about which we feel

---

1. Although, it seems to me, what people tend to feel passionate about in those cases is not so much the other person (the lover who scorns them, the spouse who flees from them, or whatever) as it is about their own sense of honor, their own pride, and their feelings that other people belong to them and have no right to exist otherwise.

I. SUFFERING

passionate. It is passion that makes us question the status quo, passion that makes us go above and beyond what others might expect from us, passion that makes us grab that which used to be impossible and make it possible, and so on.

However, it is also passion that opens us up to *suffering*. Precisely because we care deeply about ourselves and others, precisely because we wish to see our loved ones liberated from all the death-dealing forces that are arrayed against them, we *suffer alongside of them for as long as they continue to suffer*, and we also suffer as a result of our own efforts to confront forces that are far bigger than we are. To love is to suffer. Henri Nouwen states this well: "Every time we make the decision to love someone, we open ourselves to great suffering, because those we most love cause us not only great joy but also great pain."[2] This is the case, not only because sometimes we hurt and are hurt by those who love us, but because those who love us also hurt when we are hurt and because, every relationship ultimately ends with a parting (as Nouwen goes on to say, "The greatest pain comes from leaving . . . the pain of leaving can tear us apart").[3] Therefore, an openness to love requires us to be open to suffering. I wish that this was not the case, but there is no escaping it. In fact, a great deal of the harm people inflict upon others is because they have been wounded in the act of loving others and so they close themselves off to loving and being loved, thinking that this will shield them from future suffering. Unfortunately, this only further entrenches them within the suffering they have already experienced and then makes them the cause of suffering experienced by other people who deserve or desire be loved and cared for by them. Hence, the importance of understanding passion as something that we must *endure and see through to the end*. It is only by seeing it all the way through that we arrive at the destination we are seeking.

By saying this, I am neither encouraging those who are being abused to remain in abusive relationships (when you can, if you can, as soon as you can, get support that refuses to validate that abuse and that helps you explore the options you have to be free of abuse), nor am I seeking to glorify suffering qua suffering. All too often, appeals to the suffering nature of love can be deployed by oppressors, exploiters, and abusers so that they can continue to oppress, exploit, and abuse those who are encouraged to be long-suffering lovers (or children or partners or workers or slaves). I

---

2. Nouwen, *Bread for the Journey*, 254.

3. Nouwen, *Bread for the Journey*, 254. Note the distinction between "leaving" and being "torn apart." While leaving is a way of parting, it doesn't necessarily "tear us apart." It all depends on *how* we go about parting (which we may or may not have much or any control over).

entirely reject this way of thinking. I do not enjoy suffering in this way, I do not enjoy seeing my loved ones suffer in this way, and I do not think anyone should be encouraged (in any way whatsoever) to stay in a situation where they are being oppressed, exploited, and abused, simply because we recognize that suffering is connected with love. Love is a suffering that *we choose*. Oppression, exploitation, and abuse are sufferings that are *forced upon us*. Love suffers because it causes us to become increasingly inter- and intra-connected with others who are suffering. Oppression, exploitation, and abuse force some people to suffer so that some other people may experience comfort or pleasure or gratification. Love makes a choice to be vulnerable because it trusts in the beloved. Oppression, exploitation, and abuse seek out our vulnerabilities in order to take advantage of us and harm us. These are very different things.

Given that the work we do in order to be good company to and with others is up against such strong oppositional forces—composed of people who care little about being good company and who care much more about defending the wealth they steal and hoard and their ability to continue doing that (regardless of the price paid by others)—given, in other words, that this is often very difficult work, the need to step back and take a break deserves special emphasis. It is not a question of if we will need to do this. It is only a question of when and of how often. However, given the urgency of what we do, given how bereft we are of supports, given how critical we then feel our own contributions might be to the thriving of the community, we can struggle with accepting this. As a result, we can push ourselves further than we can safely go, we can take on more than we can handle well, and we can end up in a place where, instead of just parting with others for a short amount of time and returning stronger, we end up completely breaking down and then needing to part from others for a much longer time or, most difficult of all, we may then need to leave and never come back.

This is a lesson I have learned the hard way. I have taken on more than I could carry and then carried it. I could not carry it for too long and soon cracks began to appear. I became more impatient with those who deserved to be treated with patience. I became more withdrawn from those who needed a listening ear. I became more short-tempered with those who acted aggressively towards others and need special attentiveness and care. But I pressed on and on, knowing that many people were relying on me to hold a certain space in a certain way and knowing that there were other service providers who were keen to take over and dismantle or co-opt the space I helped to hold. At one time, I did so while being sexually abused by a boss and mocked by many (but not all) of my peers who worked in related programs within that agency. Still, I pressed on and on. And then I couldn't anymore. I shattered into pieces. I could no longer hold my wounds

I. SUFFERING

closed while also carrying all the other sorrows and losses and betrayals and despair and outrage that others shared with me. I had to go. And, because I had been denying my need to take a break, when I then parted from that community, I did not give them the opportunity to work through my departure with me or in advance. This mishandled way of parting with them hurt them—it hurt individuals within the community and it hurt the community as a whole. Ultimately, after my work partner could also no longer continue carrying more than she could carry (although she carried it anyway for quite a long time), the community was entirely dismantled and destroyed. By leaving, my partner and I were not responsible for the actions of those who dismantled the community. We had spent years trying (and failing) to educate them about understanding the importance of being good company to and with those who were oppressed and abandoned by others who claimed to care. But my manner of parting did add to the harm.

Therefore, it is of the utmost importance that we structure break-taking (short-term partings) into how we go about building community together. Thriving in any relationship requires some kind of space and breaks being taken between those involved in the relationship. Recognizing this, we need to face our own insecurities and pride when it comes to the reasons why we don't feel comfortable parting from others for short periods of time. Are we anxious that others will forget about us or move on from us? Are we convinced that the community will fall apart without us (and, if that's actually the case, this should make us question how we have gone about structuring the community and how realistic our language of *mutual* care and *shared* responsibility actually is)? Is our sense of self-worth entirely caught up in this work and we don't know who we are apart from it? Or are we engaging in this work so heavily so that we don't have to confront other aspects of ourselves or of our lives? Asking these questions does not take away from the observation that each one of us fills a unique niche, plays a unique role, and brings something uniquely special to the communities of which we are a part. When we take a break, our absence *is* something that will be felt. However, thriving communities can reorient themselves for a period of time to ensure that all goes well until the person taking the break returns. In other words, most of the time in a thriving community, both of these things are true at the same time: (1) you are an absolutely critical part of our thriving; and (2) we will be okay if you need to part from us for a little while. The challenge, of course, is that many of us are in communities that are struggling to thrive or fighting for their very lives. When that's the case, we become concerned that, in fact, the community might not actually be okay if we take a break.

However, it is precisely here that we should return to some of what was said above about destructive companions and refusing to be a community that holds onto those who exploit or abuse the most vulnerable members of a community, just because the abusers are prominently situated within the community. If we do not take breaks when we need to, we will end up becoming less-good company to others. In fact, if we don't stop and take a break, we can very easily become destructive companions (like so many other burnt-out service providers). For example, during the time when I should have been taking a break but was not, I had a woman I knew very well (and whom I had frequently had to ask to leave our community space for the day because of her persistent disregard for the well-being of others), come and ask me to borrow a pair of scissors to cut some thread. I gave her the scissors and she cut the thread but then she went out into the community space still holding the scissors and began to wave them around and threaten others. I knew she was not a serious risk to others but, of course, many others did not know this. Had I been feeling better, I would have deployed a more playful and distracting method to guide her out of the space and, eventually, give the scissors back to me (outside the space, I could take more time to negotiate this with her as others would not be unsettled by her swinging them around in a seemingly aggressive manner). However, I approached her in a very confrontational manner and, using an angry tone of voice, I demanded she give the scissors back to me. She did not. At that point, I felt a sudden urge to burst into tears because I instantly became overwhelmingly frustrated and angry. I had to ask my work partner, Mechele, to step in so that I could remove myself from the space to calm down. Normally, this would not have been an event worth noting. Normally, I would have joked around with the woman with the scissors, collaboratively worked out a good solution, and everyone would have gone on their way. However, because I was not working from a good place, because I needed to take a break but did not, I was reacting in poor ways, I was treating people in a way that did not affirm their specialness but that in fact reinforced the lies they had been told about themselves, I was emotionally out of control, and then I was requiring my partner to do more work than was fair for her, as well as doing the work of then attending to me to see if I was okay. Here, then, is the important lesson: sometimes we stay because we think the community can't survive well without us but, in fact, what is best for the community is for us to part from them for a little while. If we stay and don't do our best work, if we stay and harm others by doing so, then we have become like those who think it is necessary to sacrifice some (in this case, those who we are now harming). But, as I emphasized before, this is never, ever true. As soon as we choose to accept the abuse of some people for the sake of the whole group, we have entirely lost our way. Thus, taking breaks, parting for a little while, is essential to our collective thriving.

ii. Convalescing

Taking breaks is one way of convalescing. "To convalesce" means to begin to thrive again, to regain one's health, and, most especially, to begin the process by which a person grows strong. The English word, "convalesce" comes from the Latin *valescere* (the inchoative form of *valere*) with an intensive prefix added on. Significantly, the Latin word *valere* (which essentially means "to be strong") is also related to the English word "valour," which carries connotations of moral worth, merit, courage, and virtue. Understood in this way, convalescing reveals itself to be precisely the opposite of what many of us imagine it to be. All too often, we see convalescents or those who need to take breaks as failures who lack the courage or virtue needed to press on and "get it done" and so, either due to their lack of character, weakness, or inherent cowardice, a break becomes a less-than-ideal necessity. In actual fact, convalescing expresses the idea of engaging in a morally worthwhile action through which a virtuous person (or group of people) will grow strong (or recover lost strength), and which takes a notable amount of courage in order to be accomplished.

It is interesting to observe the ways in which the etymology of the word "convalescing" parallels to the etymology of the word "comforting" already noted above. Both speak to *strengthening* people. When we comfort others, we engage in a process that strengthens them. When we convalesce we engage in a process that strengthens our own selves. Convalescing, then, can also be understood as a form of self-comforting or self-soothing but as a form of self-soothing that initiates a feedback loop that makes us ever-stronger and more resilient. This directly counters other ways of self-comforting or self-soothing (say, for example, by over-working ourselves, or by isolating ourselves and shutting off our emotions, or by abusing those who are weaker than us, or doing harm to our own selves) which, ultimately, cause harm and, regardless of what momentary gratification they offer us, actually make us weaker and less resilient over time. The key point here is recognizing the legitimacy of self-soothing and self-comforting behavior. We must engage in that kind of behavior (while also opening up to being soothed and comforted by others), but we must learn to engage in this process in a way that builds us all up, instead of tearing some of us down or tearing our own selves apart.

It is also useful to relate the notion of convalescing to the theme of exile already mentioned. Taking breaks in order to grow strong is a form of self-selected and -accepted exile and, as such, it points to the potential that is contained in the experience of exile more broadly. Within the Tanakh (the Hebrew Scriptures composed of the Torah [Teaching], Nevi'im [Prophets], and Ketuvim [Writings]), exile is something that occurs when people experience when they persist in pursuing a death-dealing and death-serving trajectory. However, the motif of exile in the Tanakh is also closely related to the theme of going out into the wilderness. The wilderness is where the Hebrew slaves fled when they first achieved freedom from slavery. It is a harsh environment, but was also the pathway to their liberation, a place where they came close to their G*d, and when they were nourished and cared for in seemingly supernatural ways. Hence, also, for subsequent figures in the Tanakh, like King David, or the prophet Elijah, or Hagar and her son Ishmael, the wilderness also becomes a place where one goes when one can no longer remain in the community one loves. We see this theme continue in the Christian gospel stories about John the Baptizer and Jesus of Nazareth. Going out, being sent out, or even fleeing out into the wilderness becomes a part of a process of convalescence—of healing, of beginning to thrive again, of growing strong. In many of these cases it is worth noting that "growing strong" does not simply mean recovering strength that was lost or returning back to one's original state. Rather, "growing strong" often means *growing stronger than one was at any time before*. Taking breaks and convalescing, then, does not simply help to "get us back to our base line" (a term loved by mental health workers); rather, it is an opportunity that has the potential to help us to become wiser and stronger than ever, given that it affords us a chance to incorporate everything we have seen, learned, experienced, loved, and suffered, up until now.

Sometimes coming back stronger means coming back in new ways into new roles. Sometimes, when we take breaks, we learn that we cannot go back to doing what we were doing before—that niche is no longer ours to fill. Perhaps someone else will fill it or perhaps the community itself, as it continues to grow and develop, has shifted so that that niche does not even look the same or exist in the same place anymore. Regardless, sometimes when we take breaks, we learn that we have changed and we cannot go back to doing what we used to do before we changed. In fact, part of what was

II. CONVALESCING

driving us to take a break may have been our efforts to continue being who we no longer were. Thus, when we return (if we return—more on that in the next section), we will have to come back in new ways, in new roles, as new people. And here's the thing about that: that's *totally okay*. It bears repeating here that people change and communities change and all of us are changing all the time and, within communities committed to mutual care, ecosystem thriving, and honoring one another in all the ways mentioned above, there is more than enough room for changes like this to occur. In fact, changes like this are expected and encouraged. Thriving communities are not static or frozen in place—they are communities that are always in the process of *becoming other* and of *becoming more*. And we, too, as individuals who are member of those communities—who are co-constituted with and in those communities—are also involved in the same process of becoming other and becoming more. I may grieve the departure or loss of the person I used to be (and this grieving is often an important and necessary part of what we do when we are convalescing), but as I work through that grief, I can also end up coming to celebrate the person I now am and the niche I now fill in the community when I return to it.

Therefore, taking breaks in this convalescing way, is something very different that the ways in which many of us numb out and distract ourselves from the work we are doing when we start to feel overwhelmed by it. Technology itself—especially "smart phones," which allow us to always have games, videos, texts, apps, websites, and images, *always* at hand—makes this numbing and distraction especially easy to do. However, this way of coping is not something that makes us stronger. Rather, numbing and distracting ourselves is not so much a real break as it is a moment when we feel our lives are on pause. Pauses may help us to slow down the rate at which we are broken down, but they do not provide us with what we need in order to build ourselves back up again. As such, charity and smart phones (or 4K Ultra HDTVs) are something like neoliberalism's version of Rome's *panem et circenses*—bread and circuses. To succeed at dispossessing, oppressing, and using-up those who vastly outnumber you, dispossessors must provide the dispossessed with just enough sustenance or care to prevent the dispossessed from revolting (bread for the more impoverished citizens of Rome, social assistance for Canadian citizens today). Similarly, dispossessors must also provide the dispossessed with something to distract them from the misery of their day-to-day lives (circuses in Rome, entertainment via ubiquitous "smart technology" today). If this is still not enough, a little victim-blaming goes a long way (presenting the rulers as gods who have graced the less-deserving, barbaric poor with their presence in Rome, suggesting that people need to just practice more mindfulness, self-care, and coping skills today). Thus, it turns out that numbing and distraction, far from being things that help us to thrive, are actually things that help us to miss how much we are breaking down until we are utterly wrung-out, used-up, and then discarded and left for dead. That which numbs us and distracts us can end up causing harm to us over the long-term—even if it helps our employers boost their profit margins in the short-term.

Therefore, there is a difference between the kind of meaningful break-taking that I am attempting to describe and the numbing and distraction that many of us pursue in order to escape from our lives momentarily. Break-taking is not an escape from our lives—it is premised upon a recognition that things are happening in our lives that, in some ways, threaten or endanger them (or cause us to threaten and endanger others). Far from taking us out of our lives, break-taking becomes a means of taking account of our lives, and moving more fully, deliberately, thoughtfully, and cautiously into them, so that we can be stronger and shift our trajectory from one of decomposition to one of thriving. Of course, this is easier said than done and, in our desire to not simply pause to but to become stronger, we have to be cautious that we don't fall into making another error—that of approaching our break-taking from an overly pragmatic, goal-oriented, outcome-focused perspective, as if we can structure our convalescing in the same way that dispossessors and hoarders of wealth structure a Quality Improvement Plan for one of their businesses. When we take a break, we need to *take a break*. This can be hard for us to do. All too often, when we find ourselves outside of our usual domains of activity, we find ourselves feeling unsettled, anxious, and uncomfortable, and so we find other ways to be busy. Busyness, too, can be a way of distracting and numbing ourselves. Getting busy with "getting stronger, getting healthier, getting better" can, in fact, prevent us from convalescing. One of the things I have learned from working with people who are experiencing crises that feel overwhelming—crises wherein people are unsure of how to go forward because they don't know which way is forward because they don't even know which way is up or down or left or right anymore because everything is spinning and spinning and spinning out of control—is that people need time and space and support with *just stopping*. People need space to breath. People need to be able to have time to not do anything. And people need others who will support them, sit with them and listen to them, as they end up expressing whatever it is that they end up feeling they need to express as they sit and breath and feel and do nothing. Only after this occurs, are people able to start understanding what happened, what they need to change or how they already have changed, and what comes next.

iii. Choosing When to Stay and When to Go

We suffer and we convalesce but we do not do this as individual entities who are ultimately stable and static and unchangeable at our core. We do this as beings who are ever-changing (recall that the total changeover of all the cells in our bodies occurs within a seven to ten year time frame). We do this as beings who are constantly in motion (it turns out that not just light, but also everything else as well, exists as both a particle and a wave simultaneously). We do this as beings who are co-constituted and inter- and intra-connected with other beings, and as beings with porous boundaries who move between different environments, who discover new ways of being, who leave behind old ways of being, and who are continually broken open in unexpected ways (some wonderful, some horrible) by what the future brings in to the present (even as we continue to be marked by the futures that are now in the past). We are, all of us, always changing and we do not yet know who we will be or what will be possible to us as we continue to become both more fully ourselves and more fully other than what we have been before.

Part of what this means is that, as we change and are changed, sometimes we *cannot* continue on with communities or relationships of which we have been a part, and sometimes we *choose to* depart from some communities or relationships. These are two different roads to parting, both of which need to be worked through with consideration and care. The first road is often difficult because we come to the realization that we cannot return, *despite our desire to do so* (even if we also might feel some mixed feelings and perhaps even some relief about not returning). This difficulty is further exacerbated by the observation that kind-hearted workers often take a long time to realize that they cannot return. Because they do not want to depart, because they want to keep journeying alongside of those whom they know and love and those who know and love them, many kind-hearted workers choose not to take the breaks they need in order to sustain themselves. Or, if they do take breaks, they fail to take breaks that are long enough to permit them to convalesce and gain strength (in part because they are accustomed to "toughing it out," in part because they start missing people very quickly and start feeling better very quickly, even though, early on, this feeling is usually deceptive). Or they have not yet realized their own limits, their own wounds, or the ways in which they have been traumatized or transformed so that returning to the community and people whom they love in *any* capacity is no longer an option (all of this assumes, of course, that taking breaks or that taking breaks of a sufficient length and with sufficient security as to allow convalescing is even an option—which it is not in most workplaces wherein workers are overworked and underpaid and benefits are increasingly cut back or entirely non-existent). I have personally experienced all of these things—and watched other loved ones go through them as well. It is a hard thing to accept that you can no longer go where you desire to go in order to be with those whom you desire to be with. What kind-hearted workers all-too-frequently learn in retrospect is that they should have left a lot sooner.

A lot of the injuries sustained by kind-hearted workers accumulate and then manifest in a way that is similar to the repetitive strain injuries experienced by manual laborers. For example, when I worked as a tree planter in Wet'suwet'en, Tsek'ehne, Gitxsan, Tahltan, and Kaska territories, it was very common for tree planters to experience wrist, knee, elbow, and back injuries because they were repeating the same movements thousands of times per day (while also carrying weight on their hips and shoulders and hiking up and down mountains, through swamps, and other rough terrain). The best way to deal with those injuries is to immediately cease engaging in the activities that cause them as soon as one becomes aware that one is hurt. However, because tree planting only lasts for a few months of the year, and because people are trying to make the money they need for a lot of the rest of the year (this was how I paid for my tuition and housing while I was in college), and because a planter gets paid by trees planted (in my time, between ten cents and twenty-four cents per tree) and because they actually begin to go into debt to the tree planting company for any work days they miss (planters get charged a flat rate per day by tree planting companies in order to cover their "camp costs," even though company owners get paid far more per tree than planters do), there is a very large incentive to continue working while injured. As a result, the majority of tree planters who have worked two or more seasons will have long-term damage somewhere in their body. Tendonitis and femoral-patella syndrome are especially common. In my last

III. CHOOSING WHEN TO STAY AND WHEN TO GO

season, I was making such good money that, even though I knew my knees were blown, I kept working on them (adjusted for inflation, by the end of that season, I was earning almost six hundred dollars per day, which, for me as a young, recently homeless university student, was a *lot* of money). As a result, I injured my knees so severely, that I was not able to go back to work the next season or any other season after that. In fact, both of my wrists, both of my knees, and one of my shoulders have remained constantly prone to injury or to flare-ups of injuries that I sustained at that time because, instead of stopping to rest and heal, I chose to continue working.

Although usually driven by different motives (at least in social services where workers are massively underpaid in comparison to what social workers earn in hospitals or what social assistance workers make in government offices), kind-hearted frontline workers tend to make the same type of error. They tend to minimize their own injuries. They tend not to stop when they need to stop for as long as they need to heal, and, as a result, by the time they are actually forced to stop and take stock of their injuries, they have often crossed the line from temporary injury to permanent injury with lifelong consequences. They will never be the same, and they will not be able to do some of the things that they did before. To be clear, I do not mean to suggest that this is all their fault. In fact, kind-hearted workers face enormous pressures from their employers to work themselves to death and then keep working and then, when these kind-hearted workers finally collapse and literally cannot work another day, they are discarded and the next wave of workers is hired. Social services churn out stats and broken-hearted workers in equal measure. For the person who cannot go back to where they long to go—the person who has departure forced upon them—this is almost always a devastating process.

Part of what is devastating about this is the loss involved. Here, one experiences the loss of relationships with loved ones, the loss of one's place of belonging within a community, and the loss of familiar routines. But another important part of what is lost is the departing person's sense of self, their ability to live out their core values, and their ability to feel like they are living a meaningful life. In forced departures, we can lose the version of ourselves who we love the most and who we most desire to be. As a result, we often feel as though we have been driven into a kind of ghostly limbo where, although we have not yet died, we feel like maybe we should be dead and are puzzled by the fact that we continue to live (I suspect that anyone who has experienced significant heartbreak can identify with feeling something like this). Given the pain and loss we experience here—loss not only of others or of other things, but of large parts of the most important parts of ourselves—we feel as though we should not be able to continue to live

... and yet, somehow, we do. It feels like we're dying and yet, day after day, we're still here.

Initially, when we go through this kind of experience, we feel as though our lives have become significantly less than they were before and we, too, in this lost and ghostly state, also feel less than we were before. Losing our ability to be who we were, to do what we did, or to be where we were, feels like the fullness of life has been replaced by a great void. And, indeed, this may be true in the moment when we feel this way—but it need not be true after some time passes. An important part of moving through and out the other side of this ghostly limbo (of moving through this void that feels endless but which is not) is realizing that our inability to be who we once were or to go where we once went, does not mean we will forever be less than who we were before. It only means that we are becoming *other than who we were before*. Initially, this may feel like a lessening to us. After all, when we are living according to our values, we tend to be biased about the way we have lived up until then. But we must be cautious about such biases. They can operate in an ableist manner. A blind person is not less than a sighted person. A person with one hand is not less than a person with two hands. And so on. Each person has a different experience of the world, but each person—sighted or blind, one- or two-handed—is able to live a full and meaningful life and if they transition from being one to the other (from being sighted to blind, from being blind to sighted), they will also be able to continue to live a full and meaningful life in some new and different ways. The challenge is learning to recognize this even when that transition is forced upon us and comes within the context of injury, loss, or tragedy (as it so often does). When we have pursued a certain trajectory for ourselves, especially if that trajectory both affirms and deepens the values we hold most dearly, and when we are then thrown entirely off course, we have trouble imagining that "becoming other than" who we were before is not also and always "becoming less than" who we were before.

That is certainly how I felt when I went from living in an intentional community house in Vancouver's downtown eastside, and becoming increasingly involved in grassroots community mobilization and more militant forms of resistance, and then, in a very short period of time, transitioning to being a single dad living in an upwardly mobile neighborhood that did not welcome impoverished people (in an apartment where I could no longer see any of my old friends and companions), working nine to five for an oppressive social service, and trying to cut back from the alcohol I had started drinking in order to soothe my loneliness, and my sense of being lost and out-of-place. I thought that my life had become "less than." I felt trapped and helpless. I felt like I went from actively participating in

III. CHOOSING WHEN TO STAY AND WHEN TO GO

mutually liberating solidarity with others who were or who had been oppressed, to becoming trapped within the company of the sell-outs and the apathetic whose only response to oppression was to get as much comfort as they could afford for themselves and their family members. But I was wrong. There are many ways to live a full and meaningful and loving life. I was not trapped in circumstances entirely out of my control. I wasn't locked in a cell. I was involved in shaping the course of my life. I was an active participant (which then led me to ask why I was *choosing* to remain in a situation where I *felt* trapped—an important question to ask when it comes to trying to figure out what we really want, instead of what we say that we want). Commitments I now had—like my commitment to being a father to my children—did not compromise me. They actually gave me the opportunity to experience all kinds of other wonders, to learn all kinds of other forms of love, and to heal and be liberated in all kinds of unexpected ways (from my own childhood trauma, for example—and this liberation is something I then passed on to my children, breaking intergenerational chains of violence and ensuring that they would only ever have a father who they knew as loving and safe).

Once I chose to become a father, I fundamentally altered the relational dynamics of my life—for whom I was responsible, to whom I was accountable, and with whom I was co-constituted and inter- and intra-connected—these things all changed very dramatically. As a result, I could not live the same life I lived before. It took me some time to realize that as I tried to live both my old and new lives simultaneously and ended up doing both poorly. It also took me time to realize that the life I started to live after my kids were born, my marriage ended, and I moved away from the community in Vancouver's downtown eastside was just as worthwhile, was just as devoted to pursuing life-giving and life-affirming ways of structuring our collective life together, was just as "best" as the life I was striving to live before. For a few years, when I could no longer go back to the people and places I loved, I wasn't sure if I wanted to live or die. More accurately, I knew I wanted to live but I just didn't know if I could stay alive in the life that I was living after everything changed. Now, many years later, I could not be more delighted with the life that I have. When it comes to my life accomplishments, I sincerely believe that the most significant thing I will have done in my life is choosing and then learning to be a kind, loving, playful, and attentive father who, far from devastating his own children, actually provides them with a safe and secure home and foundation from which they can go out to explore the world and to which they can return whenever they need. Thus, I learned that becoming other is not at all becoming less. Whereas initially I felt like my life was being twisted out of shape—a painful process that made everything an unrecognizable mess—I eventually concluded that my life was being transformed into something so wonderful and unexpected that I couldn't have possibly imagined it before the change began. A true metamorphosis!

The challenge, then, when we are forced to depart against our will, is finding ways to "become other" that we find just as exciting, life-giving, and good as the way in which we believed we were living before we had to depart. This is almost always painful and difficult work. And I don't want to suggest it is always possible for each one of us to get through it. Sometimes the hurts we experience are stronger than we are. Sometimes we are too isolated to be able to come out the other side of them. Sometimes we don't have enough time to get there. All the more reason, then, for us to focus on being good company to and with others. We need to help one another through these times.

The challenges associated with *choosing to depart* from a community are different than this. People choose to depart from communities and relationships for a great variety of reasons. Some reasons appear more selfish to us than others (like, for example, a man abandoning his children in order to pursue fame or prestige or the lover he is chasing at the moment), but anytime the element of choice is more prominent, we will always be asking ourselves questions about selfishness. Furthermore, given that others involved in community spaces have different expectations of one another—and different ideas of how dedicated each individual should be to the community—we are bound to have others confront us and accuse us of selfishness (or something like that) when we consider the choice of leaving. All of this is only further problematized by the observation that communities of people who are dispossessed, oppressed, and left for dead also have considerable trauma around loved ones departing and pre-existing, completely legitimate fears about being abandoned. Thus, those who are dedicated to being good company to and with others, and most especially with those whom almost all others have forsaken, end up feeling an enormous amount of (implicit or explicit—usually some combination of both) internal and external pressure to *not* go, when they actually begin to consider the choice of departing from a community.

But people change. And the experiences people have in a community also change. Places where we once thrived can, through no fault of anyone present there, end up becoming environments where we feel like we are stagnating. Sometimes we can resolve this. But sometimes resolutions only make this more *bearable* rather than restoring us, once again, to a state of *thriving*. Sometimes we are willing to keep trying. Sometimes we are not. Sometimes we try many, many times. Sometimes we do not. Sometimes

III. CHOOSING WHEN TO STAY AND WHEN TO GO

we choose to stay and sometimes we choose to go. And here's the thing about that: if we are truly devoted to the thriving of each member of our community, if we truly desire that each person live the most abundant life that they can possibly live, then this means that, in many cases, we have to not only be okay with letting people go—we have to encourage them to go and support them to fare well. And what applies here to others also applies to ourselves as members of communities dedicated to the thriving of all people. Sometimes we, too, will choose to go. And sometimes that's okay. More than okay, sometimes that's really, really *good*.

This is a lesson I learned over the course of my marriage when both my spouse and I were choosing to remain in a marriage where both of us were not only failing to thrive but were actually unhappy and becoming increasingly unwell. What began as a beautiful thing became something else altogether. Because people change. And while many married couples will say things like, "you need to learn to change *together*" (i.e., in ways that keep you together rather than in ways that drive you apart), this is sometimes much easier said than done (I mean, it's not like we didn't spend years trying to "change together"). It felt to me like my spouse and I had been swimming down a river together—happy to discover another person in the same current, happy to discover an unexpected and welcome companion along the way (because sometimes the river got cold and rough and scary and lonely)—but the river forked and we ended up in different branches and the wedge between the two streams was growing wider and wider and the currents pushing us were growing stronger and stronger. Even then, we still tried to hold on to one another because we still cared about one another, because we had made a vow ("for better or worse . . . until death do us part") and we had made a commitment to be married no matter what. As a result, it took us years to realize that the very best way in which we could love, honor, care for, and respect one another—in other words, the very best way for us to try and honor that vow, given the reality of our situation—was for us to actually no longer be married to each other. Thus, we parted and now, I think, we are both thriving far more than we would have otherwise. And, it should be noted, the same is true of our children. This is part of the reason why I object to people saying that children with divorced parents are growing up in a "broken home" (our home was broken when we were married—we fixed it when we got divorced). Now, in my current relationship, my partner and I are devoted to one another and delight in each other's company, but we also know that if, for whatever reason, one or both of us begins to feel like we are dying in this relationship, and we are unable to work through that to a place of mutual thriving, then we are more than happy and willing to let the other person go. Life is too short to spend it doing things that make you feel miserable, just because you feel obligated to do them. Why would we wish that on anyone we love? I don't think we would. So, if we love ourselves, we shouldn't wish it on ourselves either.

This understanding also applies to the relationships we have with other individuals and communities. Some people will understand this more or less well. On the one hand, there will always be people who think you should *always* remain in a relationship, *always* stay focused on your commitment to stay there, and *never* consider leaving that relationship or community *no matter what*. On the other hand, there will also always be people who do not take commitments seriously, who take up and then abandon others all the time, who create false expectations, and who leave a trail of hurt people in their wake. We need to chart our courses between these two extremes. Having felt the pressures of the first group of people and having seen or experienced the harms caused by the second group of people, we must carefully consider what we desire, what the consequences of our actions might be, how well we can go about doing what we wish to do or feel that we must do, and then make our choice accordingly. Sometimes we will stay. Sometimes we will go. However, if we don't preclude any option from the outset, if we think through what we do with consideration not only for others, but also for ourselves, in our staying or our going, then we are more likely to arrive at a state of *mutual* thriving.

Finally, whether or not we stay or go, here and now in this moment, we *all* go eventually. We are all here only for the briefest of moments. Life is short. So short, in fact, that even just describing it as "short" does not come close to doing justice to its shortness. Not only is life short, but it is the only life that you—as the you that you are right now, with all your befores and all your afters—will only be uniquely this you just this once. And then that you will be gone forever. So treasure yourself, treasure your life. What a gift it is. There never was and never again will be a life the same as yours. If you desire to stay and you can find your way to thrive or experience fulfilment in staying, then stay. But if you desire to go and you can find your way to thrive or experience fulfilment in going, then go. We'll miss you so much. But we'll be okay. And so will you.

Conclusion
Loving and Raging in the Mean Time

D ear reader, we have come a long way together. Thank you for being my companion in producing a text with meaning (for, if any text is to have meaning, that meaning is co-produced by the author *and* the reader). At this point, I believe I have sketched out a framework for how we can go about transforming the cultures that dominate, infiltrate, or otherwise corrupt and destroy the spaces we hold or share with others, in order to begin the process of becoming ever better company to and with one another. I have chosen my words carefully, I have tried to be thoughtful but, more than anything, I have tried to speak from my heart to your hearts. As Julietta Singh once wrote, I have wanted to "burrow so deep in language with you that we exceed it."[1] By speaking excessively, I have wanted to awaken longings that so many of us have tried to deny or repress or give up on; longings so many of us have had destroyed within us; longings for a better world; longings for communities where we are safe; where we are seen, heard, and understood; where we are loved; where we know that we belong; and where we contribute in our own meaningful and uniquely special ways. I have tried to bring into the waking world the dreams so many of us had when we were children. I have tried to say and show that, yes, this really is possible. We really can do this together. And, by speaking this way, I hope you will take your own feelings and longings and transform them into actions, into conversations with loved ones, into small or big acts of coming together to care for one another outside of or underneath or hidden from the gaze and the understanding of all the structures and individuals who try to force us to give up on our dreams. I have written this text. You have read this text. Now let's act!

1. Singh, *No Archive Will Restore You*, 94.

To some, of course, this will sound outrageous. After all, in my excessiveness, I am attempting "a kind of *incommunicable communication*," and, as László Földényi explains, any effort to engage in this kind of communication faces "the danger of being labeled insanity, drunkenness, or a dream."[2] Surely a good many of the cops and the bosses and those who benefit from hoarding wealth and sacrificing the lives of many people in order to increase the profit margins of a few people would apply these labels to me and this text. They will say it is too biased and that it needs to be backed up by more footnotes referring to evidence that has been attained via best practices.[3] They will say it is too emotional. They will say that speaking from my heart to yours is not objective enough. They will say the tone is wrong (too angry, too sad, to recklessly close to the subject matter), and they will suggest I am actually harming my own cause by alienating potential allies. Essentially, they will say whatever they need to say in order not to actually have to seriously think about, engage with, or substantially respond to what I have written. As for me, what can I say in response to all of these possible objections? I say that it is very hard to speak heart-to-heart with people whose hearts are coated with the ashes of those whom they have sent to the ovens. What hope does a prisoner in a death camp have of communicating heart-to-heart with a guard who assigns thousands of other inmates to death every day? Surely, any heart-talking prisoner would be considered insane, or drunk, or a foolish dreamer. Sadly, even when speaking to other prisoners—those for whom this book is first and foremost being written—this can also be the case. So many of us have internalized the discourse, the values, the fantasies, the enframings, and the practices of our oppressors and others who leave us for dead.

One of the ways in which we internalize our own oppression is by settling for survival. In this book, I am urging us to shift our collective focus from surviving to *thriving*. Social services, healthcare, and all of the so-called caring professions are focused on demonstrating to funders and governmental agencies that they help people to receive the bare minimum needed in order to live. What a goal![4] We need to fundamentally shift our

2. Földényi, *Dostoyevsky Reads Hegel in Siberia and Bursts into Tears*, 224.

3. After all, authors like Singh and Földényi, to say nothing of the others whom I have quoted above (from Dostoyevsky to MacFarlane to Jesus to Rabbi Isaac Luria) don't count as witnesses with any kind of formally recognized legitimacy within the truth-producing apparatuses that control our officially-recognized discourse about these things.

4. And just how thin we have stretched ourselves in this regard has become lethally obvious during the ongoing COVID pandemic, although this manuscript was completed at the beginning of the COVID pandemic and before the so-called "opioid crisis" (which is really the mass production of Death that results from the criminalization of

perspective on the world and on our communities and recognize the great abundance of life. There is no natural or necessary reason for anyone to not live and thrive within that abundance. The primary reason why some of us do not experience that abundance and thriving is because some others of us refuse to allow that to happen. This is both unnatural and unnecessary. Stated frankly, it's fucking evil. But it's normalized.

In ever worsening situations like ours, people find ways to survive, to eke out existence, to not quite die just yet (for the harder Death pushes down, the more vigorously Life rises up). In this way, neoliberal administrators, public health officials, poverty pimps, and all their friends and allies, can constantly move the goal posts: "You survived on one dollar a day? I think you are taking advantage of the system—from now on we will give you seventy-five cents a day." "Oh, you survived on seventy-five cents a day? I think you are taking advantage of our kind-heartedness and generosity—from now on we will give you only fifty cents a day." And so on. When this is the case (and it *is* the case), we need to be very clear that the trajectory we are traveling is one that was both established by and culminates within the death camps. Here, it's worth noting that the administration of Auschwitz ultimately fell under the jurisdiction of the SS *Economic-Administration Main Office*. After all, even in the death camps, people found ways to survive (and so the administrators cut back rations, demanded longer hours of work, and so on). Seeing how much support we can cut to those whom we have already impoverished, forcibly deprived of housing, colonized, criminalized, pathologized, and abandoned, and then cutting more and more support all the time—this is referred to as "fiscal responsibility" but it is actually *the application and actualization of the logic of the death camps to society as a whole*. I am not being hyperbolic to say that, our entire society, in its practical outworkings, premised as it is upon neoliberal austerity, racial capitalism, colonialism, the sacrosanct nature of so-called private property, and the utterly vicious rule of law, is a Death cult. Neoliberalism and those who profit from it, more than anything and anyone else in history, have perfected the mass production of death (which is why, to this day, those who are impoverished, dispossessed, oppressed, and forcibly deprived of housing are still being told: "Arbeit macht frei!").

We, the living, must fight against this. We must reject, refuse, mock, and resist the glorification of those who perpetuate this logic and who, by tossing crumbs to a prisoner shortly before that prisoner is beaten to death by a guard, are praised as philanthropists, humanitarians, or ideal citizens.

---

healthcare and the abandonment unto death of those who are impoverished) began killing my loved ones in the hundreds (in my current city) and in the thousands (in Vancouver where I used to reside).

We must fight, not just to survive, but to actualize our right, as members of the community of the living, to participate *in all of the abundance of life*. We are not fighting for a larger piece of stale bread. We are not fighting for our right to have a shitty-ass room in a house that doesn't even meet fire code and that is filled with cockroaches and bedbugs, because that is the only alternative to freezing to death in the winter (that or smashing a few windows to get "three hots and a cot" until spring comes). We are not fighting for our right to hoard property, consume others, and get rich by exploiting those who used to be our companions. We are fighting to live a life that is liberated, that is caring, that is meaningful, and that ensures we are all, collectively, sacrificing nobody and leaving nobody behind on the way to doing this. We categorically refuse *any* vision of our collective life together, any politics or economics or community development visions, that cannot imagine that there is enough to go around, or that concludes that some people *must* have way too much while other people *must* have way too little. And we categorically refuse to acknowledge the authority of anyone who forces us to not participate in our collective decision-making, or who tells us that they'll take care of everything so we needn't be involved (apart from perhaps filling out an opinion survey in exchange for a five-dollar grocery card). We're fighting for a world that we *get to make together* and, in some interstitial spaces as we engage in this fight, *we're already making that world a reality*.

Thus we, ourselves, are the living proof that the hoarders of wealth and all the forces they deploy against us are liars. They're lying when they say, "the world *we* have created, the world that some of *you* have such a hard time accepting, is the only possible world and the least bad of all the options." Because we are the proof of their lies, they must abandon us, leave us for dead, and reduce us to bare life barely subsisting—or they must discipline us, warp us, corrupt us, and remake us in their image so that they can hold us up as proof that they are right.[5] By existing in the way that we do, we prove them wrong—about everything—and so they seek to destroy us. But we will not be destroyed. We will love and we will rage and we will build better worlds—here in this crack, there in that home, here right under their noses, there far away from them. We refuse the normalization of hatred and the cult of violence that comes with conservatism and we also refuse the equally violent bougie liberal calls for "peace and love" that are used to

---

5. On the concept of bare life, as well as how the death camps (or lagers, as he refers to them in German) can become a model for contemporary society, see Agamben's work, especially *Homo Sacer*. Unfortunately, Agamben went completely sideways in relation to COVID and has been at the forefront of anti-vaxxing efforts in Italy, leading many on the Left to appropriately reconsider his entire oeuvre.

undercut those who wish to resist oppression. No, we will not normalize hatred. We will not rejoice in oppression. But we will also not accept a false peace. We will not use our sensitivity and insights and gentleness to mask the death-dealing violence that suffuses our everyday life. *We will love and we will rage.* For as long as the current state of affairs continues, for as long as we live in what I call "the mean time" (what others, long ago, called "this present evil age"), then we have no other option open to us. We will love and rage *recklessly*. Knowing, as László Földényi also notes, that our recklessness requires us to engage in actions that are *irrevocable*.[6] We are *irrevocably committed to this trajectory*, these pursuits, and these goals. We are irrevocably committed to "experiment[ing] with our own latent possibilities, to make sure of their existence."[7] We may be wounded or die in our efforts to achieve this, we may be murdered or disappeared, we may have to continually find new ways to try and accomplish this, but *we will not be dissuaded* from returning to this trajectory over and over again.

And here, I wish to stress one last time, the importance of how *the cultures we create and maintain end up creating self-reinforcing feedback loops*. A culture centered on violence will become more violent over time and the option of being non-violent or even peaceable will become less and less possible or plausible. A culture centered on a few people accumulating possessions because they dispossess many others will lead to the development of a world where a very few people own the majority of the world's wealth and the majority of the world's inhabitants are either dead (via mass "extinction") or utterly impoverished and left for dead. A culture that values the defense of private (but actually stolen) property over human life will lead to a society with greater and greater degrees of surveillance, security, and militarization of non-military bodies like the police. A culture premised upon seeing the dispossessed as the problem instead of seeing the dispossessors as the problem will always find ever more nuanced, thorough, and seemingly admirable and commonsensical ways to reinforce this view. The deeper we go into all of these (interwoven) trajectories, the stronger the loops become, and the harder it becomes to break free of them or to imagine any kind of alternative as being possible or desirable.

However, the same logic applies to alternative cultures. A culture premised upon mutuality—mutual care, mutual respect, mutual collaboration, mutual guidance, mutual engagement—will, over time, lead to the flattening of hierarchical ways of structuring our relationships with one another. A culture centered upon liberation will lead us to become more adept at

6. Földényi, *Melancholy*, 222.
7. Földényi, *Melancholy*, 222.

identifying oppression, more aware of how oppressors try to present themselves as anything but what they are, and more active in our resistance to oppression, and this will eventually produce a more general state of liberation and make it more and more difficult for people to oppress others (imagine how different the world would be if we had been pursuing this trajectory and now lived in a world where oppression seemed almost unimaginable, rather than having spent a few centuries pursuing the opposite trajectory and now living in a world where the absence of oppression seems unimaginable). A culture that is centered upon celebrating life in all of its abundance will lead us to recognizing the indispensable specialness of every living being, will teach us to value life over the accumulation of possessions, and will make it obvious that if the choice is between breaking a life and breaking a law, you should *always* break the law. In other words, if we find ourselves focusing upon ensuring that all beings are not just barely surviving (if even that) but actually thriving, then we will build a world where that is more likely to be the case. When that is more likely to be the case, more beings will thrive. When that happens, our collective circumstances and possibilities change and even more thriving becomes possible—and on the feedback loop goes as it gathers strength until the idea of living within a Death cult is a distant nightmare about "all the meanness [that existed] in the used-to-be."[8]

Perhaps this sounds like insanity, or drunkenness, or a dream to you, but I believe that *life loves to thrive*. Living things love thriving and life, itself, thrives in all kinds of ways. It thrives in diversity and, the more you make room for that thriving, the more ways Life will diversify itself (this is why, for example, the oldest ecosystems on earth, rainforests, are packed with millions of different kinds of life, whereas the younger ecosystems, like the arctic, have much less diversity—as life persists, it diversifies, that's what it does and that's what it loves to do). Life delights in being in relationships of mutual care with other forms of life. Life delights in being inter- and intra-connected with other forms of life. Life delights in taking on another form—one never seen or imagined before (as, for example, so often happens in the process of endosymbiosis when two life forms merge and create a third, entirely new and different kind of life)—and then, after finding a niche within an ecosystem, hearing others within that ecosystem say, "Wow! It's so lovely to have you with us, that we can't remember how we ever got along without you!" Life rejoices in being alive. And there are many, many ways to be oh-so-wonderfully alive. Eurocentric scientists are only discovering this about Life—although many other cultures (cultures that Europeans

---

8. To borrow the words of Buster Scruggs in *The Ballad of Buster Scruggs* (Netflix, 2018) directed by Joel and Ethan Coen.

labeled as "primitive") have known this for thousands of years. There is life deep in the earth—billions of tons of bacteria living miles underneath us, absorbing nutrients from the rock itself. There is life not only in the forest, but under the forest, and above the forest, and *the forest itself* is so finely networked through all of its parts that it, too, is a superorganism or holobiont (just like us, human beings, and every other ecosystem). The forest is a life. This is awe-inspiring and it is good. Life is good and it deserves to be celebrated in all its diverse forms—including the very specific form that is you! If this awe-inspired celebration of Life and of all the living was at the core of how we go about shaping our collective life together, we would be in a different world today.

Alas, given the way in which Death and not Life currently rules over us, we are now living in the sixth great extinction of life. Is this an irrevocable trajectory? It certainly is and has been for some. But for who and how many? Those questions remain unanswered. There is no doubt that the self-reinforcing death-dealing and death-serving feedback loop that dominates us in the mean time is now exceptionally strong, compelling, and overwhelming. This habituated way of sharing life together is not quickly or easily overcome or reversed. But, as Aristotelian virtue ethics remind us, we can form new habits and, when we do form new habits, new possibilities become possible *for the first time*.[9] This is just as true of us as groups as it is of us as individuals. This being the case, we can never say that "it is too late to try to be good company to and with others; we're already too far gone and there's no coming back from this." Perhaps, those conclusions accurately reflect the possibilities we can imagine right now. But what is or is not possible in the future will change depending on what we do or do not do now. In other words, we strive to be good company to and with others, not just to make whatever life-giving and life-affirming changes we can make right now, but to *change the very conditions of possibility*. And here is one more lesson I have learned from my companions: it turns out that all kinds of things we thought were impossible, are actually possible. Today, we live in the mean time. Perhaps tomorrow, that is how they will speak of the past. It all depends, dear reader, on what all of us decide to do together.

Bonne chance et bon courage, mes amours!

---

9. On this ethics see, for example, MacIntyre, *After Virtue*.

Postscript

There were three fellas I rolled with who loved me and who I also loved, who also experienced what it was like to be deprived of housing when we were in our teens. I mention them first. I love you, Kurty. I love you, Critch. I love you, Egg. We didn't always have safe or welcoming homes to go back to at night and, even when some of us did and others of us didn't, we stuck together. Look at us all now! What a trip.

My brother Abe was not personally deprived of housing, but he was deprived of his brother and roommate and I know he both suffered and was transformed (although in his own way) at that time. And my older brother Jude invited me to come and stay awhile with him and his university friends in Windsor and, to a high-school kid who always saw Jude as "the cool brother" (sorry, Abe!), that really was a wonderful gift. And my oldest brother Josh always included me, was always there for me at my lowest points, and never hesitated to freeze for an hour in line for whatever punk show we were going to in the winter when we didn't want to wear jackets because we were going to spend the whole show in the pit. I love you, Abe. I love you, Jude. I love you, Josh.

After I moved to Toronto, I discovered that there were so many more of us. Literally thousands of us (approximately ten thousand youth are forcibly deprived of housing every year in Toronto). I can only name a few—both youth and adults—from the time we spent together. I love you, Anthony (Squeegee, remember when they said you were going to die on the street and instead you made them hire you? Ha!). I love you, Ivan (so much!). I love you, Shaun. I love you, Ruckus (I never pass that corner without thinking of you). I love you, Mama. I love you, Charis. I love you, Vincent. I love you, Al ("a voice from the shadows says hello"). I love you, Rev (you were one of the first to really open my eyes to a lot of things). I love you, Cory. I love you, Diamonds. I love you, Damian (I hope you fucking made it, man). I love you, Chucky. I love you, Angel. I love you, Sparkles (I mean, holy fuck, right?). I love you, Harriet. I love you Punk Ryan and Little Ryan. I love you, Sheridan. I love you, Marla (the bullies were so, so wrong about you). I love you, Little Sarah, and I love you, Sara. I love you, Moe. I love you, Trinity. I love you, Peter (remember selling fake weed to tourists to get into the Andre 3000 show? So good!). I love you, Mr. Cavalier. I love you, Dwight and Vlad and Frank and Jan (the four of you taught me a lot).

And also in Toronto, there were others who may not have been deprived of housing, but they understood oppression, they understood solidarity, they understood acknowledging and celebrating specialness, and they understood mutual caring. I love you, Andrea. I love you, Rob. I love you, Shank (and I love you, Lyf, even though we met later). I love you, Tim. I love you, Greg. I love you, Chris and Tyler (holy shit, we're still alive and we're still doing this!).

Then I was off to Vancouver, where I truly began to rid myself of the lenses of the non-profit industrial complex and finally understood that the oppressed are the best agents of their own liberation (more than that, they are the *only possible agent of our collective liberation* because nobody else is able to properly understand what's wrong and what we need to do to make things right). So many people—young and old and in between—in the downtown eastside. I love you, Christine (we love like swans—I'm glad we spoke before you died). I love you, Nicole (I can't tell you anything now that you don't already know—thanks for being you). I love you, Angela. I love you, Philemon (calling me, after so many years, was a wonderful surprise). I love you, Tim (Jesus, punk rock, and speedballs, what more could a fellow ask for?). I love you, Puneet (you made me laugh and laugh). I love you, Kaur. I love you, Kyle. I love you, Miranda. I love you, Cecelia (experiencing cruelty never made you cruel—I think about you often). I love you, Matt (remember the CPU you stuffed with weed and then used an LED light to make it look like it was still working? Brilliant!). I love you, Amber. I love you, Joe. I love you, Kelly (I miss falling asleep on the couch with you after dinner). I love you, Sandy. I love you, Summer (remember when the snake stole your wig and pulled it down the toilet? One of my favorite stories!). I love you, Yve (I regret the years of friendship that we lost). I love you, Soren (I still sometimes forget that you are dead and then it hits me all over again—that story about when you won the competition for male strippers will stay with me forever).

And in Vancouver there was also a number of accomplices and allies who taught me so much and did exceptionally good work for and with others. I love you, Jody (Valkyrie, you taught me how to be awestruck). I love you, Nicky (truly, madly, deeply!). I love you, Kirk (I miss you). I love you, Charles (my son has your name). I love you, Dave and Teresa (I will always look up to you—sorry!) I love you, Stan (stay safe, brother!). And I love all the people whose names I no longer remember who also volunteered at and helped to facilitate Boys'R'Us (a drop-in for cis- and trans-men who engage in sex work and one of the very best places in the whole fucking world—or, at least, in the whole world of fucking!).

Once I became a dad of two kids, I ended up back in London, closer to my brothers and sisters-in-law and nephews and nieces and mom. I thought I knew what "hardcore" impoverishment looked like after seven years in Vancouver's downtown eastside, but, in some ways, people who have been dispossessed, colonized, and oppressed have it worse in London (the hopelessness is palpable here, whereas the solidarity and resistance are strong there—or at least they were . . . and still are in some ways, but the 2010 Olympics started a very efficient process of hyper-gentrifuckation in order to further dispossess the already impoverished and further enrich the already bloated, and that has taken a major toll on the 'hood). I was shocked by the number of people I found on the streets of my hometown (just as I was also shocked by how many people were dying every year without anyone else seeming to find either of these observations remarkable, often assuming—quite wrongly—that, "hey, at least things aren't as bad as Toronto or Vancouver"). I have journeyed alongside so many good people here. I love you, Daniel (whose street name I will not use because it's not true). I love you Jim and Jay. I love you, George ("by Jesus!"). I love you, Diane. I love you, Ricky (trying to imitate your voice on the phone was one of the times I found myself thinking, "Oh boy, I'm for sure going to jail this time"). I love you, Joe (thanks for loving me because of the ways I love my kids—when I said goodbye to you in that hospital bed, you looked like you had been crucified). I love you, Nikko. I love you, Brenda. I love you Chylene. I love you, Clarence (even if "that's no name for a gangster!"). I love you, Rick. I love you, Pete. I love you, Two (and I know you love me, too). I love you, Omid (no one but you could have traveled that road). I love you, Jim. I love you, Shannon. I love you, Danial (you bring so much to every community space). I love you, Bart. I love you, Jimmy and Jimmy. I love you, Ernie. I love you, Maurice (I wish I had stopped for a beer with you that one day you asked me—I didn't know it was the last day I would see you alive). I love you, Gordo. I love you, Alan ("Remember, Dan, if you drink Listerine, it makes you Mr. Mean!"). I love you, Julie (you make me want to be more like myself).

But yet again, in London, there have been faithful companions who didn't all come from the streets but who came to the streets and worked wonders alongside of us. Like Mechele, my co-conspirator, whom I have mentioned many times already in this book. Without you, Mech, where would we all be and what could we have all done? And Tish who is the absolute bomb. And Karen who makes every single person know, when they are with her, that they are not alone, they are loved, and we can get through this together. And Andrea (the good doc), too. I love you all.

As I conclude this book, my son, Charlie, is fifteen years old and my daughter, Ruby, is thirteen. Nobody else in the world has taught me more about specialness, worthiness, inter- and intra-connectedness, and being honest, gentle, affectionate, kind, and comforting than they have. It is often said that children teach adults how to love unconditionally. When I first heard that saying, I thought that it meant we learn to love them unconditionally because of all the difficult things we do as we adjust to being parents—changing diapers, months or years without getting much sleep, dealing with colic, being always at-hand and always exhausted, radically changing the amount of time we spend at home versus outside the home, completely reorienting the activities we engage in, and so on and so forth—but I was wrong. Charlie and Ruby taught me how to love unconditionally (or, rather, they reminded me of how to love unconditionally) because *this is how they have always loved me*. I learn how to love unconditionally not because of what I do for them, but because of the ways that they love me. Having experienced this love, I remember that I, too, was once a child who loved in this way; I am capable of this kind of love. I am continually learning from the very best teachers. Thank you, Charlie. Thank you, Ruby. I love both of you with all of my everything and, when I am dead and we are no longer companions in the same way that we are now, the strongest and largest part of me that will remain is the love that I shared with the two of you. That love will continue to live in your hearts and it will also go out from your hearts into the world as you continue to learn how to be good company to and with others. Love and light have a lot in common that way. Stars who stopped burning millions of years ago still light up our sky at night. And so it is with our love. Even after I am gone, the love we shared will continue to shine in your hearts and, when things are especially dark, just like the stars, it will help you find your way home. And the love you put out into the world? It will do the same thing. Just you wait and see—it's going to be amazing.

Not last and not least, but with and among and alongside of everyone else, I love me, too. It took me a long time—I have often fallen back into accepting the lies abusers and oppressors told me about myself—but I don't believe those lies anymore and I really do love me now.

Thanks for being good company. Thanks for welcoming me home.

XOXO
Dan

Bibliography

Agamben, Giorgio. *Homo Sacer: Sovereign Power and Bare Life*. Translated by Daniel Heller-Roazen. Meridian: Crossing Aesthetics. Stanford: Stanford University Press, 1998.
Anderson, Paul Thomas, dir. *Magnolia*. Burbank: New Line Cinema, 1999.
Annaud, Jean-Jacques, dir. *Seven Years in Tibet*. Culver City, CA: Sony Pictures, 1997.
Arntfield, Michael. *Murder City: The Untold Story of Canada's Serial Killer Capital, 1959–1984*. Victoria: Friesen, 2015.
Atkinson, Craig, dir. *Do Not Resist*. N.d.: VANISH Films, 2016.
Barad, Karen. *Meeting the Universe Halfway: Quantum Physics and the Entanglement of Matter and Meaning*. Durham, NC: Duke University Press, 2007.
Bosch, Thomas C. G., and David J. Miller, *The Holobiont Imperative: Perspectives from Early Emerging Animals*. Heidelberg: Spring-Verlag Wien, 2016.
Bourgois, Phillippe. *In Search of Respect: Selling Crack in El Barrio*. 2nd ed. Cambridge: Cambridge University Press, 2003.
Brown, Brené. "3 Ways to Set Boundaries." https://www.oprah.com/spirit/how-to-set-boundaries-brene-browns-advice.
Brown, Vanessa. *The Forest City Killer: A Serial Murderer, A Cold-Case Sleuth, and a Search for Justice*. Toronto: ECW, 2019.
Burstow, Bonnie. *Psychiatry and the Business of Madness: An Ethical and Epistemological Accounting*. New York: Palgrave MacMillan, 2015.
Burstow, Bonnie, et al., eds. *Psychiatry Disrupted: Theorizing Resistance and Crafting the (R)evolution*. Montreal: McGill-Queen's University Press, 2014.
Canadian Mental Health Association. "CMHA Ontario Responds to the Death of Yet Another Individual Experiencing a Crisis." June 24, 2020. https://ontario.cmha.ca/news/cmha-ontario-responds-to-the-death-of-yet-another-individual-experiencing-a-crisis/.
———. "We Need to Do More and We Need to Do Better: Statement From Cmha Ontario." June 5, 2020. https://ontario.cmha.ca/news/we-need-to-do-more-and-we-need-to-do-better-statement-from-cmha-ontario/.
Carver, Raymond. *What We Talk About When We Talk About Love: Stories*. New York: Vintage Companions, 1989.
Chase, Robert T., ed. *Caging Borders and Carceral States: Incarcerations, Immigrant Detentions, and Resistance*. Justice, Power, and Politics Series. Chapel Hill: University of North Carolina Press, 2019.

BIBLIOGRAPHY

Cillizza, Chris. "Donald Trump's 54 Most Outrageously Over-the-Top Lines From His North Dakota Speech." *CNN* (June 28, 2018). https://www.cnn.com/2018/06/28/politics/donald-trump-north-dakota-speech/index.html.

Clark, John P. *Between Earth and Empire: From the Necrocene to the Beloved Community*. Oakland: PM, 2019.

Coen, Joel, and Ethan Coen, dirs. *The Balled of Buster Scruggs*. Los Gatos, CA: Netflix, 2018.

Cooper, Melinda. *Family Values: Between Neoliberalism and the New Social Conservatism*. New York: Zone, 2017.

Cordingley, Michael J. *Viruses: Agents of Evolutionary Invention*. Cambridge, MA: Harvard University Press, 2017.

crow, scott. *Black Flags and Windmills: Hope, Anarchy, and the Common Ground Collective*. Oakland: PM, 2011.

Deleuze, Gilles, and Félix Guattari. *Anti-Oedipus*. Translated by Robert Hurley et al. Minneapolis: University of Minnesota Press, 2005.

———. *A Thousand Plateaus*. Minneapolis: University of Minnesota Press, 2005.

Demas, Gregory E., and Randy J. Nelson, eds. *Ecoimmunology*. Oxford: Oxford University Press, 2012.

DeSalle, Rob, and Susan L. Perkins. *Welcome to the Microbiome: Getting to Know the Trillions of Bacteria and Other Microbes In, On, and Around You*. Illustrated by Patricia J. Wynne. New Haven, CT: Yale University Press, 2015.

Doe, Jane. *The Story of Jane Doe: A Book About Rape*. Illustrations by Shary Boyle. Toronto: Vintage Canada, 2004.

Dostoevsky, Fyodor. *The Brothers Karamazov*. Edited by Manuel Kmoroff. Translated by Constance Garnett. New York: Signet Classic, 1999.

Eubanks, Virginia. *Automating Inequality: How High-Tech Tools Profile, Police, and Punish the Poor*. New York: St. Martins, 2017.

Fellini, Federico. *Fellini on Fellini*. New York: Delacorte, 1976.

Fisher, Mark. *The Weird and the Eerie*. London: Repeater, 2017.

Földényi, László F. *Dostoyevsky Reads Hegel in Siberia and Bursts into Tears*. Translated by Ottilie Mulzet. New Haven, CT: Yale University Press, 2020.

———. *Melancholy*. Translated by Tim Wilkinson. Foreword by Alberto Manguel. New Haven, CT: Yale University Press, 2016.

Foucault, Michel. *Abnormal: Lectures at the Collège de France 1974–1975*. Edited by Valerio Marchetti and Antonella Salomoni and translated by Graham Burchell. New York: Picador, 2003.

———. *Discipline and Punish: The Birth of the Prison*. Translated by Alan Sheridan. New York: Vintage, 1995.

———. *The History of Sexuality. Volume 1: An Introduction*. Translated by Robert Hurley. New York: Vintage, 1990.

———. *Power/Knowledge: Selected Interviews and Other Writings 1972–1977*. Edited by Colin Gordon and translated by Colin Gordon et al. New York: Pantheon, 1980.

Freire, Paulo. *Pedagogy of the Oppressed*. Translated by Myra Bergman Ramos. 30th Anniversary Edition. New York: Continuum, 2000.

Government of Canada. "Indian Residential Schools Settlement Agreement." https://www.rcaanc-cirnac.gc.ca/eng/1100100015576/1571581687074.

Gelderloos, Peter. "Amplifying The Ecological Resistance." *Earth First! Journal* (March 16, 2022). https://itsgoingdown.org/amplifying-the-ecological-resistance-a-

request-for-proposals-from-biocentric-media-and-the-earth-first-journal-on-next-steps-forward/?
Graeber, David. "Concerning the Violent Peace-Police." https://nplusonemag.com/online-only/online-only/concerning-the-violent-peace-police/.
Guevara, Che. "Socialism and Man in Cuba." March 12, 1965. https://www.marxists.org/archive/guevara/1965/03/man-socialism.htm.
Haraway, Donna. *Staying With the Trouble: Making Kin in the Cthulucene*. Durham, NC: Duke University Press, 2016.
Hart, Carl. *High Price: A Neuroscientist's Journey of Self-Discovery That Challenges Everything You Know About Drugs and Society*. New York: Harper Perennial, 2014.
Haywood, William D. *The Autobiography of Big Bill Haywood*. New York: International Publishers, 1929.
Hedges, Chris. "The Cancer in Occupy." Truthdig (February 6, 2012). https://www.truthdig.com/articles/the-cancer-in-occupy/.
Heidegger, Martin. *Being and Time*. Translated by Joan Stambaugh. New York: State University of New York Press, 1996.
―――. *The Question Concerning Technology: And Other Essays*. Translated and with an Introduction by William Lovitt. New York: Grand Publishing, 1977.
Hermann, Judith. *Trauma and Recovery*. New York: Basic, 1992.
hooks, bell. *The Will to Change: Men, Masculinity, and Love*. New York: Washington Square, 2004.
INCITE! Women of Color Against Violence, ed. *The Revolution Will Not Be Funded: Beyond the Non-Profit Industrial Complex*. Cambridge, MA: South End, 2007.
Jablonka, Eva, and Marion J. Lamb, *Evolution in Four Dimensions: Genetic, Epigenetic, Behavioral, and Symbolic Variation in the History of Life*. Illustrated by Anna Zeligowski. Rev. ed. Cambridge, MA: MIT, 2014.
James, Steve, dir. *The Interrupters*. N.d.: Cinema Guild, 2011.
Jay, Dru Oja, and Nikolas Barry-Shaw. *Paved With Good Intentions: Canada's Development NGOs from Idealism to Imperialism*. With the collaboration of Yves Engler. Halifax: Fernwood, 2012.
Jenkins, Alan. *Becoming Ethical: A Parallel Political Journey with Men Who Have Abused*. Lyme Regis, UK: Russell House, 2009.
―――. *Invitation to Responsibility: The Therapeutic Engagement of Men Who Are Violent and Abusive*. Adelaide: Dulwich Centre, 1990.
Johnson, Walter. *The Broken Heart of America: St. Louis and the Violent History of the United States*. New York: Basic, 2020.
Jones, Mary Harris. *The Autobiography of Mother Jones*. Edited by Mary Field Parton. Chicago: Charles H. Kerr & Company, 1925.
Kaba, Mariame, and Shira Hassan. *Fumbling Towards Repair: A Workbook for Community Accountability Facilitators*. Illustrated and designed by Molly Costello and Rachel Hoffman. N.d.: Project NIA and Just Practice, 2019.
Karetak, Joe, et al., eds. *Inuit Qaujimajatuqangit: What Inuit Have Always Known to Be True*. Halifax: Fernwood, 2017.
King, Martin Luther, Jr. "Letter from Birmingham Jail" (April 16, 1963). https://billofrightsinstitute.org/primary-sources/letter-from-birmingham-jail.
Knott, Helen. *In My Own Moccasins: A Memoir of Resilience*. Regina, SK: University of Regina Press, 2019.
Krasznahorkai, László. *Baron Wenckheim's Homecoming*. Translated by Otillie Mulzet. New York: New Directions, 2019.

Kropotkin, Peter. *Mutual Aid: A Factor in Evolution.* New York: McClure, Philips, 1902.
Leduc, Amanda. *Disfigured: On Fairy Tales, Disability, and Making Space.* Toronto: Coach House, 2020.
LeFrancois, Brenda A., et al., eds. *Mad Matters: A Critical Reader in Canadian Mad Studies.* Toronto: Canadian Scholars, 2012.
Litz, B. T., et al. "Moral Injury and Moral Repair in War Veterans: A Preliminary Model and Intervention Strategy." *Clinical Psychology Review* 29 (2009) 695–706.
Lopez, Barry. *Arctic Dreams: Imagination and Desire in a Northern Landscape.* New York: Vintage, 1986.
MacFarlane, Robert. *Landmarks.* London: Penguin, 2016.
———. *Underland: A Deep Time Journey.* London: Hamish Hamilton, 2019.
MacIntyre, Alasdair. *After Virtue: A Study in Moral Theory.* Notre Dame, IN: University of Notre Dame Press, 1981.
Mandela, Nelson. *Long Walk to Freedom: The Autobiography of Nelson Mandela.* New York: Back Bay, 1995.
Mann, Michael. *Fascists.* Cambridge: Cambridge University Press, 2004.
Martin-Baró, Ignacio. *Writings For a Liberation Psychology.* Edited by Adrianne Aron and Shawn Corne. Cambridge, MA: Harvard University Press, 1994.
Matthiessen, Peter. *The Snow Leopard.* New York: Penguin, 1978.
Maurin, Peter. *Easy Essays.* Illustrated by Fritz Eichenberg. Chicago: Franciscan Herald, 1984.
Maynard, Robyn. *Policing Black Lives: State Violence in Canada from Slavery to the Present.* Halifax: Fernwood, 2017.
McFall-Ngai, Margaret J., et al., eds. *The Influence of Cooperative Bacteria on Animal Host Biology.* Advances in Molecular and Cellular Microbiology 10. Cambridge: Cambridge University Press, 2005.
Milstein, Cindy, ed. *Taking Sides: Revolutionary Solidarity and the Poverty of Liberalism.* Oakland: AK, 2015.
National Centre for Truth and Reconciliation. "Final Report." https://web.archive.org/web/20200505161532/http://trc.ca/about-us/trc-findings.html.
National Inquiry into Missing and Murdered Indigenous Women and Girls. "Reclaiming Power and Place: The Final Report of the National Inquiry into Missing and Murdered Indigenous Women and Girl." https://www.mmiwg-ffada.ca/final-report/.
Newsom, Jennifer Siebel, dir. *The Mask You Live In.* Culver City, CA: Netflix, 2015.
Nichols, Robert. *Theft Is Property! Dispossession and Critical Theory.* Durham, NC: Duke University Press, 2020.
Nouwen, Henri J. M. *Bread For The Journey.* San Francisco: HarperOne, 1996.
———. *Life of the Beloved: Spiritual Living in a Secular World.* New York: Crossroad, 1992.
Odling-Smee, F. John, et al. *Niche Construction: The Neglected Process of Evolution.* Princeton, NJ: Princeton University Press, 2003.
Oliver, Kelly. *Carceral Humanitarianism: Logics of Refugee Detention.* Minneapolis: University of Minnesota Press, 2017.
O'Neill, Heather. *Lullabies for Little Criminals: A Novel.* New York: HarperCollins, 2006.
Oppal, Wally T. *Forsaken: The Report of the Missing Women Commission of Inquiry Executive Summary.* The Missing Women Commission of Inquiry, 2012.
Orwell, George. *Animal Farm: A Fairy Story.* London: Penguin, 1989.

Oudshoorn, Daniel. *A Magnificent Work*. Eugene, OR: Resource, 2020.
———. "Sex Work Is Real Work: A Guide to Taking Sides." https://www.danoudshoorn.com/2019/sex-work-is-real-work-a-guide-to-taking-sides/.
Oudshoorn, Judah. *Trauma-Informed Youth Justice in Canada: A New Framework toward a Kinder Future*. Foreword by Howard Zehr. Toronto: Canadian Scholars', 2015.
Oudshoorn, Judah, et al. *The Little Book of Restorative Justice for Sexual Abuse: Hope through Trauma*. The Little Books of Justice and Peacebuilding. New York: Good, 2015.
Parsons, Talcott. *The Social System*. New Orleans: Quid Pro, 2012.
Payne, Malcolm. "Understanding 'Going Missing': Issues for Social Work and Social Services." *The British Journal of Social Work* 25 (1995) 333–48.
Potter, Andrew. *The Authenticity Hoax: How We Get Lost Finding Ourselves*. Toronto: Emblem, 2011.
Potter, Andrew, and Joseph Heath. *The Rebel Sell: Why The Culture Can't Be Jammed*. Toronto: HarperPerennial, 2004.
Potter, Shawna. *Making Spaces Safer: A Guide to Giving Harassment the Boot Wherever You Work, Play, and Gather*. Chico, CA: AK, 2019.
Rancière, Jacques. *Hatred of Democracy*. Translated by Steve Corcoran. London: Verso, 2006.
Rau, Rama, dir. *No Place to Hide: The Rehtaeh Parsons Story*. Concord, ON: Fearless Films, 2015.
Rogers, Carl. *On Becoming a Person: A Therapist's View of Psychotherapy*. London: Robinson, 2016.
Roy, Arundhati. "The 2004 Sydney Peace Prize Lecture." https://www.sydney.edu.au/news/84.html?newsstoryid=279.
Schulman, Sarah. *Conflict Is Not Abuse: Overstating Harm, Community Responsibility, and the Duty of Repair*. Vancouver: Arsenal Pulp, 2016.
Scott, James C. *The Art of Not Being Governed: An Anarchist History of Upland Southeast Asia*. New Haven, CT: Yale University Press, 2010.
Simmons, Aishah Shahidah, ed. *Love WITH Accountability: Digging Up the Roots of Child Sexual Abuse*. Chico, CA: AK, 2019.
Sinclair, Upton. *The Jungle*. New York: Penguin Classics, 1985.
Singh, Julietta. *No Archive Will Restore You*. Bolton, ON: Punctum, 2018.
Smith, Clive Stafford. *The Injustice System: A Murder in Miami and a Trial Gone Wrong*. New York: Penguin, 2012.
Solnit, Rebecca. *A Paradise Built in Hell: The Extraordinary Communities That Arise in Disaster*. New York: Penguin, 2005.
Stern, Mark Joseph. "The Police Lie. All the Time. Can Anything Stop Them?" *Slate* (August 4, 2020). https://slate.com/news-and-politics/2020/08/police-testilying.html.
Sultan, Sonia. *Organism and Environment: Ecological Development, Niche Construction, and Adaptation*. Oxford: Oxford University Press, 2015.
Taylor, Charles. *A Secular Age*. Cambridge, MA: Bellknap, 2007.
TheSomebodytoknow. "My Story: Struggling, Bullying, Suicide, Self Harm." https://www.youtube.com/watch?v=vOHXGNx-E7E&t=6s.
Tosh, Jemma. *The Body and Consent in Psychology, Psychiatry, and Medicine: A Therapeutic Rape Culture*. London: Routledge, 2019.

Turner, J. Scott. *The Extended Organism: The Physiology of Animal-Built Structures.* Cambridge, MA: Harvard University Press, 2000.

Vitale, Alex. *The End of Policing.* London: Verso, 2018.

Wang, Jackie. *Carceral Capitalism.* Semiotext(e) intervention series 21. South Pasadena: Semiotext(e), 2018.

Watkins, Mary, and Helene Shulman. *Toward Psychologies of Liberation.* Critical Theory and Practice in Psychology and the Human Sciences. New York: Palgrave MacMillan, 2008.

Weber, Max. *Sociological Writings.* Edited by Wolf Heydebrand. The German Library 60. New York: Continuum, 2004.

Willse, Craig. *The Value of Homelessness: Managing Surplus Life in the United States.* Minneapolis: University of Minneapolis Press, 2015.

Yong, Ed. *I Contain Multitudes: The Microbes Within Us and a Grander View of Life.* New York: Ecco, 2016.

www.ingramcontent.com/pod-product-compliance
Lightning Source LLC
Chambersburg PA
CBHW030821230426
43667CB00008B/1322